# MEMOIRS OF A
# MEDIEVAL WOMAN

# MEMOIRS OF A MEDIEVAL WOMAN

## The Life and Times of Margery Kempe

### LOUISE COLLIS

PERENNIAL LIBRARY

Harper & Row, Publishers, New York
Grand Rapids, Philadelphia, St. Louis, San Francisco
London, Singapore, Sydney, Tokyo, Toronto

A hardcover edition of this book was published by Thomas Y. Crowell Company in 1964 and was originally published in England under the title *The Apprentice Saint*. It is here reprinted by arrangement.

First HARPER COLOPHON edition published 1983.

LIBRARY OF CONGRESS CATALOG CARD NUMBER: 82-48226

ISBN: 0-06-090992-7

# MEMOIRS OF A
# MEDIEVAL WOMAN

# CONTENTS

6

# ILLUSTRATIONS

# CHAPTER I

## Introduction

Margery Brunham, or Burnham, was born about 1373 in Bishop's Lynn, as King's Lynn was then called, in Norfolk. When an old woman, she dictated the memoirs* on which this book is based. Her autobiography is remarkable in many ways. It is the first to be written in English. Though she wished to depict herself as, above all, a saintly woman on familiar terms with God, many of the conversations with friends and enemies are recorded in a thoroughly down to earth spirit. These are real people speaking to a real woman. They say the kind of things anyone would in similar circumstances. They are bored by continual piety. In some cases, they laugh scornfully at religious excesses. In others, they become suspicious and denounce the writer to the authorities as a detestable heretic. Yet others were fully convinced of her sanctity, declaring that a place was reserved for her in heaven. There were also those who believed in spite of themselves: if in trouble, they desired her prayers; if not, they avoided her. They may not have used the very words reported, but one can't help feeling the sense is true enough.

Her memory was extremely good. She never became literate and, consequently, had no notes or diaries to help her recall the past of twenty, or thirty, years before. She realised that she hadn't always got the sequence of events quite correct, especially in the earlier chapters. But revision is difficult, when one cannot read or write. She left it as it was, with an apology. Where her story can be checked with reference to outside events, or the names of people mentioned, her accuracy is striking. She was an honest woman with a high opinion of herself.

As she did not consider the state of childhood interesting, we are told nothing of her life before marriage, except that she committed a secret sin which filled her with horror and remorse and preyed on her mind for years. No amount of penance, good deeds, or almsgiving relieved her. In order to be absolved, it was necessary to confess to a priest and this she was afraid to do. She would

* *The Book of Margery Kempe*, ed. S. B. Meech and H. E. Allen. Early English Text Society, 1940. All quotations are from this source, unless otherwise stated.

rather risk hell. She suffered greatly from fear of eternal damnation, being a firm believer in every dogma laid down by the Church. The nature of the shameful secret is never disclosed, but it seems likely that it was some sexual adventure. She was, particularly in youth, of an amorous disposition and susceptible to flattery.

What sort of an England did Margery and her friends inhabit? The medieval system, though politically and economically bankrupt, had reached a stage of superficial magnificence and luxury. The aristocracy, the new business class imitating them as far as circumstances allowed, dressed gaily, expensively, fantastically. The young people, their slenderness emphasized by long and graceful gothic lines, their hair carefully arranged, could hardly help looking handsome. They wore jewelled brooches. They sang and danced and made up poems and jousted. Their hunting parties resembled a pageant. Their architectural setting has never been surpassed.

It is a fairytale world, somewhat removed from the actual facts of life, as though a richly gilted decoration had been applied to the exterior of things. People aspired to beauty, to chivalry and a high moral standard based on Christian principles. Yet, they were human, after all, as Margery so abundantly shows. The most cursory acquaintance with the statutes, regulations and litigation of the period reveals the gap.

Behind the chivalrous façade, the pursuit of romantic love and personal elegance, was another world of violence, cruelty, corruption and dirt. Rubbish and filth lay outside doorways where the occupants had thrown it. Plague was endemic. Even well-to-do persons had a perpetual battle with fleas and lice.

In theory, ladies were goddesses of love, to be wooed with music and song. In fact, the days of individual choice had not yet come. Marriage was a business deal, fixed up by the parents of the parties concerned, for their own profit.

The towns were supposed to be governed by a committee elected by the citizens. In practice, only rich merchants could be mayors and aldermen and only other rich merchants could vote for them. All tolls and market dues were levied by the oligarchy and they also administered the lower courts of justice.

Ideally, war was a gallant affair with proper arrangements for the treatment of the vanquished. But, unless the defeated were seen to be worth money and a good ransom, they did not qualify under the rules. The history of the Hundred Years War with France contains many incidents of this sort. Even in one's own country, one was not safe from incursions by armed bands. Towns were walled and the gates shut at night. All citizens had a duty to go up on to the battlements, if necessary.

Perhaps it is in religion that the underlying violence of medieval life came out most clearly. Hell's torments were lovingly dwelt on and elaborated. Every kind of roasting, screwing, beating, boiling, disembowelling, was described in words, paint and sculpture. The painful stories of innumerable martyrs' deaths at the hands of Romans or heathens were known by all. Pictures of them covered the walls of many churches, the actual moment of beheading or rending to pieces being meticulously portrayed. That part of the Bible narrative meditated on most strenuously by the devout was the Passion. The more imaginative felt they actually saw Christ in agony on the cross, blood trickling and splashing to the ground. The ability to have such visions seemed to them a sign of heavenly grace. This moment of torment, so clearly and persistently before them, represented Christ's love of man. The mystery plays, performed by the guilds on holy days and festivals, abounded in slaughter and damnation. Heaven, by contrast, was rather vague, a place inlaid with precious metals, full of light and divine love, with the saints and angels in attitudes of perpetual adoration.

In this atmosphere, Margery Brunham, the mayor's daughter, grew up, her education consisting of lessons in household management and polite behaviour. It is rather surprising that she should not have learned to read and write. Most girls of her class could do so. The authors of etiquette books recommended an elementary knowledge for women, on the ground that it enabled them to study devotional books and kept them out of mischief. As a girl, Margery evidently had no taste for serious pursuits. Later, she was to become an enthusiastic student of popular religious works, though she was obliged to pay someone to read to her. She was not, however, interested in secular literature. In the late fourteenth century, Chaucer and Froissart were both alive. There is no evidence that she had heard of either.

If she could have relaxed her principles slightly, one feels she would have enjoyed the *Canterbury Tales;* for she was very observant of human nature and by no means narrow-minded. History and politics, on the other hand, were definitely outside her sphere, though her father was six times Member of Parliament for Lynn. During her early life, the war with France was in a more or less quiescent stage. Various expeditions went across the Channel, took what booty they could and returned. French pirates raided the English coast at intervals. At times, there was an official truce. In 1396, Richard II very sensibly felt that the struggle was doing nobody any good. He negotiated a thirty years peace and sealed it by marrying the French king's daughter, who was only seven. The child was a widow very soon afterwards. In 1399, Richard lost his throne to Henry IV and came to a mysterious end in Pomfret Castle, a few months later.

Margery notices none of these dramatic events. Her object was to relate the process of her own salvation. What had kings and infant queens to do with that? She does not even mention the Peasants' Revolt of 1381, one of the most dangerous internal upheavals the ruling class in medieval England had ever had to face. The highlights of history are not her subject. She tells us, in detail, what it was like to be an eccentric medieval woman. No other author does precisely that.

# CHAPTER II

## Marriage and Illumination

At the age of twenty or so, that is, in about 1393, Margery was married to a 'worschepful burgess' of Lynn. This was John Kempe, son of a successful merchant and holder of municipal office. The bridegroom seems to have been in his twenties also, and to have had an affectionate and charming nature.

Margery does not describe the wedding feast, but we can assume it was a cheerful occasion with a banquet after the church service, attended by everybody John Brunham thought worth bothering about in Lynn. A great deal was drunk at such times, followed by dancing. Everyone had a right to partner the bride and kiss her, if he could.

At suppertime the dancers paused, and afterwards those who could still stand up went on with the fun. The sound of music, shouting, singing and thumping of feet must have been audible a good way off. It was often past midnight before the last round of drinks had been finished and the happy couple conducted to bed.

John Kempe owned a house in the town and here in due course Margery became pregnant, suffering extremely from attacks of sickness, though she must have been fundamentally strong and healthy. Otherwise, she could scarcely have survived fourteen births and enjoyed an active old age. Perhaps her troubles were psychological. She still had not been able to expiate the unnamed sin which doomed her to an infinity of torment in hell. Suppose she died in childbed?

The birth was very difficult and her weakness so great after it that she felt certain the end had come and sent for the priest. Now she must confess all the faults of her life in order to obtain absolution and avoid falling into hellmouth where eager devils waited with pitchforks. But long brooding had made the sin enormous and terrifying. She had never been able to speak of it to this priest, for fear of what he would say. She broached the subject with trepidation and, just as she expected, he immediately began reproving her wickedness in the strongest terms, as was his duty. He did not think it his business to sympathize with sinful girls. In his view, evidently, God was not a personification of charity and love, as some averred. He did not consider that the young soul in his charge had been through hell already. No, she was bound for the fiery pit and excruciating torture. He upbraided her so fervently that she was afraid to complete the confession. No matter how he urged or threatened her, she dared not go on.

She was going to die. It was impossible to obtain forgiveness. Overcome by physical weakness and nervous strain, she went out of her mind, believing herself surrounded by demons and evil spirits for 'half yer viii wekys and odde days'.

Her hallucinations were of punishment by devils. They came at her breathing fire, as though intending to swallow her. They made rushes at her, uttering horrible threats, dragged her about, ordered her to deny God 'hys Modyr and alle the seyntys in Hevyn'. Under their influence, she slandered her husband, her mother, her father and herself. She tried to commit suicide and bit her hand so deeply that it was scarred for the rest of her life. John Kempe engaged keepers and had her tied down to the bed. In spite of precautions, she tore savagely at her bosom with her nails.

At last the crisis came. Recovery was dramatic. The inferno of devils vanished and Christ appeared, radiant in beauty and love. 'Clad in a mantyl of purpyl sylke,' he sat down on the bed, saying, 'Dowtyr, why hast thow forsakyn me and I forsoke nevyr thee?' Waiting for no reply, he ascended to heaven on a beam of light. A profound sense of peace and happiness suffused her as she watched.

Thereafter, she was calm and clear in the head. When her husband came, she spoke sanely and asked to have meals in a normal manner. He must have been overjoyed, for he loved her passionately, as subsequent adventures show. The servants and keepers, however, were sceptical, saying she was not really lucid and certainly not fit to have charge of the storeroom. He decided to risk it and was proved right. She sat down and 'toke hyr mete and drynke' as well as her weakness permitted. She recognized everyone she had known before.

Many came to stare at her, not altogether believing that she could be recovered. Her madness had been so violent, her sanity so completely restored. A miracle had happened, as she herself explained. Jesus had rescued her from the Devil's clutches. More important, her secret sin was forgiven. God had taken her under his protection.

The next period must have been a happy time for the young couple, in spite of Margery's headstrong character. Their love life was entirely satisfactory. They had 'gret delectacyon ... eythyr of hem in usyng of other'. There was money for fine clothes in the gay new fashion imported from the Continent. Margery bought a wonderful headdress consisting of gold pipes and wires. Her cloaks were slashed, showing brightly coloured silks underneath. She doesn't mention gowns, shoes or jewellery, but they must obviously have been on the same level. We don't know whether she was beautiful. She cannot have helped appearing a striking woman, full of vigour and frank enjoyment of life, though with a hint of moodiness and withdrawal.

She was vain, too, and tended to be extravagant, buying more and more clothes and ornaments in order to outshine other merchants' wives and catch admiring eyes. When poor John Kempe ventured to say that they could hardly afford all this magnificence which, in any case, was unsuited to their junior position in society, he was 'answeryd schrewydly and schortly'. No doubt he was unworthy of notice, she said, in effect, but she had a position to keep up. Had not her father been mayor of Lynn and alderman of the Guild of the Holy Trinity? What had his family to compare with that?

His reply is not reported. Perhaps he was crushed, especially as the money appears to have belonged to his wife. Or, he may have produced accounts to prove his case, for Margery began to feel it would be a good thing to set up in business and increase her income. What could be more profitable than the drink trade? She started brewing and, at first, all went well. The town archives show that John Kempe was associated with the venture, although his wife was the principal. After three or four years, however, the firm began to totter. Whether this was due to mismanagement and lack of experience in the boss, or to dishonest servants who took advantage of her illiteracy, or to supernatural intervention, as she herself was inclined to think, cannot now be determined. Whatever the reason, her workmen thought it prudent to find other employment.

Downcast by failure, she begged her husband's pardon for not having taken his advice. It seemed certain that she was being punished for the sin of ostentation. But the mood passed. Going into business was not, of itself, displeasing to God. She must have more money and prove herself a success before the world. She set up as a miller, with two fine horses to turn the grindstones. This enterprise failed almost at once, either because her man was a crook, or else the Devil got into the horses as he declared. Some people said she was cursed and it served her right. Others suggested that Christ had chosen her specially and was summoning her to abandon all other callings and follow him. This explanation appealed to her most. The more she brooded on it, remembering the vision during her madness, the more likely it seemed.

We do not know whether John Kempe had any suspicion of what was in store for him next.

# CHAPTER III

## The Sins of Love

Margery's conscience became troublesome again. She struggled with it as best she could, doing several penances for the sins of vanity and worldliness. In due course, she received intimations of heaven: lying in bed beside her husband she distinctly heard the music of paradise. The melody was extraordinarily sweet and compelling, surpassing anything experienced in this world 'wyth-owtyn ony comparyson'. Waking fully, she jumped out of bed, exclaiming to the astonished John: 'Alas, that evyr I dede synne, it is ful mery in Hevyn.'

Though no doubt proud to think his wife had been singled out by the angelic host, he cannot have cared for the sequel. For, from this time, she began to discourage him, saying that anything which happened between them was against her will as her love had now been entirely given to God. She would weep, she records, and beg him to leave off, but 'he wold have hys wylle'. Yet, one feels he would hardly have persisted to the extent of fourteen children unless there had been something kind in her manner underneath the tears and protestations. By all accounts, though young and lively, he was a mild, devoted and unassertive man.

So now, he did not regard the situation very seriously. On being informed that his conduct was displeasing to God, he remained calm, unable to believe their mutual love an evil thing. When begged to take a vow of chastity as the only means of averting divine displeasure, he good-humouredly replied that he was sure it would be an excellent move, 'but he mygth not yett, he shuld whan God wold.'

He had to endure lesser inconvenience also. Whenever Margery heard 'ony myrth or melodye' she would be reminded of the supernatural music and burst into tears, sighing over the evils of the world, particularly if friends were present, and saying reproachfully, 'It is ful mery in Hevyn.'

'Why speke ye so of the myrth that is in Hevyn?' they protested with irritation. 'Ye know it not and ye have not be ther, no mor than we.' They thought her affected and were bored by her moralisings and continual emphasis on the special signs of favour shown her by God.

Never a woman to do things by halves, she redoubled her penances, was shriven 'somtyme twyes or thryes on the day', lingering over the old secret sin in the confessional. She fasted tremendously. Getting up at two, or three, in the morning, she hurried to church and often remained at her prayers all day, with a break for lunch. Undeterred by critics who said she was going mad again, or that she had no business to subject herself and, in some degree, her husband, to such hardship and notoriety, she bought a hair shirt. The long-suffering John, she felt, might well make a scene if he discovered such a garment. Almost certainly, he would tear it off her. So she sewed it carefully into her dress and he noticed nothing. Perhaps she explained away the marks it left on her as a rash, or a punishment from God for the sins he obliged her to commit most nights of the week.

She found these austerities very satisfying, had no inclination to sin and was, indeed, 'mych mor mery' than she had ever been in the fashionable days of the wonderful golden headgear. Especially exciting were the sneers of those acquaintances who refused to believe her conversion genuine. Had not all the 'apostlys, martyres, confessorys and virgynes' endured the same slights? She was on the right path to heaven. Christ, himself, had trodden it.

Exultation rose higher and higher. 'Wyth plentyuows teerys and many boystows sobbyngys' she bewailed her own sins and everyone else's also. Continually running over her life from as far back as memory permitted, she counted up her misdemeanours as if they were a treasure trove. Wild cries and bellowings of grief would come from her as she knelt in St Margaret's, which may be seen to this day in Lynn.

In fact, she overdid it. Her friends began to avoid her. Some 'seyd sche was a fals ypocryte', trying to draw attention to herself. Others, no doubt, were terrified: the priest of St Margaret's was the first Lollard martyr. In 1401, he was publicly burnt in Smithfield. They must all have known him, by sight at least. It was foolish to mix oneself up with anything eccentric. One could easily fall into error.

With the accession of Henry IV in 1399, Archbishop Arundel

of Canterbury resumed the position he had lost under Richard II. Having just been crowned by Arundel and being still insecure, the new king was not likely to put difficulties in the archbishop's way, provided no one important was offended. It was Arundel's firm intention to get rid of the Lollards, once and for all. These followers of Wyclif, sometime Master of Balliol, were gradually becoming more active and numerous. They wrote tracts and pinned notices in public places denouncing the clergy as unfit for their job and as liars and deceivers of the people. When arrested, they usually recanted. On being released, they relapsed, though more cautiously, into their former ways.

In William Sawtre of St Margaret's, Lynn, the archbishop found someone of whom he could make an example. Sawtre had already been tried in Lynn and had publicly renounced his opinions. In the pulpit he had been accustomed to declare it better to worship good men than the cross or the angels, preferable to give to the poor money wasted on pilgrim travel. Above all, he had denied that the bread and wine became flesh and blood during communion. He declared these things to be wrong before the assembled crowd in Lynn.

He then went to London and was soon arrested again on the same charges. Examined before Archbishop Arundel, he stood firm. An act to allow the burning of heretics was hurried through Parliament in 1401. Such was the archbishop's rage, that the prisoner was burnt nine days before the act became law. Margery took note of these events, as we shall see.

For the moment, however, she knelt passionately in St Margaret's, praying for a sign from God. She wanted a miracle, so that there could be no more arguments as to whether or not she was divinely inspired. Other saintly persons had seen the crucifix dripping blood. They had watched the image come alive as they worshipped and reach out towards them. Might not Christ come off the cross, for her alone, and administer the bread and wine?

The sequel was not as she had expected. No wonders were vouchsafed. Instead she fell into 'the snar of letchery'. Though continuing cold towards her husband, young men began to catch her eye. There was one of whom she was particularly fond. After a conversation with him outside the church, she could not 'heryn hir evynsong, ne sey hir Pater Noster'. Good thoughts could not be induced to come into her head.

The service over, she ran to him and declared they should spend the night together. To her surprise, he hummed and hawed, though he had seemed eager enough before. In spite of the rebuff, she persisted, throwing saintliness to the wolves. It was not until he fled from her, saying he would rather be cut up small and put in a saucepan, that she gave over.

It took her some time to recover from this ludicrous episode, such an impression had the young man made on her. Of course, it was the Devil's work. She was being punished for her presumption in demanding a miracle. In her usual manner, she began turning the new sin round and round, viewing it from all angles, suffering as much as possible in order to atone. Her lamentations were intense, the nervous strain almost unbearable.

Here a note of caution enters her narrative for the first time: her penances were strictly 'governd aftyr the rewelys of the chirch'. It is not quite certain what year we have reached. If one adds up the various periods allotted to her illness, business, temptations and so on, it comes to about 1406. But as she speaks always of 'ii or iij yer', or 'iii or iiij yer', the sum is very approximate. However, one can say that 1406 would be a reasonable date on which to consider taking measures to protect oneself against false accusations, particularly if one had made a good many enemies. Lollard arrests continued briskly, as the movement was still active.

In 1409, Archbishop Arundel found it necessary to issue a declaration: 'Let no man presume to dispute, whether publicly or secretly, concerning the articles determined by the church', he wrote. Let no one call them in doubt or teach or preach the contrary, unless he wanted to risk a heretic's death.

In 1410, the second martyr was burnt at Smithfield. People of humble position were especially vulnerable.

# CHAPTER IV

## The Anchorite Encourages

It seems, therefore, that as the first decade of the fifteenth century went on, Margery became alarmed at the criticism her extravagances aroused. When the effects of the abortive love affair had died down, she was able to consider what should be done. Those who thought her a false hypocrite had grown, rather than diminished, in number.

These problems in mind, she knelt in a side chapel in St Margaret's. Christ appeared and, after assuring her that she would go to heaven 'wythin the twynkelyng of an eye' on her death, gave her encouragement in present dangers and practical advice. 'Drede thee nowt, dowtyr,' he said, 'for thow schalt have the vyctory of al thine enmys.'

What she required was sound ecclesiastical backing. Her present confessor did not believe in her, was inclined to laugh. It would be best to approach a certain anchorite attached to the Dominicans in Lynn. He was a man of visions and prophecies, likely to recognize a fellow spirit in Margery or, at least, welcome her as a disciple. She should tell him everything and say that God would be speaking to him on her behalf.

On smaller matters, she could take off the hair shirt, since there were other ways of mortifying herself, equally efficacious and less showy. For instance, there was nothing she liked better than a good plate of beef or mutton. She could give up meat for the time being. She might also receive communion every Sunday. This was much more frequently than was usual in the middle ages and would mark her out as specially devout. The Lollard heresy turned, in great part, on the question of transubstantiation. With the anchorite behind her and the sacraments fervently observed, she ought to be safe.

'Than this creatur went forth to the ankyr as sche was comawndyd.' In the story as related, the holy man is immediately convinced of the genuineness of her claims, remarking, 'Ye han an ernest-peny of Hevyn.' But it is reasonable to suppose that she would not have gone to him unless some previous acquaintance had assured her of a good reception. The result was perfectly satisfactory. The new spiritual guide enrolled her at once, with instructions to relate all her visions as they occurred and he would say 'whethyr thei ben of the Holy Gost, or ellys of yowr enmy the Devyl'.

Now her reveries became long and delightful. She allowed her imagination to wander as it fancied, without worrying about vanity or egoism. She had the anchorite's certificate. Also, she felt God preferred meditation rather than the repetition of set prayers. 'Ihesu,' she sighed voluptuously, 'what schal I thynke?' 'Thynke on my Modyr,' he replied.

She seemed to meet St Anne, who was pregnant, and asked to be taken on as maid. She was appointed to look after the Virgin, when born, seeing to it that she had proper food and plenty of clean white clothes. The Virgin became much attached to her nurse and, when pregnant in her turn, retained her services. Together, they went to St Elizabeth and assisted at the birth of John the Baptist. The saint spoke highly of her efficiency.

Then they went to Bethlehem, where Margery hired the quarters and bought food. Taking the newly delivered Christ in her arms, she wept copiously, thinking of his predestined end. Thereafter, she was a lugubrious figure in the background, tears pouring down her face, as the Three Kings came and went and preparations were made for the Flight into Egypt.

This immature dream is typical of her so-called visions. God is always admiring her virtues and looking forward to the day when he can conduct her to the place specially prepared in heaven. Meanwhile, 'many hundred thowsand sowlys schal be savyd be thi prayers', he informs her. Sometimes, she worried about the life of sin John Kempe continued to demand. Might this not disqualify her from paradise? Not necessarily, God assured her. Many of the saints had committed misdemeanours in their early days. It made no difference in the end. She was, at the moment of speaking, with child, but it didn't matter. He loved her 'as wel as any mayden in the world'.

In his conversations with her, God never rises above the intellectual level of a devout mayor's daughter. Love only spiritual things, he exhorts her. Never mind what people say. You will triumph in the end. Your goodness and charitable disposition will be fully rewarded. We will have many chats together. The

Devil will never get you. Just take a few precautions, such as keeping on the right side of the church. Cultivate the acquaintance of the proper people.

One should not, however, dismiss her as a fraud, or a fool. She was part of a movement which had grown up in the fourteenth century as an answer, or alternative, to the increasing worldliness and corrupt practice of the church. People who had no thought of questioning matters of doctrine yet felt that the organized church had lost touch with God. It was not that they disbelieved in the Pope's power to grant remission of sin, for instance; but they were shocked by the way the sale of indulgences had been turned into big business. His Holiness was so obviously collecting money, especially after 1378 when there were rival popes, one at Avignon and one in Rome.

It was agreed that chastity and the monastic life were pleasing to God and should be supported by the community at large. But many monks and friars seemed to think only of the advantages their position gave them in this world. They lived very comfortably in their monasteries, where the rules had been much relaxed particularly in regard to abstinence and plain diet.

As for the nunneries, they resembled boarding schools for overgrown girls more than anything else. They were used as a refuge for spinsters of good birth. These young women, placed there with their dowry because no suitable husband could be found for them, had commonly no vocation whatever for the religious life. They gabbled through the services, if able to keep awake, their pet dogs yawning at their feet. Anxious to keep up with fashion, they introduced smart new variations of cut and material into their habits. Earnest bishops found them impossible to deal with; for they only laughed at instructions and went on as before.

People had very definite ideas about the religious state. They looked back to a golden age they thought had occurred in the early centuries after Christ's death. Then the monks really practised the poverty and humility they preached, sharing every hardship of their flock and leading the way to heaven by their irreproachable morality and closeness to God. They never thought of material things. Devoted to austerity, prayer and study, they listened for the divine word and often heard it. Whereas today, there seemed to be no difference between the lay and the ecclesiastical person, except that the one was more pampered than the other.

Again, the king used the church as a way of paying the civil service. As incumbents were often ambassadors, ministers or secretaries, deputies had to be found to look after the souls theoretically in their care. Perhaps, in some cases, the deputies were good and conscientious servants, but such a system made the church seem even more distant, wrapped away in a huge organization, far from everyday needs.

Under these circumstances, the late medieval mystics on the one hand, and the Lollards on the other, became very popular. They brought God close to the individual. One could communicate with him directly. He would listen to one's troubles in a sympathetic manner. Advice could be obtained, the tedious and often incomprehensible rituals of the church be by-passed. Private devotions became a habit amongst many of the new middle class, to which Margery belonged. Such people were accustomed to rely on their own judgement in the business world.

There had always been a place in the church for the hermit or anchorite.* Anyone could apply to be enclosed. Their prayers brought them near to God. Sometimes they could foretell the future, or heal diseases. They could guide their disciples towards those visions which were a foretaste of paradise. Their doctrine was personal and emotional. One must adore God with all the strength of one's being and meditate steadily on the Passion, that example of Christ's love of man. By means of assiduous prayer, fasting and contemplation, some reached a stage where they heard strange melodies, played, as it were, in heaven, by the angels. They felt an extraordinary warmth, as of divine fire, suffuse them. Others wept uncontrollably.

A few, who were capable of further progress, despised these outward symptoms as mere irrelevance. For God had whispered strangely to them in words they tried afterwards to understand

* Anchorites remained in their cells, studying and praying. They spoke only through a window. Hermits came out to preach and were often responsible for the upkeep of a bridge, or piece of road. See R. M. Clay, *The Hermits and Anchorites of England.*

and never quite explained. They only knew that they had some-how stumbled on a transcendent happiness. Their tiny cell was not a prison, but a new and vital world, wider and far more exciting than anything to be found in a life of ordinary adventure.

A very small number were able to pass beyond even this and attain the final enlightenment, where all thought of self, all attachment to the material universe disappeared; all the terrors of the soul's strange journey were overcome and ended in union with the godhead. This could only be hinted at in words, for it was a thing outside the realms of speech.

Margery was simply one of many who read, or had read to them, the books produced by the recluses and tried to follow the path to heaven on earth as well as their imperfections allowed. Lacking the intellect to grasp these esoteric ideas in their entirety, she mistook the wanderings of a commonplace imagination for a divine vision. She thought hysterical tears and fits were cer-tainly a gift from Christ himself. Nor was she alone in her opin-ions. Gradually, her supporters and admirers became numerous. Even the obdurate John Kempe was converted.

The Lollards, with whom it was so easy to be confused in times of excitement, represented the evangelical reaction. The sale of pardons and indulgences led them to denounce the Pope's authority. It was impossible that such a system could have God's special mandate. A man's position depended on grace. If he didn't behave as a priest should, it meant he was not one. The worship of relics and images infuriated them. It was more reasonable, said William Sawtre, to worship a temporal prince than a bit of wood reputed to be part of the true cross. The denial of transubstan-tiation followed from this dislike of miracles and the super-natural.

They laid emphasis on missionary work. 'Lord,' wrote Wyclif, head of the movement in England, 'what cursed spirit of lies stireth priests to close them in stones or walls for all their life, since Christ commandeth to all his apostles and priests to go into all the world and preach the gospel.' He sponsored a translation of the Bible into English, so that everyone might read and judge for himself what God's words were about. His followers travelled round the countryside, preaching as they went.

Many people liked the idea that unworthy priests had no right to their tithes. Taxes had always seemed immoral. The Lollards were humble and poor, as Christ himself had been. They often seemed nearer to the golden age of early Christianity than the regular clergy.

Wyclif did not invent the Lollard heresy. Such ideas had been known in Europe ever since the church had seemed to become too rich and organized; to put the enjoyment of this world before that of the next. Perhaps in the west, the Celtic church of the early middle ages came closest to the ideal of a life devoted to learning, spiritual exercise and spreading God's word by precept and example.

The authorities took action. Besides endangering a man's soul, such ideas were politically undesirable. The church hierarchy had no intention of allowing itself to be undermined. Oxford University, the headquarters of the movement, was cleaned up, Wyclif being retired to an obscure vicarage in 1382. But it was not so easy to eradicate the unobtrusive missionaries, trudging from town to town.

# CHAPTER V

## *The Visit to Norwich*

Margery continued to approach useful people. The vicar of St Stephen's in Norwich at this time was renowned for his scholarship and the propriety of his life. Some said he was a saint; and later certain miracles took place at his tomb. Margery felt sure that she would have a good reception from him, and was anxious to set off, although 'feynt and feble' being 'newly delyveryd of a chyld'. However, God said bracingly, 'Drede thee not, I shal make thee strong i-now.' Thus encouraged, 'sche toke hyr wey to Norwych-ward', dressed in black.

Arriving at St Stephen's, she found the vicar walking up and down outside, talking to another priest. She introduced herself and asked for an appointment after lunch, so that she might discuss religious matters for an hour 'or ellys tweyn owyrs'. 'Benedicite,' he exclaimed in some horror. 'What cowd a woman ocupyn an owyr er tweyn owyrs in the lofe of owyr Lord?' He had an hour free now, he said. She could tell him what she wanted at once.

They sat down together in the church and his manner was so sympathetic that she began from the beginning, relating her childhood, youth, marriage, business ventures, temptations, sins and visions. He was not bored. On the contrary, his interest encouraged her and she became more and more excited. Speaking of her meditations on the Passion, she suddenly heard such extraordinary music that she fell flat on the ground. Some time elapsed before she recovered.

They both took this as an auspicious sign from heaven. She enlarged on her visions. The three persons of the Trinity, both separately and together, used to appear and converse with her 'as pleynly and as veryly as one frend spekyth to another'. Saints Peter, Paul, Katherine and any others she might apply to, instructed her in the divine mysteries. She had had read to her a number of books written by famous recluses, such as Hilton's *Scale of Perfection*, Rolle's *Stimulus Amoris* and *Incendium Amoris*, and St Bridget of Sweden's *Celestial Revelations*. None equalled the brilliance of her own experiences.

Overcome by her eloquence and the unusual nature of the interview, the vicar seems not to have protested. Having read the books mentioned above, he knew that the last thing the mystics advocated was a boastful or competitive attitude towards God's favour. Perhaps it was impossible to get a word in. Perhaps her ardour, combined with the sign from heaven, was so impressive that it didn't occur to him to criticize. Besides, hers was a devout soul. One couldn't deny that.

She described how the Holy Spirit wrestled with her body, causing her to lie on the ground, sobbing with exhaustion and joy, 'sumtyme seying, Ihesu, mercy, sumtyme, I dey', while the unbelievers stood round, remarking that she must either be possessed by a devil, or else subject to fits. The vicar, now completely won over, expressed his abhorrence and said she was certainly 'indued wyth grace of the Holy Gost, to whom it longyth to enspyr wher he wyl'. He became her confessor for whenever she happened to be in Norwich. A few years later when she was summoned before the Bishop of Norwich to be examined on her faith, he testified on her behalf. In return, she prophesied that he had seven years left in the world and would die in an odour of sanctity.

This was a great triumph for Margery. All idea of weakness after childbirth forgotten, she hurried to William Southfield, a well-known Carmelite of Norwich. The Carmelites were the least corrupt and relaxed of the monastic orders. William Southfield spent long hours in prayer, fasting and various austerities. The Virgin Mary often appeared to him in his cell. After his death, it was said that his body remained undecayed in its magnificent marble sarcophagus.

Margery arrived 'on a fornoon and was wyth hym in a chapel a long tyme'. Again, she explained her whole life history and begged the friar to say whether or not her visions emanated from the Devil. Southfield recognized a congenial spirit. 'Ihesu mercy and gremercy,' he exclaimed. 'Syster, dredyth ye not of yowr maner of levyng.' She was certainly being prompted by the Holy Ghost. He addressed her in a short sermon. Many sins were forgiven for the sake of 'good creaturys' like Margery. She should receive God's gifts 'as lowly and mekely as ye kan', he admonished her and enlarged somewhat on this aspect of things, with several quotations from the scriptures to strengthen his case.

'Mech comfortyd' by these two certificates, Margery felt she could approach the most famous woman of Norwich, Dame Julian, the anchoress. This lady, now nearing seventy, was a true mystic. Unconcerned with signs and wonders, she meditated on the nature of divine truth, the meaning of the scriptures and the fate of humankind.

As a young woman, she had been troubled by doubts and conflicts which culminated in a severe illness at the age of thirty. When on the point of death, as it seemed, the image on the crucifix became the dying Christ in person. Blood flowed from his wounds as he answered her questions by means of sixteen sets of enigmatical pronouncements. The visions connected with these conversations were the only ones she ever had. The rest of her life was spent in trying to explain them to herself and every-one; for God had spoken to her merely as a representative of His creatures. She did not regard herself as having been marked out as someone superior, the recipient of special favour. 'Because of the shewing I am not good,' she wrote in her *Revelations*, 'but only if I love God the better.' Visions were nothing unless they led to understanding.

Her central feeling was that God is perfect love and charity. Though a masculine deity, his nature could be expressed in the phrase, 'our mother in all things'. She was troubled by the idea of sin and damnation. How could a God, in essence a universal mother, permit wickedness in a world he had created in his own image? It must be that evil was only relative, a necessary, but subordinate part of the scheme of things which would be ab-sorbed in the end. 'I will make all things well,' God assured her, 'and I shall make all things well; and thou shalt see for thyself that all manner of thing shall be well.' 'A kind soul hath no hell but sin', she notes in another place.

Though she did not explicitly deny any of the tenets of the church, it can be seen that Dame Julian had individual leanings. As the decades passed, her meditations grew more abstruse. The understanding she attained was beyond reach of words. 'And for the ghostly sight,' she wrote in this connection, 'I have said somewhat, but I may never fully tell it.'

To this venerable intellect came Margery Kempe in search of

approval and a good reference in case of need. Were her 'many wondirful revelacyons' divinely inspired, or not, she demanded, 'for the ankres was expert in swech thyngys.'

Since she had a reputation for giving 'good cownsel', many people must have visited Dame Julian, asking advice in their troubles, a cure for diseases, or, simply, a blessing. Over the years, she must often, on looking out of her cell window, have seen a woman dressed in black, pale and haggard from fasting, penance, disordered nerves and recent childbirth. She had her answers ready for these women who poured out their history with the greatest volubility. Yet, the others were not quite like Margery: they didn't afterwards write books.

Having listened patiently to a full account of her visitor's conversations with divinity, the old recluse replied in general terms. One could easily tell whether a vision was genuine. God was 'al charite' and a revelation which contained anything uncharitable, or to the detriment of a fellow Christian, must be the Devil's work. Margery should be obedient to God's will and steadfast in her faith. Everyone following these principles could be certain 'that the Holy Gost dwellyth in hys sowle'.

Yes, chastity was much esteemed by God. On the question of tears for Christ's death, there were precedents. Both St Jerome and St Paul said devout weeping incommoded the Devil. As for her enemies who disbelieved in her piety, saying she was an actress, or worse, she should take no notice of them. Let her patiently pursue her faith, listening for God's word, and all would be well.

Margery records that she returned to Dame Julian 'many days', perhaps in the hope of obtaining some more definite recommendation. If so, she failed, though the discussions they had were very agreeable.

She had now three useful acquaintances, honest people, who, she hoped, would help if her enemies should lay complaints before the Bishop of Norwich, for instance.

# CHAPTER VI

## The Widows of Lynn

She returned to Lynn greatly encouraged and less afraid of scoffers. The anchorite stood up for her stoutly. He 'toke it on charge of hys sowle' that hers was a genuine case, whatever anyone, including her other confessor, might say. She discussed with him the possibility that she might, one day, visit Jerusalem. Surely it would come about, he said, in a sudden spirit of prophecy, as it seemed. She would have servant trouble on the journey, but God would look after her among the foreigners.

She became a tremendous partisan of the anchorite's and wanted to do something for him in her turn. She thought of a rich widow of her acquaintance and hurried to her house. God had sent instructions, she said, that the widow should change her priest and go to the holy man for confession. The lady's priest, naturally, was against the idea and cast doubts on Margery's authority to interpret the divine wishes in this, or any other, matter. The interview grew heated, each lady promoting the claims of her favourite. Finally, Margery was thrown out and forbidden the house.

Since it was not in her nature to take things calmly, Margery went to 'a mastyr of dyvynite' and dictated a letter full of insults to her former friend. One clause was that 'the wedow shuld nevyr han the grace that this creatur had'. Another paragraph declared that God would be 'ryt wel' pleased if Margery never set foot in the lady's house again.

As for the priest, she accosted him, saying she had a message from God: it had been divinely decreed that he would be suddenly parted from his patroness at some unstated future date. Whether this would be due to the sack, or something worse, had not been revealed to her. She only knew that he would now laugh at her words. Let him wait and see how it would work out.

Many people took his side, however, calling her a mischief maker and other names. But she did not care. She had forces behind her, too. Every day God's special favour became more apparent. It seemed clear that she had been marked out for an exciting spiritual career, perhaps on the lines of St Bridget of

Sweden, who had also been afflicted with a husband and children in her early days. Like Margery, she had been subject to holy tears at the mere thought of the Passion. Christ and the Virgin, particularly, had frequently appeared and addressed her in a kind of sermon. In this manner, she often learnt what was to happen in the future. Taking a strong interest in church politics, the saint wrote letters to the Pope in 1370, saying that if he fled to Avignon, he would come to a bad end. Sure enough, he died within a month. She also founded a new order of monks and nuns. The Mother of God had explained the rules to her in the greatest detail. In 1373, she died in Rome.

Margery had no desire to found an order, but in all other respects, she felt herself the equal, or superior, of St Bridget. When, one day, she saw the blessed sacrament fluttering like a dove as the priest held it up, God remarked that St Bridget had never seen this miracle. It was no good Margery watching for it to happen again, he added. It was a particular manifestation and meant vengeance. 'A, good Lord, what veniawnce?' she cried avidly. An earthquake, she was informed. Furthermore, God continued inconsequently, he spoke to her 'rygth as I spak to Seynt Bryde'. Every word of the saint's revelations are as true as the fact that Margery will get the better of her enemies. The more she suffers from them, the greater the reward in heaven.

It is her duty to save people from sin, to tell them how they should behave, to communicate her visions. It's all part of the scheme of things. There is 'prechyng and techyng, pestylens and bataylys, hungyr and famynyng', loss of goods, general tribulation and the advice of selected persons, such as Margery. Nothing seems to make much difference to a wicked world, but she must persevere. He has a message for another widow.

Alarmed by her visitor's appearance, manner and reputation, the widow refused to speak to her alone. Her priest was sent for and all three went into a chapel where Margery 'wyth gret reverens and many teerys' announced: 'Madam, owyr Lord Ihesu Crist bad me telle yow that yowr husbond is in Purgatory.' It would be a long time before he worked off his sins and qualified for heaven.

The lady was affronted. Her late husband, she said, 'was a good man'. He had never gone to purgatory at all. The priest, however, was more cautious. Evidently, he did not wish to be cursed by a woman whom some well-informed people said was high in God's favour. Or, it may be, he thought the widow ought not to express so decided an opinion on a theological matter. Or else he saw a bad fight coming and hoped to avert it. Whatever the reason, he said soothingly that one couldn't be certain in these cases. It was, possibly, as Margery said. There were precedents. These he related at length.

The widow had by no means cooled down when he finished. Having got rid of Margery, she sent a deputation, led by her daughter, to the anchorite, saying that he should expel Margery from the circle of his disciples, unless he wished the widow to withdraw the support she had previously given him. Although, we must suppose, his patroness's alms had been generous, the anchorite remained loyal. 'Sche was Goddys owyn servawnt,' he repeated to all enquiries concerning Margery's character, 'sche was the tabernakyl of God.'

This made an impression. Another widow, feeling her conscience, asked Margery to pray for her husband's soul and find out 'if he had ony nede of help'. Yes, he had, Margery replied, he would 'be xxx yer in Purgatory les than he had bettyr frendys in erthe'. An expenditure of three or four pounds in masses and alms was required. This was a considerable sum of money. What were thirty years in purgatory, compared with an eternity of bliss afterwards? It was not a matter of hell's torments. The widow replied vaguely and did nothing.

Though discomposed, Margery was not discouraged. Flat on the ground in St Margaret's, she continued her devotions unabated, the spirit of prophecy often falling on her. Sometimes her words came true and sick people lived, or died, as she had declared. Once the anchorite asked her to pray for 'a woman whech lay in poynt of deth' and find out whether she was destined to recover. Anxious friends and relations of ill people would come to her, begging to know the worst, or else be relieved of their fears. She would then consult God and report his answers which, besides the required information, often contained agreeable remarks about herself.

Gratifying though this sort of thing was, there were dangers. She was not always right. Then the humble inquirers became

33

angry and said she had listened to the Devil and mistaken him for God. All those she had offended with unwanted advice began murmuring again: she gave herself the airs of a saint, yet did not enter the religious life fully in the recognized manner; she went about moralizing and preaching; she was a Lollard.

She knew she was not a heretic, but it was possible the Devil had deceived her. The saints were full of warnings on the subject. The whole of Satan's superhuman ingenuity was especially directed against men and women who strove to follow God and were the elect of this world and the next.

The anchorite advised her not to despair. He believed in her. Frequently, her predictions had been correct. Perhaps, on the other occasions, she hadn't understood God properly. It was not easy. The divine intentions were not always expressed in plain language. Her friend Dame Julian had had similar experiences. She should take comfort and keep calm.

She did so. The mood passed. She was fighting fit again.

# CHAPTER VII

## John Kempe's Bargain

Meanwhile, John Kempe had been living tenaciously in the background. Though threatened with instant death from supernatural causes if he didn't desist, he continued to make love to her. The children mounted up to the number of fourteen. As Margery had very little time to devote to the business of wife and mother, the household must have been rather free and easy, in spite of the continual sermonizing and pious exhortations which she must have lavished on the family. She was often out and that made it easier to stand the strain. Also, she must have had moments of warmth and charm, or John Kempe would not have remained so devoted.

We don't know how he made his living. By 1413, he had run into debt and his business required no supervision, since he was able to wander about on pilgrimage for months with his wife. If employed, he must have had the sack. If his own boss it would seem the enterprise had failed. His marriage, also, had entered a new phase. He began to think Margery might really be under God's protection. Quite a number of highly respected people now said so. There was something earnest and sincere in her manner. She had never wavered all these years.

His doubts and fears reached their culmination in Easter week, 1413. As he moved towards his wife, she shouted, 'Ihesus, help me,' and his manhood died away. 'He had no power to towche hir at that tyme in that wyse.' A few days later, the matter was clinched by a miracle.

'It befel on a Fryday befor Whytson Evyn, as this creatur was in a cherch of Seynt Margarete' at mass. Suddenly, there was a tremendous roaring, rumbling noise. Some members of the congregation called out in their fright that God's vengeance was about to fall on Margery, the Devil's servant. As she crouched down shielding her head and praying for safety, a large stone and piece of wood from the vault hit her. Partially stunned, she lay on the ground muttering, 'Ihesu, mercy.'

It seemed certain that she must be badly injured. John Wyrham, a well-known mercer of the town, stepped forward and pulled her sleeve anxiously, saying, 'Dame, how far ye?' To everyone's astonishment, she got up. Nothing was broken. Many of those present thought it a miracle. But the sceptics said, on the contrary, it showed the extent of God's wrath with this presumptuous woman. All one could say was that he hadn't actually killed her this time, as she deserved.

Both sides agreed that it was a supernatural event. They went away talking about it. The news spread through the town, particularly exciting Master Alan, a Carmelite and doctor of divinity of Cambridge University. He had written a number of books elucidating certain passages of scripture, theological problems and Aristotle's theories. He had also indexed the revelations and prophecies of St Bridget. Being a methodical and somewhat scientific man, he obtained a statement at once from Margery as to the circumstances of the miracle. Then he found the stone which had fallen on her back and weighed it. The scales showed 'iij powne'. The beam that had crashed down on her head had just been thrown on to a bonfire by the churchwarden. Master Alan snatched it off. The weight was seven pounds. 'And this worshepful doctowr seyd it was a gret myracle and ower Lord was heyly to be magnyfied.' It showed God intended to preserve her from every danger. Many people were deeply impressed by this authoritative statement. Yet, still, the sceptics stuck to their own opinion and would not shut up.

John Kempe's comments are not recorded. Perhaps words failed him. We only know that shortly afterwards he was persuaded to accompany his wife on a pilgrimage in order to give thanks for divine favour, 'fully trostyng it was the wyl of God'. They set out for York, he turning things over in his mind, she in her uppish mood, relating her experiences to anyone who would listen. Audiences were mainly appreciative and she found herself 'wolcomyd and mech mad of in dyvers placys'. God dissipated her suspicion that she might have been a little boastful, saying, 'Thei that worshep thee thei worshep me.' Anyone modelling his conduct on her advice might be sure of reaching heaven.

We must imagine Mr and Mrs Kempe, then, trudging through the summer countryside of 1413. Part of the way they certainly walked, though they may sometimes have hired ponies. There were frequent inns on the main pilgrim routes. Shrines and chapels were dotted everywhere.

This was the period of the Perpendicular style in architecture. The Church, rich and decadent, was adding to the splendid monuments she already had. How much better would the money have been spent, said those of puritan temper, in hospitals, schools and preaching to the ignorant.

The Kempes must have passed through Lincoln while the scaffolding was up for the chantry chapels. The choir stalls and misericords were finished recently. Margery was not interested in these, but in the shrine of St Hugh's Head, where miracles had been known to happen. St Hugh, who died in 1200, was Bishop of Lincoln and chief architect of the cathedral as it now stands.

Equally efficacious, from the pilgrim's point of view, was the shrine of Little St Hugh. In 1225, it was said he had been murdered by the Jews during abominable secret rites to which they were thought to be addicted. Another sacred spot was the well in the town where, according to legend, the child's mutilated body had been discovered.

Having prayed at the right places, made the right offerings and, perhaps, bought some relics, the pilgrims pressed on to York. Margery's conversation was always elevating, unless she had been crossed. It was also copious. Either John was a good listener, or else he let his thoughts wander quietly on their own. Had he reached the final crisis of his marriage? He was still impotent.

Entering York Minster, they found a good deal of confusion. Though the choir and famous east window had been completed, the central tower was still under construction. The two western towers were not yet begun. Behind the high altar stood the shrine of St William of York. Here miracles, of healing particularly, had been known to happen.

We are not told how often Margery fell down in fits, burst into tears, impressed, bored and offended people. We can assume she attracted a certain amount of attention. As on her journey to Norwich, one of her objects was to seek out substantial people and win them over. Thus, she spoke to 'ankyrs and reclusys . . . many worthy clerkys, doctorys of dyvynyte and bachelers'. To each she related her entire history and all her visions. One feels it throws an agreeable light on the fifteenth century that these persons should have had the patience and politeness to listen for hours to a garrulous woman talking about herself. One suspects, too, that her vehement style must have had a persuasiveness which has evaporated in the printed word.

The most important moment of the pilgrimage now occurred. It was midsummer eve and a heat-wave as they trudged over the wolds towards Bridlington, where the local saint had died only in 1379. Margery had 'a botel wyth bere in hir hand and hir husbond a cake in hys bosom'. Suddenly, he propounded an elaborate question: suppose an armed man appeared with orders to cut off his head, unless they made love together? 'Seyth me trewth of yowr consciens,' he cried passionately, 'for ye sey ye wyl not lye.' Would she allow him to be executed before her eyes rather than be his true wife?

'Alas, ser,' said Margery, 'why meve ye this mater?' They had been chaste for eight weeks. Couldn't they simply go on as they were? But he insisted on an answer. He must know 'the trewth of yowr hert' once and for all. Had she any love left for him? 'Than sche seyd wyth gret sorwe' that she would rather see him dead 'than we schuld turne agen to owyr unclennesse.' 'Ye arn no good wyfe,' he said abruptly. However, it was more or less what he had expected.

As they continued in the boiling sun, she asked him how it was that they had been chaste for two months, considering that they got into the same bed every night. A sort of horror came over him when he went to take her, he replied, and he couldn't do anything.

'Now, good ser, amend yow and aske God mercy,' she cried earnestly. It was a sure sign that the supernatural death she had foretold would have fallen on him if he had touched her. Let them take a vow of chastity, she urged, 'and I schal pray for yow that ye schul be savyd.' He would gain more reward in heaven than if he wore a hair shirt, or coat of mail, next to his skin. Let him name a bishop and they could go immediately and register their vow.

'Nay,' he objected, 'that wyl I not grawnt yow, for now may I usyn yow wythowtyn dedly synne and than mygth I not so.' He must have recovered his spirits sufficiently to make a pass at her, since, as they went on, she was very much afraid he would throw her down in the grass.

38

As a matter of fact, he had accepted the position and was only wondering how to turn it to his own advantage. By the time he had made up his mind, they were passing a wayside cross. Here they sat down and he said: 'Margery, grawnt me my desyr, and I schal grawnt yow yowr desyr.' Firstly, they should still sleep in one bed. Secondly, she could go to Jerusalem if she paid his debts. Thirdly, she must give up fasting on Fridays.

She could not abandon her fasting, she said, because God had enjoined it on her. Well, then, he retorted, he would have her at once. This alarmed her. Feeling it not prudent to rely on supernatural protection alone, she begged a few minutes to consider the matter. With his permission, she would kneel in front of the cross and consult God.

'Wyth gret habundawns of teerys', she concentrated her mind. God announced that the purpose of fasting was to obtain her husband's consent to a vow of chastity. Therefore, she could now properly leave off. On the question of money to pay debts, she did not require divine guidance. Her father, the wealthy merchant, had just died.

'Sere,' she said firmly to the expectant John, 'yf it lyke you, ye schal grawnt me my desyr, and ye schal have yowr desyr.' She would pay his bills before going to Jerusalem, on his promising that they should have separate beds. She would eat and drink on Fridays if he took a vow of chastity with her. He gave his word.

Full of delight she 'thankyd God gretly' and suggested they should 'sey iij Pater Noster' before the convenient cross. 'This was on a Fryday on Mydsomyr Evyn.' They began the new life at once by opening the beer and unwrapping the cake 'togedyr in gret gladness of spyryt'. This was her most triumphant moment. The road to sainthood had been finally cleared. All her intimations of a glorious career on earth, crowned by an infinity of bliss in heaven, would come true. What more could an ambitious woman ask?

# CHAPTER VIII

## Escape From Burning

They continued their travels 'to divers placys of relygyon', Margery conversing, instructing and explaining. John supported her as well as he could 'for he was evyr a good man and an esy man to hir'. If things looked very threatening, he would take fright and hide for a time. Yet, unlike some, he never denounced her and always returned when danger had passed, speaking up for her as loudly as he dared. In this he was superior to a certain disciple of the anchorite at Lynn who gave himself holy airs and professed the highest regard for Margery. At a bad moment when the crowd shouted that 'sche was a fals ypocryte . . . and thretyd hir to be brent', this man had deserted to the other side with alacrity. Whereas John 'was redy when alle other fayled and went wyth hir . . . alwey trostyng that al was for the best and shuld comyn to good ende whan God wold.'

We can admire John's courage. 1413 was a dangerous year. In the spring, Henry V succeeded. Among his plans and resolutions for the future were measures for dealing with Lollards. Of strong religious feelings, he was convinced that these heretics were inspired by the Devil. Also they had certain socialistic aims, such as disendowment of the church and appointment to priestly office on merit only, which were politically undesirable. How could a man embark on the conquest of France leaving such people at large in his kingdom? There seemed to be more and more of them each year.

Under Henry IV only heretics of humble position had been prosecuted. Archbishop Arundel had been eager to do more, but the king thought it inexpedient to molest prominent men like Sir John Oldcastle, Member of Parliament and personal friend of the Prince of Wales. Oldcastle, therefore, was not in the least alarmed by the laws against his sect and entertained Lollards openly at his house. But, no sooner had his friend the Prince of Wales been crowned, than the archbishop was unleashed. Oldcastle was summoned to Windsor and examined on his faith. The king professed himself shocked by his answers to the questions put, though they can hardly have been a surprise to him.

In September 1413, Oldcastle was arrested, tried, convicted and put in the Tower of London to await public burning in November, unless he should recant. In October, he managed to bribe his gaolers and disappeared. Great excitement and alarm prevailed. Secret messages circulated among the Lollards, who gathered in all parts of the country for a march on London. Oldcastle intended to seize the government. The plot was betrayed, however, and the rebel bands crushed before they had time to unite into an army in January 1414. Oldcastle escaped once more.

Against the background of these events, Margery and John arrived in Canterbury, to give thanks at the shrine of Thomas Becket, premier saint of England. Though the town was strongly anti-Lollard, Margery made no concessions. Why should she, an accredited holy woman and favoured candidate for sainthood? Only shortly before she had been received most respectfully at a monastery and sat at the abbot's table, entertaining the company with parables and stories of a religious nature. One suspicious monk, in particular, had been completely won over by her spirit of divination. Tell me, he had said to test her, what is my secret sin? Lechery, she had replied, lack of faith and accumulation of goods. 'Wyth wyfes er wyth sengyl women?' he had cried, astonished. 'Ser, wyth wyfes,' she had said. Thereafter, he had thought it prudent to reform and follow her spiritual advice to the letter.

So now, in Canterbury, she threw herself down in the church, wailing and sobbing, swaying, writhing, and exclaiming, as her manner was when indulging in 'hy contemplacyon'. Public comment was extremely unfavourable. She was creating a disturbance. There was a devil in her, or else she was putting it on. She was some sort of heretic. She ought to be thrown out, arrested, got rid of. John Kempe slunk away 'as he had not a knowyn hir and left hir aloon among hem'.

She continued her prayers indefatigably. Hours passed. At last they called a senior monk to deal with her. This man had had a distinguished secular career before retiring to the religious life. As chancellor to Queen Joanna, wife of Henry IV, he had been a rich and powerful official. He knew the world and had often been sent abroad as special ambassador. Though now, in theory, a humble monk, everyone, naturally, deferred to his opinion. He made her stand up and said: 'What kanst thow seyn of God?'

As her book proves, Margery's was an excellent memory. She had no difficulty in relating a story from the Bible, almost word perfectly, it seems, to prove her knowledge. It would have been better to answer in more general terms. To have read the scriptures was one of the distinguishing marks of a Lollard. His suspicions confirmed, the ex-chancellor declared she ought to be shut up and prevented from corrupting the populace. God forgive him, Margery said earnestly. It was surely his duty to protect God's servants.

A young monk stepped forward, taking his tone from the other, and said: 'Eythyr thow hast the Holy Gost or . . . a devyl wythin the, for that thu spekyst her to us, it is Holy Wrytte.'

Still not realizing the danger, Margery retorted: 'I pray yow ser, geve me leve to tellyn yow a tale.'

The monks seem to have hesitated to prolong the scene, for the crowd which had collected cried: 'Late hir sey what sche wyl.'

This was the sort of invitation Margery never could resist. She addressed the audience in a parable of her own composition about a man who, as a penance for his sins, paid others to abuse him and was always very glad to meet disagreeable people, because it enabled him to get through a part of his punishment free of charge. In her own case, she thanked them for the disgraceful treatment she had received, since the more she suffered for the love of God, the sooner she'd go to heaven.

This tactless oration can scarcely have conciliated the monks; and to the congregation it proved her a heretic. As she marched out of the church they followed, shouting: 'Thow shalt be brent fals lollare. Her is a cartful of thornys redy for the and a tonne to bren the wyth.'

'And the creatur stod wythowtyn the gatys at Cawntyrbery, for it was in the evenyng.' The strolling crowds were glad of a diversion. 'Tak and bren hir,' they screamed, ferociously surrounding her.

Margery 'stod stylle tremelyng and whakyng ful sor in hir flesch', wondering desperately where her husband had got to. 'Blyssed Lord, help me and have mercy on me,' she prayed.

Rescue came in the form of two superior young men who,

taking charge of the situation, asked her to declare whether, or not, she was a heretic. 'No, serys,' she managed to answer firmly, 'I am neyther eretyke ne loller.' Evidently the people were mollified by this, for no objection was raised as the young men asked where she lodged. She couldn't remember the street, she said, but the inn was run by a German. Recognizing the description, they quickly conducted her to the place, cheering her up as best they could on the way. There they found John Kempe, waiting inconspicuously. Margery does not record what she said to him then.

# CHAPTER IX

## Audience with the Bishop of Lincoln

John must surely have begged her to moderate her devotions. However, his protestations, if he really dared to make them, were quite useless. Encouraged by sundry conversations with God, Margery continued, on their return to Lynn, to reprove sinners, exhort to virtue, explain the scriptures and exhibit the most extravagant piety.

She lingered over dreams of a martyr's death by fire, execution, drowning and hurricane – without explaining to us how the last was to work. These imaginings were particularly delightful since Christ himself had assured her that she would never come to harm at any man's hands. At the same time, he thanked her for her willingness to suffer for his sake. It showed the great merit of her soul, he said.

Fortunately, there were many practical matters to attend to besides these masochistic thoughts, inspired both by her own experiences and the many bloodthirsty accounts in the lives of the saints. At last she could embark on the great adventure she had so long desired. She had the money for a trip to Jerusalem, Rome and Compostela in Spain. This was the regular grand tour of the middle ages. Her husband had agreed to let her go. She was about forty, strong, vigorous, individual. Her marriage had ended, for all ordinary purposes. She wished to symbolise the new purity by wearing white. Widows who took vows of celibacy assumed a special mantle and ring. This she would do also.

She hesitated slightly here, for a certain heretical sect wore white; and those who accused her of ostentation would regard the unusual outfit as a further attempt to draw attention to herself. But she knew her wishes were perfectly right. God had said so. Banishing all doubts and fears, she set off for Lincoln with the patient John. They intended to make the vow of chastity formally in the bishop's presence and ask him to authorize the white mantle and the pilgrimage to the Holy Land. Margery's papers would thus be in order, in case of emergencies. Strictly speaking, Norwich was their bishop, but it so happened that the previous man had died and the next was not yet appointed.

On reaching Lincoln, they found the bishop was not in his palace and had to wait three weeks before his return. We are not told how they passed the time, but Margery must have caused the usual mixed reaction, judging from the account of her interviews with the bishop.

Philip Repingdon of Lincoln had, in his youth at Oxford, been a fervent supporter of Wyclif. Later seeing the error of those doctrines, his ardent temperament had carried him to the extreme orthodox position.

Margery's presence among the suppliants outside excited him. It seems that he had heard of her before, since, on learning that she had been at his gates for three weeks, he sent for her at once, saying 'he had long desyred to speke wyth hir.' Taking advantage of his politeness, Margery said she wished to recount her whole spiritual life and all 'the secretys of her sowle'. She had better have an appointment, he said, realizing the interview would not be short.

'Whan the tyme cam', she appeared and harangued him in such a manner on her visions, revelations and those of her prophecies which had turned out to be correct, that he was overcome by enthusiasm. She was in direct contact with the Holy Ghost, he cried. She ought to write a book at once. God had not yet said anything about authorship, she replied, but there was another matter. She had been instructed to ask him for licence to wear the mantle and ring of celibacy and to dress entirely in white. 'If ye clothyn me in erth, owyr Lord Ihesu Cryst shal clothyn yow in Hevyn, as I undyrstond be revelacyon,' she added persuasively.

Here Repingdon became a little less spontaneous. With his history and the present state of alarm about heretics, he dared not support anything eccentric. What about John Kempe, he inquired tactfully? Hadn't they better have his opinion?

All this time, John had been cooling his heels outside in his best suit, no doubt. Let him be brought in, his wife agreed. 'John', said the bishop, 'is it yowr will that yowr wyf shal take the mantle and the ryng and levyn chaste?' 'Ya, my Lord,' he replied obediently, and placed his joined hands between Repingdon's. By this simple ceremony, they were formally separated.

The matter of the white mantle was held over until the bishop could consult with his council. For the moment, he made them 'rygth good cher and seyd we wer rygth wolcome'. A few days later, he invited them to dinner. Before sitting down, he distributed thirteen pence and thirteen loaves to thirteen paupers. The sight moved Margery to the most extravagant applause. Tears poured down her cheeks as she thanked God for having endowed the bishop with such a singular grace and charity. In their astonishment, several members of the episcopal household asked whether she was ill.

To show that he, at least, took her demonstrations as a compliment, Repingdon sent special dishes from his own table to the Kempes. As they ate, some of the officials cross-questioned Margery on her faith. Here she could never be faulted. All her ideas were strictly orthodox. She accepted every dogma, every institution, the whole extent of church authority in this world and the next. Her only claim was that God spoke directly to her in visions and also 'in hir mend', or 'in hir sowle'. There was nothing heretical in that. Unusually violent devotions might be a symptom of deviation, but they were not proof. The clerks were surprised at the readiness and good sense of her answers.

But their misgivings were not entirely overcome. After dinner, the bishop retired to his private room and sent for Margery. His council, he said, had advised that he should not authorize the white mantle without the consent of his superiors. She had his blessing for the journey to Jerusalem. Let the question of wearing white be held in abeyance until her return, when she would be 'bettyr prevyd and knowyn'.

The whole conception of diplomacy was foreign to Margery and she left his presence in a rage. This bishop worried more about what people would say of him 'than the parfyt lofe of God'. 'Owyr Lord Ihesu Crist' directed her to tell him so. God would have forgiven him if he had overstepped his parochial authority in order to oblige a faithful servant. She obtained another interview and informed him of the divine message.

Always courteous, Repingdon replied simply that she was not of his diocese, but that if she got licence from Archbishop Arundel of Canterbury, he would be happy to perform the necessary ceremony.

She had to be content with this and went away, despising him as a weak character, unlike herself who did and said exactly what she thought right, regardless of the consequences. She had other, private matters to discuss with the archbishop, she said grandly, on leaving. Besides, God had told her to receive the mantle from Repingdon only and his words could not be tampered with.

The bishop was not even now offended. He gave her twenty-six shillings and eightpence towards a pilgrim's outfit and asked her to pray for him. Perhaps he admired her courage. At any rate, he wished, as far as circumstances permitted, to keep on the right side of a woman with supernatural gifts.

# CHAPTER X

## Interview with the Archbishop of Canterbury

Margery now had certificates from a variety of respectable religious persons, some reputed holy, like her anchorite confessor at Lynn; some learned, such as Master Alan, Cambridge graduate, author and indexer of prophecies. These were scattered over the parts of the country she had visited during her pilgrimages to English shrines. Though fortified in her way of life and well provided with sympathizers, recent experience had shown that this was not enough. Absolutely first-rate credentials were essential for safety in the present anti-heretic atmosphere.

Anyone could see that Bishop Repingdon would not support her if it came to getting her out of prison, or giving evidence at a trial. But if she could catch the ear of the great Arundel himself, chief persecutor of Lollards and most powerful man in the country after the king, she would have nothing to fear.

'Than this creatur went forth to London wyth hir husbond unto Lambhyth, ther the Erchebisshop lay at that tyme.' She does not record what impression the capital made on them with its walls and gates, its river full of ships, the palaces of lords and merchants which, though only a pale reflection from Italy, were far more impressive than anything at Lynn. She does not mention the Tower, one of the oldest and strongest fortresses in the kingdom, where Henry V often lived, dreaming ambitiously: when he had conquered the whole of France, he would be the most powerful king in Christendom. Then, gathering all his wealth and strength, he would lead a last crusade and rescue the Holy Land for ever from the infidel. Here, too, Oldcastle the arch-heretic awaited execution after his trial in September 1413. It may have been September as the travellers passed.

Disregarding all that as irrelevant, Mr and Mrs Kempe made straight for the archbishop's hall. It was afternoon and the place was full of servants, followers and people who had business with the prelate. There was a tremendous din of conversation, shouting and, in particular, swearing and quarrelling. In her usual manner, Margery went up to the dissident group, and exhorted them to decent behaviour, otherwise they would certainly be damned.

No doubt she enlarged on the theme with scriptural allusions, since she found it difficult to stop, once started, even though she knew it gave the impression that she was a woman preacher, a thing forbidden by the church and often regarded as a mark of heresy.

However, the address may not have been as long as usual, for a woman in a furred coat connected with the fight, found this sanctimonious interference too much. Stepping up to Margery, she cursed her, furiously shouting: 'I wold thu wer in Smythfeld and I wold beryn a fagot to bren the wyth! It is pety that thow levyst,' she screamed, beside herself with rage. The worst had happened. John Kempe was terrified and didn't know what to do. 'This creatur stod stylle and answeryd not', with belated caution. Luckily no one took the woman's side. A nasty moment passed off. The Kempes settled down to wait until their name was called.

It must have been a fine, warm evening, for the archbishop was receiving in his garden. 'Whan sche cam to hys presens, sche salutyd hym as sche cowd.' Beginning with less important questions, she asked for a letter giving her authority to choose her own confessor and to receive communion every Sunday, should God 'dysposen hir therto'. She had, of course, been doing these things for years, but now, feeling herself a marked woman, thought it advisable to have proper licence.

There was nothing heretical in this request and Arundel ordered his clerks to write and seal the letter at once. No, he said, he would take no fee; and the clerks were not to be tipped, either.

Finding him benign, 'sche was wel comfortyd and strengthyd in hir sowle' and ventured to move on to the next subject. Would he confirm her belief that her visions and especially her weeping, to which many people took exception, were true gifts from God? He was ready to listen, in spite of pressure of business. For, though the classes were fixed in their different positions with great distances between them and an archbishop kept the state of a prince, it was possible for a woman of Lynn to gain admittance without ceremony and be treated with all the courtesy and patience which would be extended to a lady on a social call.

So she described her religious experiences in detail, with particular reference to the crying fits. She had often begged God that they might be moderated, since they caused such inconvenience, even danger, sometimes. Christ had replied that he gave, or withheld, his gifts as he pleased. She must be prepared to suffer for his sake.

As her monologue rolled on, Arundel saw there was nothing individual or heretical in her ideas. He had examined many Lollards, but she was not like them. Fervency and imagination had not led her astray. When she had finished, he complimented her on her devotion and encouraged her to continue on her way, devout, celibate, a careful follower of God's word.

Now quite at ease, Margery decided to forestall any complaints about the scene with the fur-coated woman in the hall. He had not been given his great position in the world, she said in her governessy manner, in order to support people who offended God every day by swearing horrible oaths. He would have to answer for it in heaven unless he corrected them or, better still, gave them the sack. He heard her out politely and made an agreeable reply.

Their discourse then continued on general subjects 'tyl sterrys apperyd in the fyrmament'. One feels they must have spoken of pilgrimage and the Holy Land and also of whether white could properly be worn by a wife in Margery's position. One cannot know for certain because her book records merely the extreme length of the conversation. We can only deduce that Arundel realized he was talking to a remarkable woman. Whether he guessed that literature, rather than saintly life, was to be her claim to distinction, we may doubt.

On leaving the archbishop, the Kempes went back to London and stayed for a short while. They must have visited the shrines and relics in the numerous city churches. When people heard what an impression Margery had made on Arundel, 'many worthy men' came to consult her on spiritual questions. People were eager to hear of her visions and other strange experiences. Appreciative crowds watched her tears and contortions as she entered the divine presence. No one inquired if her inspiration was of heaven or hell. On the contrary, all were moved 'to wepyn ryt sadly', such was the general rush of pious emotion. It was a wonderful holiday and must have seemed almost a miracle to poor John Kempe who, for the first recorded time, found himself admired and made much of because he was Margery's husband.

# CHAPTER XI

## Preparations for the Journey

The Jerusalem Journey, as it was called, was the greatest tourist attraction of medieval times. One saw the very places where Christ, the apostles and everyone else mentioned in the Bible, actually lived and worked their miracles. Naturally, ground so sacred had powerful emanations. People returned wiser than they had been before, able to 'argue about the Gospel and the prophets ... and sometimes overcome and set right learned divines in their interpretations of difficult passages of Holy Scripture', wrote Felix Fabri, another fifteenth-century pilgrim.* Prayers were almost bound to be heard, and answered, offered at such favourable sites as these. The mere fact of having knelt at every shrine and dipped oneself in Jordan, was sufficient to assure a man of a straight passage to heaven when the time came.

On the lighter side, there were the excitements of foreign travel, seeing the most interesting parts of the known world and having agreeable adventures with the ladies. There were books which, besides giving information about necessary equipment and rates of exchange, included in their list of useful phrases in Albanian, Arabic, Greek and Turkish, such items as: 'Woman, shall I sleep with you?' Or, more seductively: 'Beautiful maiden, come and sleep with me.' Or, if she proved dilatory: 'Woman, I am already in your bed.'†

'That many are prompted ... by sinful rashness and idle curiosity cannot be doubted', remarks Brother Felix sadly. But, even for those who could afford to travel first class, so to speak, the journey was difficult and sometimes dangerous. Though some pilgrims arranged for bills of exchange, most carried their money on them and were an attraction to robbers. One couldn't be sure that all countries and cities along the route would be at peace.

* *Book of the Wanderings of Brother Felix Fabri.* Palestine Pilgrims' Text Society, 2 vols, 1892. A German Dominican who travelled in 1480–3.
† See *Pilgrimage of Arnold von Harff,* ed. and trans. Malcolm Letts, Hakluyt Society, 1946. Though Fabri and von Harff are somewhat later in date than Margery Kempe, their descriptions are often based on accounts published earlier. They merely add further details and personal notes.

There were pirates on the Mediterranean. Storms might cast one away on an uninhabited, or hostile, shore. Calms might reduce the whole ship's company to starvation. Always one was strenuously on the move, by ship, on foot, or on horseback.

Long before Margery Kempe set out, the crusader kingdom in Palestine had fallen to the Moslems. In the fifteenth century the rulers were the Mamluk sultans of Egypt. Finding themselves the owners of so valuable a property, they organized its exploitation systematically. The different denominations of Christians were allowed to establish small communities to look after the holy places and were obliged to tolerate each other, an attitude which did not come easily to the western medieval temper. From the moment the pilgrims disembarked at Jaffa from Venetian galleys, their board and lodging, outings, tours, guides, devotions and whole timetable were strictly arranged. There were hundreds of sites to be visited and all had to be seen in three weeks at the most, after which the travellers were delivered again to their ships and sent home.

The Moslem government thus made itself responsible for the upkeep of the Holy Land and for visitors' safety in a thoroughly modern and businesslike way. No one could be further from this sophisticated attitude than Margery Kempe, burning with pious fancies, chattering with God, sermonizing everybody, whether they liked it or not. She caught no echo from the Renaissance, now in full swing in Italy. Petrarch had died in 1374, Giotto in 1337. Luca della Robbia and Donatello were her contemporaries. Her ideas and outlook were all of the past. Yet she was by no means unobservant in a general way. Her book shows that. She just found speculation about other possible points of view uninteresting. She could not allow that an alien faith might have merits. In this she was at one with her fellow pilgrims. Though the Moslems had made it possible for innumerable Christians to enter heaven, they were infidels, in league with the Devil, devoted to wickedness.

Before one could set out on the great adventure, there was much to be done. First, as to practical matters. Master Robert Springold, of St Margaret's, announcing her departure from the pulpit, declared 'that yf any man er woman . . . cleymyd any dette of hir husbond or of hir' they should come to her at once and state their case. She does not say how many came; only that she satisfied them. It is reasonable to suppose that she had to see to the sale of property in order to raise the necessary cash for this and her voyage.

Though never yet abroad, she was already an experienced traveller. Indeed, the dangers of foreign parts were not to equal those she had known in Canterbury. Perhaps she bought a new pilgrim's outfit for the occasion with the Bishop of Lincoln's gift. This consisted of a long grey robe with a hood, a broad-brimmed hat marked with a red cross, the scrip, or little satchel for provisions, a water bottle and long staff to lean on at rough places, or at the end of the day. She had to book a passage across the North Sea and join a regular party of pilgrims, as it was not safe to travel alone. She arranged to take a maid with her. John Kempe declined to come, evidently preferring to look after his soul's health at home.

She began her good-byes, visiting all her friends, especially 'the holy ankyr'. He had been particularly staunch, repulsing persistent overtures from the prosperous widow, of whose deceased husband Margery had made disparaging remarks.* He had been promised 'gret frenschepys' if he joined the lady's party, he told her. But he had loyally replied: 'I wyl not forsake hyr for no lady in this reme.' He was not going to abandon 'a lovere of God', one 'hyly inspyred wyth the Holy Gost'.

On these warm terms they parted, recalling certain prophecies he had previously made about difficulties she was to experience with her maid during the pilgrimage. She would be rescued, he said, by a man with a broken back. She was never to see him alive again.

'Than sche toke hir leve of Maystyr Robert' who gave her the special pilgrim's blessing for the voyage. Next, she made a quick visit to Norwich where the vicar of St Stephen's lived, one of her early supporters. She could not ask Dame Julian's blessing, for the famous anchoress had died in 1410, still wrestling unsuccessfully with the problem of putting her spiritual discoveries into words. But William Southfield the Carmelite, to whom the Virgin had frequently given advice, was still there. No doubt she saw him once again. She needed the most efficacious prayers it

* See Chapter Six.

53

was possible to arrange. This friend also, she was not to see again. Finally, she made an offering at the Holy Trinity altar in Norwich cathedral.

Preparations were complete. The ship lay ready at Yarmouth. She said good-bye to her husband and departed. We hear nothing of the fourteen children. Perhaps not all had survived to pray for their mother's safety on this auspicious occasion. Maybe some, in sheer desperation, had gone to the devil.

On reaching the port, she made a last offering to an 'ymage of owyr Lady' and went on board. It was midwinter 1413/14.

# CHAPTER XII

## Misadventures on the Road to Venice

The next day, they docked at Zierikzee, in Zealand 'wher owyr Lord of hys hey goodness vysited this creatur wyth abundawnt teerys of contricyon'. If she had confined her emotional outbursts to thanking God for a safe sea passage, her fellow travellers would have had no complaint. But, as they struggled on, day after day, through every kind of winter weather, traversing the Netherlands and Germany, following the Rhine valley, they became more and more irritated.

One of many practical tips given by contemporary guide books is the absolute necessity of keeping on good terms with one's company. Pilgrim quarrels were notoriously bitter. Give offence to no one, the prospective traveller is advised, for you will only get the worst of it. But Margery was of the opinion that, on this journey above all other occasions, people should try and reach perfection in manners, conversation and general behaviour. Were they not bound for the very spot where God himself had given the supreme demonstration in right thinking? She had always felt it correct to mourn for Christ's sufferings. How much more so now? It was quite wrong to laugh and joke at dinner after the day's journey was safely done. One should speak perpetually on religious subjects and exhort backsliders to better conduct.

To her companions, she seemed to go too far. They felt that there were many interesting subjects to discuss besides heaven. Particularly at dinner, they objected to her monologue. They were sick of her visions and boastings of holiness. What could one expect from a vegetarian and teetotaller? If she could be got to take a drink, or two, there might be some amelioration. A priest of the party, who acted as her confessor, undertook to try his best. He actually managed to persuade her to moderate her fasts. Unfortunately, she could never resist what she believed to be God's will for a mere question of expediency. She reverted.

Things went from bad to worse. 'Thei wer most displesyd for sche wepyd so mech and spak alwey of the lofe and goodnes of owyr Lord as wel at the tabyl as in other place.' They became

55

abusive, saying they were not going to put up with her nonsense as her husband did. She should remember that she was not now 'at hom and in Inglond'. 'Owyr Lord almygty God is as gret a lord her as in Inglond,' she replied sententiously, 'and as gret cawse I to lofe hym her as ther.'

This pious sentiment, so correct in a pilgrim, so impossible to answer without putting oneself in the wrong, enraged them beyond bearing. A bad fight ensued, which was a grief to her, she notes, since they were supposed to be 'ryt good men', and it was her intention always to be agreeable and elevating. Addressing herself to 'oon of hem specyaly', she protested at their violence. But he only shouted that he prayed God the Devil would remove her quickly, 'and many mo cruel wordys he seyd to hir'.

We don't know in exactly which part of Europe the crisis arose, but the account reads as though it were an explosion after weeks of friction when, what with the fatigue of travel and the small effect remonstrance had on Margery, patience abruptly came to an end, it may be over some quite unimportant point. In view of subsequent developments, it seems likely that they were in south Germany, a few days march from Constance, on the borders of Switzerland.

The company had by no means calmed down by the time the night's lodging was reached. The prospect of another dinner with Margery was more than they could stand. She was confronted by a deputation, including her maid: nothing would induce them to have any more to do with her. She could go her own way. The maid was staying with them, feeling herself not sufficiently perfect to accompany so holy an employer. The treasurer of the party, who had charge of her money, threw her a noble,* saying she could shift for herself in future.

By next morning, the less violent began to feel that it was scarcely possible, as Christians, pilgrims and decent men, to cast away a woman in the middle of nowhere, tiresome though she might be. Perhaps they explained her as a penance, sent from God for their sins. Whatever the reason, one of them came to her, saying that if she apologized on all points and promised to reform, they would allow her to go with them as far as Constance. Further they could not endure.

* Six and eightpence.

Peace was patched up, but reluctantly. They did not trust her protestations and she must surely have given reason for the brutal treatment she received on the next stages of the road. They may also have been afraid of her excesses. In 1413, the Pope had denounced the doctrines of Wyclif and Hus, the Bohemian heretic, in strong terms. The main reason seems to have been, however, that they hated the sight of her, yet felt obliged to escort her safely to the city where she could make other arrangements.

Margery always had a ready answer and an apt quotation and must have addressed the people of the villages they passed – necessarily in English which they couldn't understand – in the hope both of edifying her hearers and rallying admirers to her side in order the better to refute the wounding accusations of her companions. She only succeeded in enraging them to such an extent that the more moderate were unable to exert any influence.

Her gown was cut short below the knee and they obliged her to wear a canvas apron, like a working woman. She was always talking of purity, wasn't she? Let the apron be white, then. In such a get-up it would be impossible for the villagers to take her for a person of importance, as had happened. At meals they were determined to enjoy themselves in a normal manner. Instead of a seat appropriate to her station, she should take the bottom of the table 'benethyn alle other' and keep her mouth shut.

These moves she countered by so successful an air of resignation and forgiveness that innkeepers were sorry for her and did surreptitious little services, such as giving her extra good helpings, 'and that grevyd hir felawshep ful evyl'. They redoubled their insults and shocked onlookers, who predicted that they would certainly be murdered in the next lonely place, unless they reformed.

Much alarmed by the prediction, which she considered only too likely to come true, Margery went into a church and 'preyde wyth al hir hert, wyth gret wepyng and many teerys' for divine help. 'Drede the nowt, dowtyr,' said God bracingly. He did not promise that her companions would, or could, mend their ways, but punishment would be deferred until she had parted from them.

She continued the journey with some confidence, therefore. Suffering for the love of God had always given her the deepest satisfaction. Her visions were stronger and more direct at such times. Christ came at once and listened to her complaints. She was assured of heavenly bliss and a magnificent posthumous career as a saint. Nothing could be more appropriate than that these trials and triumphs should happen on a journey to the Holy Land. After all, she need not have driven the party mad with irritation. It would have been possible to demonstrate her superiority without provoking extreme reactions.

It must have been with a great sigh of relief that the travellers sighted Constance, standing splendidly on the head of a peninsula at the end of the lake. The Bishop of Constance was a prince of the Holy Roman Empire. His city contained a magnificent cathedral and many ecclesiastical establishments. Here the Holy Roman Emperor Sigismund was to hold an international conference later in this same year, 1414, and force the whole of Catholic Christendom to agree on the election of a single, legitimate pope. At the beginning of the schism in 1378, there had been two popes. Now there were three. It was unanimously felt that something must be done. In the end, after tremendous discussion, the three popes were persuaded to resign and a fourth, to whom everyone swore obedience, was installed in 1418.

Preparations for this famous Council of Constance had already begun when Margery's company booked into their inn. Preoccupied with her quarrels and, indeed, the problem of reaching Jerusalem at all, she had no leisure for international affairs. On enquiry 'sche herd tellyn of an Englysch frer, a maystyr of divinite and the Popys legat, was in that cite'. He was the man for her. She had never had difficulty in explaining herself to educated people. Her sentiments were so admirable, her views so orthodox. She knew how to flatter, asking spiritual advice humbly, as a woman ought. She had received treatment calculated to shock anyone who had not had to endure her conversation on top of the rigours of midwinter travel across Europe.

Sure enough, he was quite won over. She described the revelations she had experienced, the prophecies she had made and the very deep sorrow she suffered at the thought of the Passion and of a sinful world. Sometimes, she said earnestly, she tried not to have visions, fearing they might be devilish emanations. He was a learned man, close to God. Would he say whether, or not, her apprehensions were justified?

Certainly not, cried the priest, enthusiastically. 'It was the werke of the Holy Gost.' 'The Devyl hath no powyr to werkyn swech grace in a sowle,' he assured her. He would come to her rescue. It would be best to have a plain demonstration of her companions' treatment. Let them invite him to dine.

A dinner was arranged. 'The worshepful legat and doctowr' sat down first, being the most important person present. The others took their places in order of precedence 'and at the last the seyd creatur at the bordys ende syttyng and no word spekyng'. In a way, the occasion was a success. Everyone became cheerful, but why was Margery not joining in, her new friend called down the table? 'And sche sat stylle and answeryd not.'

The fellowship realized what was happening. When the dishes had been cleared away, they put their side of the quarrel. It was beyond human nature to stand her company for another day, they said, unless something was done about it. He seemed to have influence over her. He had also the ecclesiastical authority to order her to give up being vegetarian and teetotal, to leave off the tears of devotion and continual improving lectures. All these things were driving them mad.

The worshipful legate and doctor, however, was unable to oblige them. Firstly, the matters they complained of were all admirable. To be abstemious, faithful and full of pure thoughts were the goals to which everybody ought to aspire. Secondly, it appeared to him that an excellent, even saintly, woman was being disgracefully bullied. If he asked her to cease her exhortations, he said hotly in conclusion, it would only be because they were not worthy to hear them.

'The company was wroth and in gret angyr.' Let the legate take charge, since he admired her so. They would have nothing further to do with her. He could take her money on the spot. Here it was, twenty pounds. No, there was not another sixteen pounds due to her, as she alleged. The maid was staying with them.

The servant seems to have made a few half-hearted protests, for the sake of appearances. Had she really wished to accompany her mistress, what could have prevented her, in the circumstances?

Margery's new friend 'ful benyngly and goodly receyved hir as thow sche had ben hys moddyr'. It was a welcome improvement after the dicipline to which she had been subjected. He put her up and changed her gold into the proper currency. They must have had many delightful talks on theological subjects. Having been vindicated, Margery was, no doubt, especially pious in her own noisy manner. But, charming though this interlude might be, it could not continue long. She must get to Venice in time to catch the galley for Jerusalem.

'Than this creatur went into a cherche and preyd owyr Lorde' to provide her with an escort and guide on the next stage of the journey. She felt sure God would not forsake her at this crucial point. Nor did he. 'An olde man wyth a whyte berde' presented himself. 'My name is Willyam Wever,' he said. He came from Devonshire and was ready to accompany her, if they could come to an agreement about salary. As she had plenty of money, this was soon fixed.

They decided to start immediately. She said good-bye to the legate who had proved a real Samaritan. It was her habit to approach the Deity on behalf of anyone showing her kindness. The most exquisite after-life in heaven was invariably promised. We can assume that they parted with expressions of mutual regard. If a coolness had developed between them, she would have noted it down as one more delightful misfortune redounding to her spiritual credit.

Next, she made a special point of seeking out her late companions to take leave of them. They could see that all their malice had made no difference. She had simply made new arrangements. God was with her and she could not fail. They might, however. For the divine protection only covered the whole party while she was present. This she had had by revelation during the first crisis of the quarrel. She then turned to the servant girl, reminding her that she had broken the solemn contract of service sworn between them.

Most of the pilgrims were not impressed. They did not think much of old William Weaver as a defence against robbers. This was Margery's feeling also, in spite of a brave front. Further, neither of them knew a word of any foreign language. It was true there were vocabularies of useful phrases, such as: Which way? How much? Give me bread, wine, chicken, eggs and so on. But how to pronounce such words, even supposing the authors had heard them correctly? Besides, we do not know that William Weaver was literate. It is no wonder she started out 'wyth ful hevy cher and rewful'.

Nor was Mr Weaver optimistic. As they went along, he began to consider his age and infirmity. In a burst of enthusiasm he had taken on the job. Now he began to be nervous. Suppose they met bandits. 'I am aferd,' he trembled, 'thu shalt be take fro me and I shal be betyn for the.' Gloomy visions of himself lying unconscious and stripped naked by the roadside assailed him.

'Willyam, dredyth yow not,' Margery said briskly. 'God shal kepyn us rygth wel.' She was not as easy as she sounded. The story of the woman taken in adultery kept coming into her head. 'Lord,' she prayed, 'as thow dreve awey hir enmys, so dryfe awey myn enmys.' She was very alarmed by the thought of rape. She had vowed her body to God. Surely he would not allow her to come to a bad end on this lonely mountain track through the Alps.

Thus, they crept along precipitous paths together. The wind must have been piercingly cold, the mountains covered with snow. On some days, perhaps, there were blizzards, or icy rain, or mist. Darkness came down early and, if they lost the way, they might fall over a cliff, or simply freeze to death in this desolate robber country. There were certain pilgrim hymns sung particularly at bad moments to keep the spirits up and call God's attention to his servants' need. One would think that Margery and William must have sung them now.

In the villages, however, everyone was most agreeable. No objections were raised to Margery's habits. On the contrary, innkeepers hurried to put meat and drink before them and their wives often took Margery into their own beds. Either it was due to God's direct protection, or else there was something so forlorn about these two lonely travellers coming through the winter dusk that people pitied them. They must have admired Margery's courage. Also, since they did not know a word of English, it was impossible for her to hector them. In some places, no doubt, they believed her to be a holy woman, possessed of supernatural powers.

This was the most difficult part of the journey. They were following the Inn valley into the heart of the Alps. Finally they came to Resia, where it was necessary to cross over the pass (4944 feet) to the valley of the Adige. The long descent began from here, through ravines, past cascades and overhanging rocks. The scenery was magnificent, but the fifteenth century romantic fancy did not dwell on landscape. It must have been a great moment when they sighted Bolzano, chief centre of trade between Venice and the north, set in a wide basin of luxuriant fertility.

Here they would lie up for a while and recuperate. Some days later, a group of pilgrims came down from the snows. It turned out to be Margery's late companions. When they saw her already comfortably installed in Bolzano, 'than had thei gret wondyr'. Only a miracle, they felt, could have brought her and feeble old Mr Weaver safely over those terrible passes with such expedition. Perhaps she had travelled by supernatural means, flying through the air for instance. Was it a good thing to have cast her off? An emissary was sent to ask if she would consent to apply to be received again into the party.

As she agreed, we must assume that William Weaver had had enough. It may be he had contracted only to go as far as this. Or, he may simply not have been able to stand her undivided attention longer. Or the fatigue was too much for him. We do not know what he was doing so far from Devonshire, unless he was returning from the Holy Land himself. Business may have called him back.

In any event, Margery thought it prudent to take the opportunity of rejoining her former friends. But they, though glad to make use of her as a kind of spiritual insurance, were determined to start with a proper understanding. If they were to receive her, they said, 'ye must makyn a new comnawnt, and that is this, ye schal not speke of the Gospel wher we come, but ye schal syttyn stylle and makyn mery, as we don, bothin at mete and at soper.'

She agreed to observe these rules. 'Than went thei forth to Venyce and thei dwellyd ther xiij wekys.' They had been travelling for about two months.

# CHAPTER XIII

## Venice

In the early fifteenth century, Italy consisted of a number of independent dukedoms and city states. These were perpetually at war, but the fighting was of a particular kind. The ordinary Italian citizen had no taste for military service, so that the armies were made up of mercenaries under their own captains, the condottieri. Since every soldier hoped to live to a respectable age and retire on his savings, it was understood that battles were not to be bloody. Campaigns resembled a game of chess, where certain moves were taken to indicate victory and others defeat. Nor could the loyalty of the captains be relied on in all circumstances, as their connection with Venice, Genoa, Milan, or whatever state it might be, was purely monetary.

It was a civilized way of adding to one's principality and rested on a solid basis of the profits of trade. The Italians were the richest merchants and bankers in Europe and the most educated. They covered their country with the palaces, statues, frescoes, paintings, which have supported the tourist business ever since. Venice had trading posts all over the Levant, even as far east as the Sea of Azov and was beginning to conquer Lombardy at this date. The whole oriental trade was carried in Venetian bottoms; for nobody had yet rounded the Cape of Good Hope. The major part of the pilgrim traffic to the Holy Land took passage in Venetian galleys.

To this unique city, appearing then substantially as it does now, sailed Margery Kempe, restraining floods of holy tears and exhortations as best she could, remembering the covenant made at Bolzano. Her companions were bearing up; she had managed to keep quiet at meals, the point on which they felt most strongly because, if she broke out then, they were cornered.

On arrival, pilgrims were met by touts sent out by the hotel proprietors, eager to attract custom with every variety of sales talk. No one could say how long the stay in Venice would be, as the galleys left, not on a fixed date, but some time between April and June, or even later. The inns of Venice were rough and of doubtful reputation. Rich travellers were usually put up privately.

Members of religious orders were fitted into the appropriate monastery. Merchants were obliged by law to live at the *fondaco*, or trading post, of their nation.

After they had settled into their quarters, the visitors were free to embark on a tremendous round of sightseeing. Every day one could hire a boat and row to a different church containing marvellous relics, often decked with jewels and gold. There was 'an entire hand of the most blessed virgin, St Catherine of Sienna, very large and beauteous with all its flesh and bones';* the arm of St Damian embedded in a golden bowl; the whole remains of St Zacharias, father of John the Baptist, 'with his mouth open'.*

Some relics were puzzling; for instance at S. Giorgio Maggiore, they had 'the head of St James the Less, which I saw also later at Compostela in Galicia. These muddles of the priests I leave to God's judgement.'† Others were delightfully miscellaneous: a thumb of the Emperor Constantine, St Mary Magdalen's breast-bone, a portrait of the Virgin painted by angels, the pitcher used by Jesus when turning the water into wine, a piece of the sponge used to wipe His face on the cross 'and many other famous relics',† each of which the pilgrims reverently kissed. It was also usual to bring one's jewellery, and that of one's friends at home, and press it against the relics.

'I myself', wrote Fabri, 'was . . . the poorest of all our company, yet had I many precious jewels . . . lent me by my friends, patrons and patronesses, in order that I might touch with them the relics and holy places . . . receiving a reward for so doing.' These gems were afterwards incorporated in rosaries where the peculiar sanctity they had received would be most efficacious. One had captured the saint, as it were, and obliged him to second one's prayers.

The surrounding islands were also extremely interesting. At Murano, for example, there was a mass grave containing a great number of the Holy Innocents, as well as the famous glass works. 'There are no such workers in glass anywhere else in the world', was the general opinion, noted by Fabri. 'They make there costly vases of crystal.' 'It is said,' adds von Harff, who was always

---

* *Book of the Wanderings of Felix Fabri*. In 1414, St Catherine was not yet canonized. Evidence of her sainthood was being busily collected in Venice.
† *Pilgrimage of Arnold von Harff*.

Jousting. (From a 15th century copy of Froissart's *Chronicle*. Harley 4379.)

Archbishop Arundel reading a forged papal bull in Canterbury Cathedral. The story that Arundel forged a papal bull in order to further the cause of Henry IV is not corroborated by other writers of the period. (From Créton's *Histoire du Roy d'Angleterre Richard II*. Early 15th century. Harley 1319.)

A queen and her attendants. (From a 15th century copy of Froissart's *Chronicle*. Harley 4380.)

careful to inquire the price of things, 'that one man's stock was valued at 10,000 ducats.'*

The profusion of relics was such that they were stored in heaps, 'laid one over the other without respect, as is the case generally in Lombardy'.† One could buy them, even from the very shrines. At Ravenna, for instance, von Harff was shown 'St John's head, St Pantalaon's head and the head of Jonas who spent three days inside a whale'. He was given 'three pieces of these heads, which I saw him break off'.

In St Mark's, however, they were not fortunate enough to have the apostle's body, as it had been stolen by a German and taken to an island in Lake Constance. Instead, one could see 'the treasure of St Mark, which is of inestimable value in gold, silver and precious stones',† set out on the altar on feast days. There were 'for instance, twelve crowns and twelve stomachers made of gold, pearls, sapphires, balas rubies and emeralds . . . six rare golden crosses . . . the Doge of Venice's hat . . . a large and long unicorn's horn, most highly chased'.†

Next, one could adjourn to the Doge's palace, noting on the way two columns between which criminals were hanged. Visitors were conducted 'by someone belonging to the Doge's court round all the inner chambers of the Doge, even to the Doge's treasury'.‡ If it happened to be the women's festival, one could admire 'a display of women's worldly ornaments so costly'‡ that one was astonished, even after viewing St Mark's.

On the piazza outside, one could watch the Venetian ladies strolling about, wearing a fortune in jewellery, their dresses cut daringly low, their faces painted, their feet in curious, thick-soled shoes. 'I was informed by a merchant', notes von Harff in his practical way, referring to a young woman they saw, 'that in his opinion (her) jewels were worth more than 600,000 ducats.' It was almost as marvellous as the relics.

Tourists were also shown round the arsenal. There one saw innumerable swords, daggers, pikes, crossbows, coats of mail, slings and guns. One could admire the galleys on the stocks, the

* About £1,600.
† Von Harff.
‡ Fabri.

gunpowder factory, the rope works, employing a hundred women, the sail works, the foundry. 'We came next to the government wine cellar where they gave us excellent wine to drink.'* From this store the workpeople in the arsenal drew their rations. It was a strenuous outing: 'we reflected that we had spent four full hours in this place, going about without ever standing still.'*

Those uninterested in military matters and wanting a change from the religious atmosphere might stroll to the Rialto where 'the merchants assemble daily about nine or ten o'clock for their business ... Close by the square sit the money changers who have charge of the merchants' cash.'* One could 'see daily much traffic in spices, silks and other merchandise packed and dispatched to all the trading towns'.* In the streets leading from the Rialto were many shops, 'such as goldsmiths and jewellers selling pearls and precious stones'.* Another street was full of 'tailors, cobblers, rope sellers, linen and cloth dealers and others, trading there without number'.* Above the shops were warehouses, each 'like a monastery dormitory'.* Here every 'merchant in Venice has his store full of merchandise, spices, rare cloths, silk draperies and many other goods'.* The impression of wealth and sophistication was overwhelming, even to Italians from other rich centres, such as Canon Pietro Casola of Milan.†

'I will not attempt to describe the number of large and beautiful palaces splendidly decorated and furnished,' he cries, 'worth, some a hundred, some fifty, some thirty thousand ducats ... The said city, though it is in water has so many beautiful piazzas, beginning with that of St Mark, that they would suffice for any great city placed on the mainland.'

The stocks of tapestries, brocades, silks, carpets, spices, groceries, drugs and wax stupefied him, he records. No less astonishing were the food markets: 'I never saw such a quantity of provisions elsewhere.' In the bakers' shops round St Mark's even the over-eaten were tempted to start again, so appetizing were the loaves. The meat was not much good, true, but the huge quantity and the quality of chickens, butter, cheese, vegetables, fruit, wine,

* Von Harff.

† *Canon Pietro Casola's Pilgrimage to Jerusalem*, 1494. M. M. Newett, Manchester University Press, 1907.

especially from Greece, made one's mouth water. With fish, one was rather let down again. But what was that in the midst of so much excellence?

The only thing in short supply was fresh water, particularly in summer. There were no springs and though people collected every drop of rain from roofs into cisterns, and special barges came from the river Brenta, there was not enough for washing clothes. This made the laundry arrangements not as satisfactory as at Milan.

The spectacular variety of this city was still not exhausted. One could go up the famous campanile, for instance, and obtain a bird's-eye view of the whole island. The stairs inside were so large that it was possible to climb them on horseback. But, perhaps, the various ceremonies in which the Doge himself took part were most satisfying to the tourist eye.

'I saw him going in state to St Mark's church in this manner', relates von Harff. 'First they carried before him eight golden banners, of which four were white and four brown.' Then came 'a picture which was borne on a golden standard', a golden throne with cushion, his hat 'with which he is made a Doge, which is valued at 100,000 ducats'. Directly after this followed the Doge himself, 'most gorgeously dressed, a white lighted candle in a silver candlestick' being held in front of him. Behind 'was carried a sword in a golden sheath'. The procession was headed by 'fourteen minstrels, eight with silver bassoons, from which hung golden cloths with the arms of St Mark, and six pipers with trumpets, also with rich hangings'. The rear was brought up by 'eleven chief lords with the other gentlemen richly attired, fine stately persons'. Thus, the music playing, they passed into the church's dim interior.

It is most probable that Margery's company was in Venice on Ascension Day 1414 and stood among the crowds watching the festival of the wedding of Venice to the sea. This curious ceremonial was held to celebrate a great victory won more than four hundred years previously. After a service in St Mark's, 'The Patriarch with his clergy and the religious from all the convents and the Doge with the Senate and all the guilds',* emerged on to the piazza 'with banners, torches, reliquaries and crosses'.* To the

* Fabri.

sound of bells, trumpets and hymns, the procession moved to the Grand Canal, where ships waited. The Patriarch, Doge and Senate embarked on the great state barge called *Bucentaur*, which, painted, gilded and with its silken hangings and golden figure-head, is still preserved in Venice.

An immense fleet, estimated by onlookers at 'about five thousand'* set sail, to the accompaniment of cannon, trumpets, drums, shouting and singing that seemed 'to shake the very sea'.* At the appointed spot, the Patriarch blessed the waters and the Doge took a gold ring from his finger and threw it overboard 'thereby espousing the sea to Venice'.* Immediately, a host of Venetians tore off their clothes and dived for the ring. The finder kept it and lived tax-free for the rest of the year.

A little later in the month, Corpus Christi Day was almost as exciting. Pilgrims had not seen it celebrated like this anywhere else in Europe. 'The procession was marvellous and contained a vast multitude of priests and religious ... wearing their sacred vest-ments and carrying most precious reliquaries.'* They came out of one door of St Mark's, the Patriarch bearing the host 'and by his side walked the Doge in his costly ducal cap',* followed by the abbots in their mitres, the Senate, the guilds, each presenting a pageant 'with singing and every kind of musical instruments, interludes and spectacles of all sorts'.* No one felt capable of adding up the value of 'so much gold and silver, so many precious stones and costly dresses'.* It was the custom for pilgrims to join the ranks as this dream of oriental splendour wound its way round the decorated square and back into St Mark's by another door.

Nor was this the end. After dinner, there was 'a superb proces-sion with the Corpus Christi, reaching a long way upon the Grand Canal, with many pageants'.* The whole city, it seemed, was on the water, bound for the church of Corpus Christi which belonged to 'rich and noble Venetian ladies, who are nuns of the order of St Dominic'.*

We don't know how many of these possible shows, outings and beauties Margery allowed herself to enjoy. In her book she mentions none of them, though no one was more partial to processions than herself. 'This creatur was howselyd† every

* Fabri.
† Received communion.

Sonday in a gret hows of nunnys,' she notes severely, 'and had gret cher among hem.' She was able to let herself go 'wyth gret devocyon and plentyuows terys' which were appreciated, 'the good ladys of the place were mech amerveylyd therof.' They could not object, being nuns. As rich Venetian ladies, such extravagant piety amazed them. For they had passed beyond the middle ages.

Margery was an antique from a provincial place, two months journey to the north-west. Yet, one must not think of all Italians, or even the majority, as modern and forward-looking. The educated class, who employed the great artists as interior decorators, garden and public square furnishers, was extremely small. But the Italian atmosphere was very different from that of Bishop's Lynn. Here, one was at the centre of civilization. The best minds were finding inspiration not in God, but in pagan Rome. Margery does not mention a classical author anywhere in her book. If she had heard of one, she thought him unworthy of notice. All the splendour of Venice did not rouse her to a single comment, enthusiastic, or otherwise.

She was, however, in a state of excitement, due, perhaps, to the great spread of relics, the innumerable churches in every one of which God might speak to her privately, in English, in the middle of the foreigners; or else the nuns' encouragement made her bold. Whatever the reason 'it happyd, as this creatur sat at mete wyth hir felawshep, that sche rehersyd a text of a Gospel . . . wyth other goode wordys.'

When the company remonstrated, she replied that it was impossible to keep quiet longer. God had commanded her to spread his word. In that case, they said, she would have to make arrangements to dine separately. 'And than sche toke hir chawmbre and ete alone vj wokys', at which date, she was struck down by an illness and thought she might even die. But she recovered, in spite of total neglect from her perfidious servant girl, who was ready enough to cook and wash for the rest of the party.

Thus, in one way and another, Margery and her associates passed their three-months wait in Venice. Pilgrims were always glad when the time of embarkation came. They had spent a lot of money and seen everything worth looking at long before their stay was up.

# CHAPTER XIV

## *Taking Ship*

Although pilgrim accounts of Venice remark on the enormous quantities of valuable merchandise to be seen in the city, none mention the fact that they, themselves, represented an important department of trade. The Venetian government were fully alive to this aspect of things and many enactments were passed to ensure the smooth passage of travellers to the Holy Land and back. The trouble they took was rewarded by an almost complete monopoly of the pilgrim traffic.

Specially licensed guides were on duty all day in the Piazza San Marco and at the Rialto. They must have been linguists and it was their business to help pilgrims in difficulties, finding lodgings, changing money, advising on the purchase of stores and provisions for the voyage and helping to bargain and make a fair contract with the ship's captain. It was their particular charge to see that pilgrims were not cheated. They were expressly forbidden to take commissions from money-changers, or shops. Their wages were regulated by statute. They were to receive whatever tips were offered gracefully and without trying to extort larger sums.

The existence of these fatherly arrangements indicates both the abuses which had become prevalent and the importance attached to revenue from tourists. Nor was this all. Only registered captains could carry pilgrims. Ships must be seaworthy: newly painted alone would not do. Copies of contracts made with pilgrims must be deposited with the magistrates. The agreed date of departure was to be strictly adhered to. The captain was not to put into extra ports on the voyage for purposes of trade. The exact amount of merchandise that could be carried was laid down, along with the number of sailors, their equipment and pay. Clerks were to be employed to make careful notes of everything during the passage. The boats had a cross painted on the hulls at the waterline to prevent overloading.

It can be seen that the Doge and Senate did what they could to remedy the discomforts and dangers of an arduous journey. Every type of rapacity brought to their notice was laboriously embodied in a corrective statute: berths were to be at least eighteen inches wide and long enough to accommodate the feet. All complaints were promptly attended to by specially appointed magistrates. Pilgrims could feel assured that in coming to Venice they were making the most sensible and economical arrangement. Even so, the expense was great. The ticket cost about eight or nine pounds, and as much more again was necessary for incidental expenses. On the Jerusalem journey, experienced travellers advised, one must be prepared to keep one's purse open.

Sailings were twice a year, in spring and autumn. When a sufficient number of pilgrims had gathered in the city, two banners would be set up in the Piazza San Marco. This meant the galley captains were signing on the crew and waiting on board to show prospective passengers over the ship, extolling its comfort, speed, seaworthiness, and the remarkably low price for which parties could be conducted even as far as Jordan, if necessary. For the contract was inclusive, covering all meals, hotel charges, entrance fees, guides and so on, from Venice back to Venice.

One hired a boat and rowed out to the galleys. The captain, who was also the owner, or part owner, received one affably, with drinks, if one seemed likely to pay extra for first-class accommodation and food. The ships were two- or three-masted and propelled by sails, except in harbour, when oars were used. At the bow was a figurehead with a large beak. Aft, was a high poop where the captain lived in an expensively furnished cabin. Under this was a private hold, containing his money and plate, which also accommodated ladies travelling first-class.

The general cabin for pilgrims was the hold under the rowing deck. There were no portholes. Light and air came only through the hatchways. A berth consisted of a space big enough to lie down in chalked on the boards. This would be one's only private place during the voyage. Here, one spread one's mattress, piled one's luggage at its foot and tried to sleep through the noise of snoring, cursing, talking, the sailors running about overhead, the animals in pens on deck stamping, all the creaking and movement of a ship at sea. The heat and smell were horrible.

But this was in the future as the pilgrims surveyed the galley, noting what an excellent boat she was, as the captain said. He was an experienced seaman; had been to the Holy Land many times; knew how to manage the Saracens; was acquainted with every port on the shortest route, there and back. The other galley was extremely inferior. He would not advise anyone to take passage in her. He spoke as a sailor and an honest man.

The next stage was to draw up a contract, in order to bind one's captain to observe certain elementary decencies. The guide books gave examples. One should try and get him to agree to a definite date of departure and the exact price for which he would undertake to sail to Jaffa, the port for Jerusalem, and conduct one round the necessary sights at a reasonable pace, so that one was not utterly exhausted by heat and continuous travel. One should insist on the full complement of mariners being taken, in particular the twenty crossbowmen stipulated by law in this very year, 1414, as a protection against pirates and Turkish war galleys.

It was a good thing to have it in writing that the meals were to be fit for human consumption and regularly served. Should the pilgrims wish to bring their own chickens, space must be reserved for coops on deck; and they must have the right to go into the cookhouse and do their own cooking, as there were those who couldn't stand Italian food day after day. Continual salads dressed with oil were found particularly unappetizing.

A further set of clauses could be inserted with advantage to restrain the captain from trying to combine pilgrims with merchandise, which was, in any case, forbidden by law. Chests of goods were not to be intruded into the pilgrims' cabin, taking up space already paid for dearly enough. Extra ports were not to be entered, unless the pilgrims especially wished.

On account of seasickness, overcrowding, rats, lice, fleas, maggots, foul air and general debility, travellers often fell ill. One should try to provide for such times: the captain must definitely concede the right to come up on deck for air at any hour and to remain there until revived. If the worst happened and one died, one's belongings were not to be seized from those to whom one had willed them. Also, a proportion of the passage money ought to be returned. It might not be possible to get him to agree to carry one's body to the nearest land for proper burial, because a corpse on a ship was considered unlucky by sailors. They preferred to pitch it overboard forthwith.

Lastly, the captain should be asked to give protection against violence from the crew, especially the oarsmen. These were not usually slaves in the fifteenth century, but a sort of conscript, notoriously rough, brutal and inclined to settle any argument in the most primitive manner.

These matters being all agreed and signed, the intending passenger took his contract and had it registered with the proper authorities in the city. There was now no more time for sightseeing or marvelling at shows. Much prudent shopping had to be done before embarkation. On this subject, also, the handbooks gave advice.

Change your money into newly minted Venetian coins, they said; the Moors will accept nothing else. Go to the shop near St Mark's where you can buy 'a fedyr bedde, a matres, too pylwys, too peyre schetis and a qwylt'* and sell them again for half-price on your return. A few pairs of linen drawers are recommended for coolness. On the other hand, it can be very chilly at sea and the careful traveller provided himself with a long warm overcoat.

Laxatives were necessary to combat unhealthy airs, such as those at Famagusta, in Cyprus, which were particularly deadly to English people. The captain should be prevented from putting in there, if possible. One needed a covered pail for the night and in case of seasickness. Although meals were included in the ticket, 'ye schal oft tyme have nede to yowre vytelys'* and it was wise to provide biscuit, bread, wine, water, cheese, eggs, fruit, sausages, sugar, sweetmeats and syrup of ginger to settle the stomach in emergencies. 'Also by yow a cage for half a dosen of hennys',* and a bag of millet for them.

Don't forget to lay in a good restorative, the pilgrim is urged, also rice, figs, raisins 'whyche schal do you gret ese by the wey',† pepper, saffron, cloves and mace. Remember to take a saucepan, frying-pan, plates, cups, saucers, glasses, knives, 'a grater for brede and such nessaryes'.† Above all, have a chest with proper lock and key. There is something about shipboard life that affects men's morals. As a result, it's not safe to leave anything down. Even one's own friends can't be relied on.

Margery's party scurried about from shops to lodgings, gathering provisions. Being very anxious to shake her off, they

* See *Itineraries of William Wey*, 1458. Roxburghe Club, 1857.
† Wey.

did not book her a place on the galley, nor offer to buy her things with their own. So, she had to make separate terms with the galley captain and bargain with the seller of bedding and clothes near St Mark's. In this she could have asked help from the piazza guide on duty in the square at the time. With some triumph, then, she 'cam wher thei weryn and schewyd hem how sche had don'.

This was bad enough. They could hardly have expected the sequel: 'as this creatur was in contemplacyon, owyr Lord warnyd hir' to transfer to another ship. At first, no doubt, her unwilling companions thought it a splendid stroke of luck. God had taken pity on them at last. As the days went by, however, they became less sure. Suppose it was a true message from heaven? Everyone had heard terrible stories of storms, pirates, shipwreck, prolonged calms, murder and supernatural happenings of all sorts. In the end, much against their worldly judgement, they felt obliged to change to the ship divinely chosen for Margery, even though these last-minute re-arrangements meant extra expense, as the captain made difficulties.

The prospect of a month's voyage with a woman who had overcome every effort to dislodge her, put them in an extremely irritated frame of mind, especially those whose pilgrimage was not, strictly speaking, religious. They had come to see the world, to prove themselves well enough off to pay the fare, to enjoy the respect given to a returned traveller from the Holy Land. A hard fate obliged them to listen to incessant homilies whether or not they deviated from certain puritan standards to which they subscribed only in theory. 'Thei durst non otherwyse don'.

It remained only to visit those churches dedicated to saints likely to take a benevolent interest in one's journey over the sea and through the Holy Land. There was St Raphael, the archangel, for instance, who had guided Tobias with such solicitude; St Michael, the slayer of dragons, enemies and all evil things; St Martha, the perfect housewife of the gospels who, if she could not always provide a good inn, would at least give them patience to endure bad ones with suitable Christian resignation; St Christopher, whose sole duty in heaven was to smooth the path of mortal travellers.

At last the time came to hire a boat and row to the galley with one's bedding, pots and pans, food, medicine and hens. Fortified by having kissed a hundred relics and prayed to all the saints, one clambered aboard on the last leg of a journey which was to give one not only social status in the material world, but also a reserved seat in heaven. The flags of the Pope, the captain and the city of Venice were hoisted. The pilgrims sang an appropriate hymn. The sailors chanted orders and responses. The oarsmen sang their rowing song as the ship moved out of harbour and caught the wind in its sails.

# CHAPTER XV

## On Shipboard

The course was southward along the Dalmatian coast, east through the Greek archipelago, Crete, Rhodes, Cyprus, the shores of the Holy Land. It took about a month. Numerous ports were entered in order to take on fresh provisions and to trade. Sometimes the pilots were not as skilful as they ought to have been and the ship struck rocks, or sandbanks, and had to be repaired. Or a sudden storm might come up and split the sails. These adventures were very frightening for the pilgrims, many of whom had never been to sea before. They could not judge how dangerous the situation was, nor had the crew time to explain. Margery and her companions, however, were experienced voyagers in that they had crossed the Channel, at least.

Although it delayed the journey, everyone was glad to put into harbour for a short break. The various cities seemed marvellously beautiful as they approached over the water. The walls were so fine, they thought, the churches so magnificent, the people delightful, the flags and banners welcoming. It was reassuring to feel the solid ground under one's feet again. There was a rush to land, even for an hour or two, in spite of the enormous fares charged by small boatmen who rowed out and offered to ferry them to the quay.

The stay might be extended to a few days. In that case, passengers took the opportunity of lodging in the town to recover health and spirits away from the communal cabin which, for those not fortunate enough to obtain a berth near the hatchways was 'ryght smolderyng hote and stynkyng'.* When the ship dropped anchor, 'be ye sped afore other', advises the practical William Wey, or else the best rooms will be taken and the freshest provisions already bought before you get there. In some places, it was well to be suspicious of fruits, as these were not suited to the English constitution and might cause serious illness. In others, especially Rhodes, the wine is particularly recommended as cheap and good.

Margery does not record places visited en route for Jerusalem,

* Wey.

but we can easily picture this vehement mayor's daughter of Lynn tearing into the churches of Dalmatia and the Greek islands, falling flat on the pavement in the jewelled Byzantine interiors in lakes of tears, with roaring fits, listening to the divine voice issuing from some bright mosaic figure with words of comfort in the East Anglian speech.

She needed support, for her travelling companions were mad with irritation at her and at themselves, no doubt, for having been persuaded to come on this ship simply because she declared the other unsafe. It was impossible to get away from her voice in the cabin and they began to harry her in small, but explosive ways. During the day, the pilgrims' bedding had to be rolled up and hung by a rope from a nail at the head of the berth. One evening, on coming to lay out her mattress, she found they had removed it. When she got it back, a further quarrel blew up. 'A preste wech was in her cumpany' declared one of her sheets was his. 'Sche toke God to wytnesse that it was hire schete.' He swore on a holy book that she lied. 'And so sche had evyr mech tribulacyon tyl sche cam to Iherusalem.' Sometimes she would try and smooth things over, saying: 'I prey yow, serys, beth in charite wyth me, for I am in charite wyth yow.' Let each side forgive the other. It was God's will that they should live in harmony. Perhaps her overtures had a short effect, but the gulf between them was too wide for permanent reconciliation.

Besides, life on board ship got on people's nerves at the best of times. The days were long and empty for the passengers who had no work to do. At dawn there were short prayers before a picture of the Virgin, held up by a sailor. These over, trumpets sounded and the crew began the day's tasks. The pilgrims had to try and think of some distraction. The oarsmen all had jars of wine for sale under their benches. Some bought a good supply and drank all day. Many gambled with dice and cards. The younger and more light-hearted danced, sang, lifted weights, turned somersaults, ran up the rigging, played on bagpipes, flutes, zithers, lutes and whatever other musical instruments they had in their luggage. The serious-minded read improving books, meditated, wrote memoirs, prayed and exhorted their fellows to use this unique opportunity to turn over a new leaf.

At about midday, the boatswain's whistle sounded for prayers again. This time, a chest was converted into an altar near the mast and mass was said, except for the actual sacrament, which was not given at sea, for various practical reasons: the ship did not carry an official priest; the host would not keep fresh in damp weather; there might be a sudden lurch of the ship at the most solemn moment and everything be pitched on to the deck; a worse omen for the voyage than that could scarcely be conceived of; there was not a single inch of space on board that could be dedicated as a holy place; people had sworn, quarrelled, and perjured themselves everywhere, and the sailors could be relied on to kick altar, priest and holy vessels out of their way if an emergency arose; in rough weather, one might sick up the holy sacrament, a thing to be avoided at all costs.

Meals provided a welcome interlude. On the trumpets sounding, everyone rushed to the poop at full speed and sat down, the first comers in the best seats, no matter what their rank in life. Those not quick enough had to dine on the rowers' benches, unprotected from sun, wind or rain, as the case might be. First there was an aperitif. Then salad, mutton, or fish on fast days, pudding, cheese, bread, or biscuit, followed in rapid succession. The various courses, uniformly stale and adulterated, were planked down in front of the diners with the greatest celerity and, as soon as they had swallowed them, trumpets blew and the table-cloths were snatched off.

Dinner for the captain, senior officers and first-class passengers was served immediately afterwards. This was a more stately affair, brought in silver dishes, though the helpings looked smaller. The captain's wine was tasted by a servant before he drank, as if he were a prince. The inferior members of the crew cooked their own food and gnawed it brutishly on deck. Women did not come to table, which must have been a great joy to Margery's companions. They ate at their berths.

As only two meals a day were provided for in the ticket and as one sometimes couldn't face Italian cooking for a bit, the pilgrims often had recourse to their own provisions. Getting out their frying pans and the eggs which were keeping cool in the ballast sand under the cabin floorboards, they would go to the cookhouse where the cooks were cursing, swearing and falling over each other in the small, hot space. It was not easy to obtain permission to do a little private frying from these irate beings. Substantial tips were necessary.

After eating, one might doze for a time, being careful to secure one's money to one's person; it was unsafe to lay down even a pen on board ship, if one hoped to see it again. There were days when everyone seemed to be in a happy dream and an almost celestial harmony to descend on the decks. On other days, tempers were lost on the smallest provocation, knives snatched up and damage done. The crew did not intervene in really fierce fights. It was not wise to do so. Never make enemies at sea, advise experienced travellers, the memory of these fatal disputes before them as they write. Never occupy another man's place unless he has expressly allowed it, or you will be taken for a thief and dealt with accordingly. Make yourself agreeable even to slaves, for you can't tell when you may have need of help. The prudent man, who hopes to survive the perils of the sea, is always watchful, not sitting down anywhere without first testing for soft pitch, keeping away from ropes, above all, not fancying his skill as a sailor and offering to help during storms. On the other hand, one should be manly and not spend one's days miserably taking every medicine recommended by the doctors and poking suspiciously at food in the fear of being poisoned. Moderation and tact are the supreme virtues in these circumstances. One wonders that Margery came through alive.

At sunset, the last public prayers were said. After the first part, the passengers were wished goodnight and sent below. The service then continued in Italian for a further quarter of an hour, ending with a prayer to the parents of St Julian. No one knew what connected this venerable couple with a seafaring life, but the crew could not safely face the night without having addressed them.

Indeed, night contained many trials besides the dangers of sudden shoals and rocks. Everyone was struggling in the hot dark space to lay down his mattress. Perhaps the ship was heeling sharply under a stiff breeze. A shouting match about sheets, such as Margery records, was a mild occurrence. Blood might be shed over accusations of theft, or of taking up more than one's allotted space. Some pilgrims were drunk. Others wouldn't stop talking, or put out their lights until the contents of chamber pots were poured over them. Even then sleep was difficult for anyone of sensitivity. The noises of the sea and wind were almost drowned by snoring, chattering nightmares, the smell, the heat, the vermin, the rats methodically feeding on the cheese and biscuits, bread and sweets with which the passengers hoped to assuage their hunger on succeeding days.

With regard to the vermin, however, there was one interesting point, duly noted in memoirs of the period: none were poisonous. Every known kind of horrible worm and biting creature could be counted in idle moments, except scorpions, toads, vipers and snakes.

Can one wonder that on those glorious days when the anchor dropped at some Calypso isle, people thumbed the phrase books eagerly and practised stuttering Greek for: 'Beautiful maiden, come and sleep with me'? In these places, all the inns were brothels. Women leaned invitingly from every window and beckoned from the doors. Of course, they would rob one, if they could. There was even a chance of being murdered, as these same books remarked. One did not care. One had escaped. Later, at the holy places, on one's knees, one could obtain remission of all sin in perpetuity.

# CHAPTER XVI

## *Jaffa to Jerusalem*

At last, the ship approached the sacred shore. Long before anything could be seen from the deck, the look-out in the crow's-nest shouted down the news. There was great excitement. Everyone scrambled for the gunwales to stare across the water. A Te Deum was sung and certain special hymns. Then all those with musical instruments played them, and those fond of exercise danced with joy. Many people prayed continuously, tears of happiness and thanksgiving pouring down their cheeks. Gradually, the mountain tops came faintly into view. It was like an indistinct vision of heaven.

A glance at the guide books, however, brought one back to reality. Get the captain to make himself responsible for your gear during your absence from the ship. Take a cushion. Take wine, for the Moors don't drink and you won't be able to buy any until you reach Ramleh, first stop on the road to Jerusalem. Take water; the heat and dust are frightful in the desert. Don't let the Saracens jostle against you, or you'll find they've picked your pocket. Don't try and argue with them on religious subjects; you'll only get into trouble. Never make passes at their women. Speak sweetly to all infidels and pay them what they ask, for you are at their mercy, far from home, and many pilgrims have been imprisoned, beaten, tortured for minor indiscretions. Don't stray from your party, either by hurrying ahead in your eagerness to see the holy city, or by lagging behind.

Full of pious emotion and practical advice, therefore, the pilgrims leaned curiously over the side as the ship came to Jaffa, the port for Jerusalem. It had been a 'fine large city, but now it is totally uninhabited'.* One could trace the broken lines of walls and towers and try to imagine how it must have appeared when St Peter lived there, performing famous miracles, especially the raising of Tabitha, his handmaiden, from the dead. 'In this city I did not see any living man,' remarks John Poloner who visited the place in

* *Le Saint Voyage de Jherusalem du Seigneur D'Anglure*, 1395. Société des Anciens Textes Français, 1878.

81

1421.* It was only a sad remembrance of the old crusaders' kingdom.

As soon as it was known that the ship had arrived, however, the scene became less dismal. People from local villages gathered, some with camels, on the shore. The various officials who had to receive and register the pilgrims pitched their tents and set up an office on the quay. After a last meal of tired salad, stringy mutton, mouldy bread and watered wine, the pilgrims prepared to disembark. As they came on deck, the entire crew was lined up, drinking-mugs in hand. It was expedient, the guide books said laconically, to drop something into each of these receptacles.

One landed in small boats and was met by the Prior of Mount Sion, the Franciscan monastery in Jerusalem, and by the Emirs of Gaza and Ramleh, whose clerks immediately wrote down each traveller's name. This was not an easy task. A queue was formed while the officials struggled to pronounce and to transliterate intractable northern names, such as Margery Kempe.

Once entered in the books and given a ticket, the pilgrims were immediately thrust into certain vaults, known as St Peter's Caves. These apartments, dripping with damp and decay, were ordinarily used by animals. The smell was frightful, even to people accustomed to the communal cabin on the ship. There was nothing for it but to shovel the dung into a corner and reflect on those passages in the scriptures describing the great benefits to be obtained from lodging humbly on a dunghill – the story of Job, for instance, who had actually lived in this city for a period, it was said.

It soon became apparent, however, that comfort was only a matter of money. A regular bazaar was established outside the caves. Saracens arrived from all directions with rushes and branches to make beds; scents and sweet-smelling ointments to combat the stench; Arabian gums to burn; rolls of muslin; soap; even precious stones, though these might turn out to be coloured glass on later examination. Everyone began to feel much better. More Saracens came, this time with bread, cool fresh water, hot cakes, fruit, salads and frying-pans in which they would cook you a supper of eggs.

The infidels were very ingenious in their ways of making money.

* *John Poloner's Description of the Holy Land, c. 1421, trs. Aubrey Stewart.* Palestine Pilgrims Text Society, 1894.

They might suddenly demand a penny from everybody as the price of a night's lodging in the caves. As they were numerous, armed and extremely fierce, it was safest to comply. Under a regulation introduced in order to prevent incidents, the pilgrims were supposed to stay in the caves. Interpreting this literally, the Moors had been known to demand another penny from anyone wishing to step outside for a moment during the night.

Another tactic was to bait the Christians with jeers, indecent jokes,* tripping them up, grabbing their cloaks and so on, with the object of provoking an assault which would then have to be paid for very heavily to prevent arrest, imprisonment, torture and heaven knew what more, for the unfortunate offender. Urchins were particularly fond of this game.

Sometimes a few wretched Christian prisoners would be produced, their captors threatening to flay them alive on the spot unless a ransom was paid. If their co-religionists seemed to hesitate, the victim would be pegged out on the ground and the instruments got ready. It seemed certain that these savages would do as they said. Were they not all agents of the Devil? It was impossible to refuse the demand.

One could only turn to the scriptures once more, musing on such holy aphorisms as: 'Of him that taketh away thy goods, ask them not again.' And: 'I say unto you that ye resist not evil.' And: 'Whosoever shall smite thee on thy right cheek, turn to him the other also.' 'Whoso is unable to follow this counsel,' remarks Fabri, 'he cannot pass through the Holy Land in peace.'

Several days might be spent in the caves before the authorities were ready to take the pilgrims on. From dawn, they were be-seiged by what seemed to be hundreds of Saracens, some wishing to sell a great variety of goods; others cooking all kinds of provisions. There was also a large crowd of the curious, come to stare at the Christians, their dress and behaviour. These were often moved to extravagant laughter by what they saw. It was difficult to discover a quiet place in which to say one's prayers. Perhaps Margery did not find this such a hardship, accustomed as she was to the attentions of a hostile audience and the luxury of suffering for the 'lofe of God'.

* Fabri tells of one young man of effeminate appearance who was so upset by this that he stayed on the ship, abandoning the rest of the journey.

Fortunately, there were certain things to be said for Jaffa. The tumbledown vaults in which the pilgrims spent so many damp and smelly hours were part of the house of Simon the Tanner, host to St Peter during his visits to the town. A prominent rock off-shore marked the very patch of sea where the saint pursued his avocation as fisherman. Among these breakers, too, Jonah was pitched down the whale's throat and vomited on to this very beach after three days.

Perhaps the story of 'the virgin giantess Andromeda'* shows the medieval fancy most delightfully at work. The tragedy took place at a remote date, before the age of Noah. 'Her parents stood weeping on the shore'* as their enormous daughter, bound to a group of rocks in the harbour, awaited her fate. Pilgrims could testify to the fearful currents that eddied round her and the breakers' roar, because they had to row through them in a small boat when disembarking. But Perseus slew the dragon just in time and lived happily ever after with his bride in Persia. The monster's bones remained on the beach, objects of admiration to all visitors; 'for every one of its ribs were forty-one feet in length.'*

Eventually, certain saints destroyed them, in case pilgrims should waste their time on heathen marvels. Similarly, the huge chains and iron bands mentioned by ancient authors were not now to be seen. There remained only the bare rocks as a source for speculation. Some people thought the vanished bones had been those of the virgin giantess herself. The more analytically minded pointed out that this could not be so, since she had definitely ended her days in Persia with her husband.

Reading these emendations to the classical story, one can't help feeling that an antediluvian giantess with forty-foot ribs agrees very well with a tale of supernatural monsters, human sacrifice, and figures gliding through the air on magic wings, wearing divine helmet and shield. These old-fashioned pilgrims seem closer to the legend than their modern contemporaries who, discovering Greece and Rome in secular mood, portrayed the familiar shrinking maiden, naked and inviting on her rock.

Interesting though local history might be, it was not for this that the travellers had journeyed so far. At last formalities were

* Fabri.

84

completed and the captain finished haggling with the emirs over port dues and the price of transport to Jerusalem on donkeys. 'We therefore arose with joy and came forth from our prison, even as captives do from the place of their captivity.'* It was advisable to hurry at this point; 'for and ye com by tyme ye may chese the beste mule ... for ye schal pay no more fore the best then for the worst.'† Only if one were superior and expensively connected, like Canon Pietro Casola of Milan, could one say: 'I always let the Ultramontanes – who trod on each other's heels in their haste to leave – rush in front.'

The path to the place where the donkeys were gathered was narrow and steep. At a certain point, officials stopped the travellers and laboriously checked them against the list. At the donkey pound, there was pandemonium. Although the captain had contracted for a suitable number of beasts, every owner for miles around had turned up in the hope of being hired. Lying in wait at the end of the path down which their potential customers came, several of them seized each one as he appeared and tried to drag him towards different animals. It required a good deal of physical force to extricate oneself from this situation.

At last all were mounted and the baggage loaded. Although the drivers had been paid according to general contract, they had to be tipped as well, if one wanted to be sure of their good nature. A huge cavalcade was now formed. There might be two hundred pilgrims and their drivers, the two emirs and their suites, the Prior of Mount Sion and his servants, the galley captains,‡ a detachment of soldiers in the van and rear in case of attack by wild Arabs. Everyone was in great excitement, especially the unsophisticated ultramontanes. The climax of this most expensive adventure would be reached in a couple of days. Jerusalem was thirty-nine miles to the east. It was as if one were riding to heaven: the prescribed trip round the holy city meant a reserved seat in paradise, when the time came.

They observed with interest fields of cotton on the plain and villages where natives poorer than any they had seen came out to beg, making them appreciate the superiority of their own

* Fabri.
† Wey.
‡ There were usually two galleys.

Saracens whom, before, they had regarded as a low lot of infidels bound for hell, whose misery, taking the long view, could scarcely be equalled. Other things, too, made them thoughtful. The inhabitants of the countryside were fanatical Moslems and, plainly, only the sultan's troops saved the travellers from a violent death. It was not in order to insult the Christian religion that the Moors made it impossible for the pious to walk the road to Jerusalem barefoot, a course which would have reflected much glory in this life and secured privileged treatment in heaven, for those hardy enough to persist in it. Everyone could now see what practical considerations guided the authorities in the rule which laid down that if people walked, they must keep up with the donkeys.

On entering towns, however, the regulations were different. It was not seemly that Christians should ride into Moslem towns, through the cemeteries outside. Hot, dusty and fatigued after a day in the saddle, one had to dismount, shoulder one's baggage and march the last mile or so to the gates where more dues had to be paid and the pilgrims usually counted and checked against the official list.

The first night's stop was Ramleh, at the foothills of the mountains. Later in the fifteenth century, the Duke of Burgundy had a hospice built for pilgrims, to save them from the dangers and inconveniences of lodging in the public inn at the market place. In 1414, they had to brave Moslem hostility at the caravanserai as best they could. The thieves were terrible everywhere. Knowing that their victims dared not retaliate, their boldness and insolence was unbounded.

Sometimes it was necessary to halt a day or two at Ramleh for reasons that were not clear to the pilgrims, but were perhaps connected with the state of the road ahead and the gathering of provisions. If he had not done so at Jaffa, or on the galley, the Prior of Mount Sion now addressed his co-religionists in a series of practical exhortations, designed to keep them out of trouble in the holy city. He spoke in Latin and educated members of the audience translated into all necessary languages as he went along. One feels that many unfortunate incidents must lie behind these careful precepts which urged a meek and lowly conduct, not for religious reasons, but from prudence. Thus one would acquire spiritual merit, the prior said, and also live to see one's home again. For the Saracens were, above all, violent and disinclined to make allowances for natural ignorance. It was as if one were Daniel at the entrance of the lion's den.

One should never go out except with a party conducted by an official guide. Deportment should be serious: the Saracens were very suspicious of merriment and apt to think they were being made fun of, a thing they particularly hated. Every effort must be made to keep a straight face if confronted with absurd antics by infidel men or boys: 'the pilgrim ought to turn himself away and remain grave and so he will have peace.'*

It was dangerous even to look in the most innocent manner at passing women, 'because all Saracens are exceeding jealous'.* Should a woman beckon from a window, one could be certain it was a robbers' trap, set by her men. The pilgrim would be lucky to get out of her house alive.

If begged for a drink by a Saracen, one should beware of offering wine in the hope of making oneself agreeable, 'because straightway, after one single draught thereof, he becomes mad and the first man whom he attacks is the pilgrim who gave it him'.* Such was their fanaticism on this subject, that it was unsafe even to have a drink oneself in public. However, if he couldn't manage without it, the pilgrim should 'ask his comrade to stand before him or let him cover himself with his cloak'.*

It was possible to become friendly with a Saracen, but only to a certain extent. They were, by nature, treacherous and their touchiness was beyond belief. Nothing could be more dangerous than to tweak one's supposed friend's beard, or flip him over the ears in the genial European manner. He would at once become a raging fury and one's life might be endangered. Nor should one have financial dealings with him, unless it was absolutely impossible to be cheated.

To enter a mosque was certain death. To step on a grave most unwise, as it was thought to disturb the dead. If assaulted, the right course was to complain to the authorities and if they did nothing to put up with it. It was a mistake to try and avoid payments, no matter of what sort. Remember always, said the prior, that all Moors are dishonest and also all Jews and eastern
* Fabri.

87

Christians. Such people simply have no conscience, especially the last.

Those of noble birth were advised to keep their station secret for reasons too numerous to list. They should refrain from scratching, or painting, names and coats of arms on the monuments. Similarly, the infidels objected to the chipping off of pieces of the holy places, or to any marks, such as the boring of holes, being made on them.

Everyone, in short, should try and behave with decent restraint, queueing up in an orderly way at the shrines, instead of rushing them in a herd so that no one could comfortably perform the proper devotions.

The next item must have made Margery feel that God had prompted the bishops in a faraway England in their refusal to let her wear a white widow's mantle. She could now reflect that, although she had not understood it at the time, she was wearing the regulation pilgrim's uniform by divine decree: 'Let no pilgrim put upon his head white turbans when there are Saracens present,'* or wear white clothes, though it is unreasonable for them to object to this as the Koran contains approving references to Christians in white robes. But, since they have taken up this attitude, one can only comply. In the same way, one must endure one's donkeyman, whatever his character. One can't change to another, 'save with the consent of the driver, because otherwise disturbances arise'.*

Finally, the prior begged his hearers not to forget the poor monks of Mount Sion in Jerusalem. And, should anyone have incurred excommunication by coming to the Holy Land without the Pope's licence, the prior himself would fix it, here and now.

So ended this remarkable sermon, founded on centuries of melancholy experience. Sometimes, no doubt, the Moslems passed through fiercer periods than others. But the ordinary man in the street must always have been dangerous on account of his ignorance of western manners and because the unarmed and helpless pilgrim was a constant temptation to rapacity and violence. On their side, the Christians had all the failings attributed to the Saracens, but, as the prior and all the memoirs and guide books continually emphasized, they could not afford to lose control of

* Fabri.

themselves in the smallest respect, even for a moment. To behave always with the utmost decorum and circumspection was their only sure safe conduct.

With these exhortations and warnings fresh in their minds, the pilgrims laid in hard-boiled eggs, cheese, water and wine for the second and third stages of the journey. One night would be spent camping near some village and supplies would be difficult to renew.

Once more mounted on their donkeys, they began to climb the barren hills of Judaea by precipitous paths, through rocky defiles strewn with boulders, behind which bands of robbers often hid. On these occasions, the travellers would have to halt while the escort drove off the bandits. Then the cavalcade would clatter over the dangerous pass as fast as their mounts could trot. It might not be safe to stop before dark and they would continue winding along some narrow place, hardly able to see the man in front. The donkeys, however, seemed to know the road tolerably well and somewhat calmed a feeling the travellers had of being cast away in a terrible wilderness with a lot of murderous infidels. Could this really be the promised land, flowing with milk and honey? It was so far from conceptions formed in the woods and greens of northern latitudes.

Such a doubt upset the pious. How could anything in holy writ not be true? It must be that the sins of mankind had blighted the countryside. Had not the supreme crime of history been perpetrated here? What more fitting than that the very earth should mourn the Crucifixion? It was a land under a curse. The remains of castles and settlements with their gardens gone to waste proved that the ground had once been fertile. Perhaps, even now, it could be moderately so, were the Saracens not such abominable husbandmen. Or, one could also argue that descriptions of the promised land referred to heaven and not to any terrestrial spot. St Jerome had suggested as much in one of his epistles.

Thus, they tried to comfort themselves, eating cheese and hard-boiled eggs on a stony field in the middle of nowhere, the escort standing guard on the perimeter, for fear of marauding savages. Next day they would see the walls and gates of Jerusalem.

It was now almost midsummer, 1414. The heat and dust of the promised land were greater than anyone had imagined. There were no fruit trees to shade the way, Canon Casola notes complainingly. 'Nor did we come across any beautiful fountains. These are not like the countries of Italy.' Towards evening, they arrived at what they thought was the foot of Mount Shiloh, home of the prophet Samuel, though it seems actually to have been Mount Gibeon, six miles north-west of Jerusalem, an equally sacred spot; for here the Lord appeared to Solomon and the seven sons of Saul were hanged. But, for some unexplained reason, the names had been displaced.

If time and circumstance permitted, the pilgrims were allowed to climb the hill which was also called 'the Mount Joy, a full fair place and a delicious; and there lieth Samuel the Prophet in a fair tomb. And men call it Mount Joy, for it giveth joy to pilgrim's hearts, because that there men first see Jerusalem.'* Everyone felt great rush of emotion. Some knelt in the road and prayed while pious tears fell down their cheeks. This was a proper thing to do and the guide books recommended it.

It seems from Margery's account that her party did not halt on sighting the holy city. Probably, therefore, it was not possible to ascend Mount Gibeon because it was too late in the day; or, the travellers were judged too weary to stand a detour; or, the local inhabitants couldn't be relied on. They must have been quite close before they saw their goal below them. At all events, 'whan this creatur saw Ierusalem, she then rydyng on an asse, sche thankyd God wyth al hir hert.' Such were her fervour and excitement, that a perfect vision of the heavenly Jerusalem burst on her. She saw God's many mansions and the streets paved with gold and precious stones. 'Than for joy . . . sche was in poynt to a fallyn of hir asse.'

The English party were prepared to let her break her head, but two German pilgrims, one of them a priest, caught her as she swayed and gave her spices from their store 'wenyng sche had ben seke'. These charitable Germans found they had to support her the rest of the way to Jerusalem. Perhaps in their weariness they became impatient of her devotions, more sympathetic towards her countrymen; for, on reaching their destination, she felt obliged to say, 'Serys, I prey yow beth nowt displesyd thow I wepe sore in this holy place wher owyr Lord Jhesu Crist was qwyk and ded.'

* *The Marvellous Adventures of Sir John Maundevile.*

Having dismounted, bowed their heads, crossed their hands and, in some cases, taken off their shoes, Margery Kempe and her unwilling companions passed under the gate at that time called 'David's Gate, because the Tower of David overhung it. It was also called the Fish Gate'* as it gave on to the road to Joppa and the sea. 'Through it also came merchants bringing divers stuffs from Ethiopia and Egypt.'*

Singing a Te Deum, they stepped into the place on which the dreams and visions of the saints had centred for fourteen hundred years. Every stone was sacred. Every street had received the footprints of 'owyr Lord Ihesu Crist', his friends, followers and relations. 'Lo, here is the city of the Great King, whose likeness all the churches of the world are not able to present.'* It stood on a bluff above the junction of the two precipitous valleys of Kidron and Hinnom. The lower city was full of steep alleyways. The upper, more level, was at an altitude of about 2,400 feet. 'Round about its walls there once stood eighty three towers and seven fenced castles, whose ruins may be seen to this day most clearly on the north side.'* The walls one sees today had not yet been built.

* *John Poloner's Description of the Holy Land*, 1421. Palestine Pilgrims Text Society, 1894.

# CHAPTER XVII

## The Holy Places

The mere fact of having arrived in Jerusalem earned each pilgrim a plenary indulgence. 'From the gate we went through a long street'* admiring this 'very large and beautiful city ... the fine well-paved streets'* the impressive buildings. Only the presence of innumerable Saracens marred the view. A short walk brought them to 'a fair large courtyard, paved with polished marble of exceeding whiteness.'† This was the forecourt of the church of the Holy Sepulchre, which contained the sites of almost all the events of Christ's last days.

'When we heard this, we flung ourselves down ... before the door of the church and prayed and kissed the earth many times.'* Now began what seems to modern eyes a most extravagant scene. In the fifteenth century, at this spot, it was the regular thing. It gives one some idea of Margery's excesses that, even here, people were astonished and thought she went too far.

As the pilgrims lay on the pavement, the divinity with which it was impregnated entered them. Some remained 'powerless on the ground, forsaken by their strength'.* Some got up and wandered about 'beating their breasts as though they were driven by an evil spirit'.* Others knelt on bare knees 'and prayed with tears, holding their arms out in the form of a cross'.* A certain number sobbed so violently 'that they could not hold themselves up and were forced to sit down and hold their heads with their hands'.* Or else they staggered round, not knowing what they were doing, making 'strange and childish gestures'.* 'The women pilgrims shrieked as though in labour, cried aloud and wept.'*

But, as Margery's career shows plainly, there was always a dissident party. These were people often of a calm, or reserved, temperament. They were not unbelievers. It was just that they found it repulsive to express their devotion thus. Supporting this side, for their own reasons, were the snobs. They felt it showed an illiterate and unsophisticated spirit to be carried away by emotion.

* D'Anglure.
† Fabri.

They were modern, touched by the Renaissance; their beliefs being tinged by the new outlook, it was impossible for them to fall on the ground in floods of holy tears. They had come, perhaps, more from a wish for adventure and to see the world than anything. Lastly, there were the professional pilgrims. These were hired men, travelling in the name of a rich employer who did not fancy the discomfort of a personal journey, but wanted to collect rewards in heaven. They were old hands at the game and could not hope to be overcome by pious feelings. Besides, they were notoriously of bad character.

The collective opposition stood in the courtyard of the church of the Holy Sepulchre, surveying the scene with aversion, superiority or indifference. Most of them 'held such devout people to be fools, hypocrites, vain-glorious, deceivers',* and probably heretics. Afterwards, they usually scorned the devotees, 'disdained to converse with them and disparaged them'.* Some of Margery's party were evidently of this opinion.

When the transports had somewhat abated 'we went up to the door of the church where we looked in through'* hatches used for passing food to the guardians of the Holy Sepulchre who were locked inside. The interior was dark, but they could vaguely see the mound of Calvary 'and we were again thrilled by devout feelings'.* Pious howls and contortions were renewed in full strength. One can hardly imagine what state of hysterics Margery had reached. People threw themselves on the marble footprints marking the place where Christ had sunk down under the cross to rest. There were even traces of blood to be seen.

By now, the pilgrims must have been absolutely exhausted. All day they had been travelling in the heat and dust with in-creasing excitement and nervous strain, culminating in these emotional outbursts. In spite of a desire to remain flat on the ground, penetrated by divine essences, they cannot have been altogether sorry when the Saracens firmly herded them into the Hospital of St John where they were to lodge during their stay in the city. This large building, dating back to crusader times, was adjacent to the church. Those unable to enjoy the holy emanations in a vociferous spirit, must have been delighted at the prospect of supper and bed.

* Fabri.

The supreme experience in Jerusalem for pilgrims was the night's vigil in the church of the Holy Sepulchre. This could not always be arranged immediately, since it depended on the unpredictable Moors, but there were more than enough other sites, almost equally holy, to be visited meanwhile. Indeed, the only question was whether one had sufficient stamina to get round.

Rising 'erly in the morwenyng', perhaps before dawn, the party would set out singing hymns, or murmuring the various rhyming couplets thoughtfully provided by the guide books as an aide-memoire:

> By nethe the cherche and thys auter
> Kyng David lyeth that made the Sawter.
> Nys to thys auter the Apostlelys sett
> When owre Lorde Cryst dyd wasche here fete.'*

These lines refer to the Franciscan church on Mount Sion in the south-western corner of the city. Here also, the Last Supper had been held. 'And evyr this creatur wept abundawntly al the wey that sche went for compassyon of owyr Lordys Passyon.' She received communion in the church, 'for in this place is plenyr remyssyon'.

Other interesting things could be seen there. The upper room of Pentecost, for instance: 'And whan this creatur cam into the place . . . owyr Lord gaf hir gret devocyon.' The pillar to which Christ was bound for scourging; a stone where he stood when preaching. 'Twelve feet from this inscribed stone there is another stone fixed in the ground on the place where the Blessed Virgin Mary sat and listened to her Son's preaching. Also, five paces off, is the place where her cottage stood, wherein she dwelt after her Son's Ascension.'†

One could admire the rocks with which St Stephen had been done to death and peer into a dark opening where martyrs were buried. Everything was close together, ten paces this way, forty paces up, or down, fifty to the left and so on. 'I counted with the greatest care that I could', remarks John Poloner in his *Description of the Holy Land*. His efforts to make his guide correct were methodical and thorough to the last degree.

* Wey.
† Poloner.

94

To help in keeping one's bearings among innumerable points claiming attention, the books listed Latin abbreviations one could mutter as one proceeded. 'Que scola. Domus. Her. Symonis pharisey',* for instance, signified four stopping places: the house where the Virgin went to school; Pilate's house; Herod's palace; Simon the Pharisee's house. This was the Via Dolorosa: 'And her gydes teld wher owyr Lord bare the cros on hys bakke.' 'Forty paces further to the right, nearer the road, is the place where the Blessed Virgin stood'† watching. Here the guides described 'how sche swownyd and how sche fel down . . . and so lay till she was lifted up and carried away by the other women'.† Once the church of St Mary of the Swoon had marked the spot, but it had 'been destroyed by the traitorous Saracens'.†

The party crowded into every shrine, the guides calling for order so that each should be able to see properly and offer at least a prayer. For time pressed. They must hurry on to the Mount of Olives, the Garden of Gethsemane, stopping on the way at the fountain where the Virgin washed the infant Jesus' clothes, the Virgin's tomb.

At this point, Margery had a vision, kneeling 'on hyr knes the tyme of tweyn Messys'. Christ himself addressed her, remarking that all her sins had been forgiven long ago. She could only enlarge her spiritual merit by pilgrimage. Her confessor had been trying to dissuade her from going on to Rome, saying so pure a soul didn't require it. Relations with the English pilgrims continued very bad and the thought of travelling all the way to Rome with her was more than they could bear. 'Notwythstondyng al this,' said God, 'I comawnde thee in the name of Ihesu, dowtyr, that thu go vysite thes holy placys.'

Then the Virgin spoke up and adjured her to be brave. She should not be ashamed of the great gifts God had given her, nor be deflected from her weeping by unworthy criticisms. 'Thes swet spech and dalyawns had this creatur at owyr Ladijs grave' in the valley of Kidron.

The shrines were endless: the Pool of Siloam, the Mount where the Sermon was delivered, Caiaphas' house, places where the Virgin had sat or stood. No wonder the pilgrims complained of

* Wey.
† Poloner.

heat, fatigue and being driven backwards and forwards through dusty streets at top speed. Many, no doubt, were relieved to learn that the Moors made it impossible to visit some places, either because they had become private houses, or else, like the Temple, they had been turned into mosques. These could be ticked off as one hastened to the tree under which Judas had hanged himself, the field bought with the thirty pieces of silver, the exact spot where Peter stood when the cock crowed for the third time.

Those not overwhelmed by piety found opportunity to observe the Moslem scene as they went along. The women, they saw, always wore veils, the men turbans and both sexes long white robes. The houses had flat roofs, they noted, on which the men would sit in the evening coolness. Sometimes women might be seen dancing there to a strange music of cymbal and drum. But the men never joined them in their figures, as was the European custom. At the appointed hours, the Saracens could be seen prostrating themselves in an easterly direction. Their prayers were fervent and decorous, more so than those of many Christians. Some were saddened by the sight. For, the greater the devotion with which the poor infidels worshipped their false god, the worse would be hell's torments hereafter.

The covered bazaars impressed them particularly. Besides carpets, silks, gems, scented ointments and gums, one could buy every kind of cooked food: rice pudding, chickens, fried eggs and many other tasty titbits of unknown name and provenance. They noticed the schools attached to the mosques, where crowds of little boys chanted their lessons in a shrill soprano. 'Ha y la Haylyl la lach,' they seemed to sing as well as foreign ears could understand. 'Ha y la Ha lyl la lach.'*

There were many other inhabitants of Jerusalem, besides the ubiquitous Saracens. Each group had a special quarter to live in, if numerous enough. All the various sorts of Christians were represented by at least one monastery and their spheres of influence in the shrines were carefully regulated: how many masses they were to say and at which altars. Western Christians were obliged to endure these arrangements as best they could, though it was against every tradition of militant Catholicism to allow the open expression of opinions contrary to their own.

* Fabri.

A medieval public house. (From a collection of stories intended to illustrate the four cardinal virtues. Late 14th century. Additional 27695.)

Pilgrims setting off by land and sea. (From a book of 28 miniatures, without text, illustrating chapters 1–5 of Maundevile's *Travels*. Early 15th century. Additional 24189.)

One could only pray that God, in his wisdom, would mend their ways. Meanwhile, one observed with sorrow the Greeks, once a learned and holy Church, 'but now it is darkened by numberless errors';* the Syrians 'who in truth are not Christians but children of the devil';* the Jacobites and Abyssinians who circumcised their children like Saracens; the Nestorians 'led astray by errors of the worst kind';* Armenians, Georgians, Maronites, all wearing enormous beards and full of detestable heresy. These were among the melancholy sights of the holy city, worse even than those ruined streets where the houses were untenanted, except by dead 'camels, horses, asses, dogs and the like',* thrown there because it was more convenient than dragging them outside the city precincts.

* Fabri.

# CHAPTER XVIII

## The Holy Sepulchre

Margery does not tell us whether her vigil in the church of the Holy Sepulchre took place at the beginning, middle, or end of her stay at Jerusalem. Sometimes pilgrims spent several nights in this most holy spot. It all depended on the Moors, who had the keys, and on the degree of piety experienced by the majority of the party: for some, once was quite enough. Margery seems only to have achieved one visit which, she says, lasted from evensong 'til the next day at evynsong-tyme'.

Twenty-four hours was an exceptional vigil. Most travellers speak only of a night, though the Seigneur D'Anglure mentions an almost equally long period in 1395. 'After returning from the above mentioned holy places,' he says, 'all we pilgrims went into the holy church of St Sepulchre together, at the hour of vespers; and we stayed there the whole of that night and the next day until none, when the Saracens opened the doors.'

In Margery's time, this famous church was mainly a twelfth-century building in the romanesque style of southern France, put up by the Latin kings of Jerusalem. They had enlarged the previous structure, incorporating into the main church various adjacent holy sites, such as the mound of Calvary, which had been commemorated by separate chapels. There were mosaics and decorations in the Byzantine manner, as well as the delightful little reliefs characteristic of the French architecture of the time: the raising of Lazarus, for instance, where the spectators, vigorous, square, large-headed figures, were holding their noses in the background.

Attached to the church was a small convent of Franciscans who shared the care of the holy places with some of the despised eastern Christian sects. European pilgrims were specially warned not to encourage heresy by putting offerings into the wrong collecting boxes.

After a day on feet and knees, punctuated by emotional scenes of different kinds, then, the pilgrims gathered in the forecourt of St Sepulchre's towards evening, buying food and drink for picnic meals, as the doors were locked during the vigil. Very respectable and dignified Saracens were stationed at the entrance, Fabri noted, to take the fees. They scrutinized everyone carefully and sometimes checked names against the official list.

Once in, the pilgrims began kissing the nearest holy places incoherently, but were soon called to order by the presiding Franciscans who, first of all, delivered a short homily, running over the rules of good behaviour which were to be observed during the vigil. Some points had already been put in the address at Ramleh: keep a sharp eye on your property, for instance; no carving, or chipping, of holy objects; no pushing and shoving at the shrines. Other annoyances, peculiar to the Holy Sepulchre, were also dealt with. Priests among the pilgrims were not to fight round the altars for the privilege of saying mass at them. Everyone was to take a full part in the programme of devotions arranged.

The procession was then formed and 'the frerys lyftyd up a cros and led the pylgrimys abowte fro one place to another wher owyr Lord had sufferyd ... every man and woman beryng a wax candel in her hand.' As they walked, they sang appropriate hymns 'and the frerys alwey as thei went abowte teld hem what owyr Lord sufferyd in every place'. Thus they wound slowly past the many altars, paying their devotions. Sometimes the precious relics had iron gratings over them for protection and one could only just touch them with one's fingers. This was the case with the fragment of the pillar to which Christ had been bound during his scourging. The stone was of a purple colour, sprinkled with red spots, due either to its own nature, or else to a miracle; opinion was divided.

Singing, sobbing, staggering, weeping, conversing, holding up their lighted tapers, the worshippers revered the spot where a dead man was raised by a touch of the true cross, thus proving its authenticity beyond doubt; where Christ appeared as a gardener to Mary Magdalene; Christ's prison after judgement; the place where the soldiers gambled for his clothes; and the stone on which he sat while crowned with thorns.

Sometime they plunged underground, to the chapel of St Helena, for instance, that magnificent Byzantine princess, in later life at least, mother of the Emperor Constantine. The pillars here, miraculously covered with drops of water in eternal grief at the scenes they had witnessed, had been brought by St Helena from the hall where Christ was judged. Also in this chapel was an enormous shell at which the careful listener could hear groans, shrieks, grindings, the roaring of terrible fires and all the other noises one would expect to rise up through a vent leading directly to hell. Calmer and more reflective pilgrims, however, were inclined to think it a collected echo of what was going on in the church above. The deepest point was reached at a cave, cut out of the rock, where St Helena had unearthed the true cross.

After these subterranean excursions, the procession ascended to ground level and from there to the rock of Calvary, fourteen and a half feet above the pavement. The history of the sacred mound went back to the earliest times, for Adam had died on it and Isaac been brought to it for sacrifice. But these events, though important, were strictly subordinate. Margery had little thought to spare for them. Her moment of supreme vision came at this appropriate spot. For years, she had dwelt on Christ's suffering on the cross, turning it backwards and forwards in her imagination, finding emotional satisfaction in the grisly details of the scene. This was perfectly usual in the middle ages, as were the howls and tears of piety, she so frequently records. But now, she experienced something altogether more intense, which surprised onlookers by its violence, even though it happened in the middle of a crowd of excited devotees.

Holding out her arms in the form of a cross, she fell on the ground in convulsions. The spirit 'walwyd and wrestyd wyth hir body' so that she 'mygth not stondyn ne knelyn'. Extraordinary screams broke from her: 'the cryeng was so lowde and so wondyrful that it made the pepyl astoynd.' Nor could she refrain 'fro krying and roryng thow sche shuld be ded therfor'.

Enveloped by divine essences rising from the opening into which the cross had been inserted, she was overcome by 'holy thowtys and medytacyons and holy contemplacyons'. More plainly than in real life, she saw Jesus nailed to the cross. Rivers of blood flowed 'plenteuowsly' from every part of his 'tendyr body', oozing under the crown of thorns, pouring out of his many wounds, more numerous, by far, than the holes in a dovecot.

This was stronger stuff than anything vouchsafed to Dame Julian at Norwich, or St Bridget of Sweden. The blood was so lifelike. More convulsions followed, 'wondyrfully turnyng and wrestyng hir body on every syde'. And how, she asks, pausing in her narrative, can people say such expression of sorrow is too violent to be genuine? 'We may se eche day . . . both men and women, summe for los of werdly good, sum for affeccyon' giving way to the most extravagant grief, 'cryen and roryn', wringing their hands, seeming quite out of their wits. If anyone advises a woman who has lost a lover to pull herself together and be sensible, he gets the usual answer: 'thei loved ther frend so mech and he was so gentyl and so kende to hem that thei may be no wey forgetyn hym.' Obviously, the greatest possible feeling, properly vented, is obligatory for the death of Christ, our heavenly lover.

Thus fortified by the essential rightness of her conduct, she continued her demonstrations unabated, particularly at the place where Jesus was nailed to the cross and the stone on which his corpse was laid when taken down. Here, also, red spots were to be observed. Nearby was the holy sepulchre, surrounded by lighted lamps. As Margery 'entyrd that holy place, sche fel down wyth hir candel in hir hand as sche shuld a deyd for sorwe'. When she recovered sufficiently to stand, her grief was as great 'as thow sche had seyn owyr Lord berijd even befor hir'.

Masses were sung at regular intervals and everyone could receive communion, as Margery did, in the chapel on the rock of Calvary.

'When the procession was over, the pilgrims drew together according to their several companies into the various corners of the church . . . for we were wearied and worn out, and we made a sober meal. After we had eaten, we leaned our heads against the wall for a short rest and lay asleep on the pavement.'*

There was still plenty of time to fill in before the Saracens unlocked the doors. One could visit all the shrines again and many did so. The quieter spirits preferred this second round. The meaning of things and the truths of religion seemed nearer than 'in the general procession in which there is much pushing and disorder and disturbance and singing and weeping'.*

Distractions were still numerous. One could not help noticing the eastern heretics performing their abominable rites at the altars in their charge. Perhaps, on reflection, these were less reprehensible than the priests among the Latin pilgrims fighting

* Fabri.

to say mass at the holy sepulchre. At times, they came even to blows. For it was a most useful certificate at home to have succeeded in taking one's place before so holy an altar. Some had been paid to do so by patrons. Others were overwhelmed by zeal. A mass performed here did more good to the celebrant and to souls in purgatory than any other. As soon as one had finished, his vestments were torn off him by the impatient queue.

The vigil was much too long. Only the most ardent and holy spirit could sustain a rapt devotion for hours on end. Lesser people found their mundane thoughts and feelings creeping back, despite the divine exhalations rising on every hand. Knights who had churches on their estates to which offerings were not largely made sometimes took this opportunity to slink about with a secret hammer and chisel. A chip off the holy sepulchre, a scraping from the true cross, would draw the congregation at home. Miracles might even happen and the happy knight would live richly ever after.

Persons with a head for business thought it safer and, probably, equally profitable to buy from the eastern Christian traders who had spread out 'precious stones . . . cloth of damask, of camlet and of silk'* just inside the door. They had got in by paying large fees to the Saracen guards and their keenness to drive a bargain was extraordinary. 'They never even sleep during the time that the pilgrims are in the holy land', remarks Fabri. The noise of haggling echoed through the church.

As noisy, though less venal, were those who strolled about talking in loud voices of fights they had been in; or places visited; or tight corners cleverly got out of; or gossip of mutual acquaintances. They would stand in front of the shrines, laughing and arguing, without the slightest regard for anyone on his knees before the holy mysteries. Yet, such behaviour was preferable to those who wandered round with a piece of chalk, or charcoal, or a bottle of ink, idly writing their names on any flat surface, to show subsequent travellers that they had been there; and also from a vague feeling that God would notice it and give them credit in heaven. Many of the mosaics had been damaged by knights nailing on to them representations of their coats of arms.

On the whole, those who sat in a corner and got drunk were

* Fabri.

less obnoxious, provided they didn't become quarrelsome. The most perfect solution to boredom and too high a spiritual standard was found by pilgrims overcome with exhaustion from heat and sightseeing: these lay motionless on the floor in a dead sleep, in spite of the myriad bugs that lived in every crack.

We can assume that Margery spent the hours staggering from altar to altar, screaming the new scream, writhing in the grip of divine spirits, conversing agreeably with God, the Virgin and all the saints, experiencing such piercing visions 'that sche cowde nevyr expressyn hem aftyr, so hy and so holy thei weryn'. While, all around, the vaults re-echoed a confusion of shouting, haggling, swearing, laughing, snoring, the chink of money and many foot-steps tramping to and fro and up and down.

Suddenly it was over. The Saracens flung open the doors, crashing them back on the hinges. Some pilgrims ran quickly round the nearest holy places, kissing them once more. But the Moors were impatient of delay and took strong measures. Banging the doors sharply against the wall so that none could fail to hear, they rushed into the church bellowing incomprehensibly, seizing the pilgrims and driving them out. When they had cleared the church, they locked up 'and went their way, leaving us in the courtyard outside',* rather dazed.

* Fabri.

# CHAPTER XIX

## Excursions

The list of sights was by no means exhausted once the pilgrims had seen everything in Jerusalem. One feels for the galley captain, to whom the mere thought of another holy place, another lot of Saracens, fees, donkeys, lodgings, provisions, miracles, devotions, must have become altogether repugnant. With what boredom must he have listened to the naïve excitement of outer barbarians from the fringe of Europe who had never been anywhere or seen anything. A smart man could make money in the tourist business, certainly, but he had to work for it. If the Moors were awkward and the programme was held up, his charges immediately turned on him, brandishing their contracts with accusations of theft, bribery, sharp practice and corrupt dealings with infidels. He had to calm them as well as he could, trying to prevent violence which, at best, made the Moslems put the price up, seeing that he was under pressure to settle matters quickly; or, at worst, caused disagreeable incidents.

Margery, however, had no complaints of this sort. Compared with the sufferings she endured at the hands of her English companions she found the Saracens distinctly sympathetic. They 'mad mych of hir,' she notes, 'and conveyd hir and leddyn hir abowtyn in the cuntre wher sche wold gon.' For there were several excursions to be made in the neighbourhood of Jerusalem.

One was to Bethlehem, five or six miles south of the city. Mounted on donkeys, the pilgrims 'went along a very gay and beautiful road, with beautiful gardens on both sides'.* Much else of interest was to be seen. Three springs, for instance, which had begun to flow as the three kings followed the star along this very road. One could trace the ruins of a tower 'where Jacob wrestled with the angel'† and admire Rachel's tomb 'finely built by the Saracens'.‡

As they jogged on, with halts for prayers at the various shrines, the Franciscans, accompanying the party, recalled other

* Casola.
† Poloner.
‡ Von Harff.

illustrious travellers of the Bible age: 'Isaiah, Elijah and many of
the holy prophets';* Abraham, Lot and their respective wives;
above all, the Holy Family. Places were pointed out where the
Virgin, when pregnant, had sat down to rest, not so much on
account of her own fatigue, but out of pity for Joseph who, being
less closely connected with divinity than herself, felt the heat
more.

Further on, they passed 'an ancient building'† marking the
spot where 'the angel took Habakkuk by the hair and carried him
to Babylon, which is called Cairo, to the lion's den where Daniel
the prophet was imprisoned'.†

With all these diversions, it is not surprising that the journey
took three hours. But, at last, across the deep valley where the
shepherds watched their flocks on the night the star appeared,
they saw Bethlehem standing on its hill, 'a little city, long and
narrow and well walled and on each side enclosed with good
ditches.'‡ The pilgrims got off their donkeys and said an appropriate prayer. Remounting, they hurried over the last stage,
while 'some wept for joy and piety; some in their mirth sang the
well known Christmas hymns'.§

The church of the Nativity of St Mary, though rather dilapidated, was large and striking. 'It was more beautiful formerly
than at present', remarks the Seigneur D'Anglure sadly. Nevertheless, one could still get a wonderful impression of grandeur
and richness. Dating from the time of Constantine, the nave
contained 'forty-four marble pillars in three rows'.|| The roof was
made of precious woods from Mount Lebanon and covered with
lead. Within were twelfth-century Byzantine mosaics in 'gold,
silver, azure and other colours'.‡

A number of Saracens waited at the church, some with candles
for sale and others ready to collect entrance fees. Having paid and
bought, the pilgrims went in, the more emotional among them
in an extravagant state of devotion. For, as the Holy Sepulchre
contained almost everything connected with Christ's last days,

* Poloner.
† Von Harff.
‡ Maundevile.
§ Fabri.
|| D'Anglure.

St Mary's at Bethlehem enshrined the story of his birth.

In the main church was the altar where the holy infant was circumcised: 'While a man stoops down to kiss the place, an unusual odour is breathed out towards him, which delights him and inclines him to worship.'* The effect of this on Margery must have been terrific. It was not possible to circumcise the child in the stable, explains Fabri reasonably, 'because of the darkness; and it may be that the circumcisers disliked the smell of the stable.' Also in this part of the church, was a chapel commemorating the place where the three kings, Caspar, Melchior and Balthazar, got off their camels, unpacked the presents, and put on their best clothes.

The most exciting places were underground. One descended stairs and came to a magnificently decorated chapel where the Virgin had been delivered, 'adorned with marble and full richly painted'.† A stone was shown where the newly born Christ had been laid. Here also, strange scents intoxicated the devout. A scientific examination showed no earthly source from which they could have emanated. 'So we . . . remained for a long time kissing the sacred stone and received plenary indulgences.'*

'And three paces beyond is the crib of the ox and the ass',† a fine marble affair, bathed in divine essences and so highly polished that, by a trick of light, an extraordinary illusion was produced: 'If carefully and minutely looked at, there appears in it the figure of an old bearded man, lying on his back on a mat, in the dress of a dead monk and beside him the figure of a lion. This picture is not produced by art, or work, but by simple polishing alone.'* Some regarded it as a miraculous portrait of St Jerome, who had lived here a long time, translating the scriptures into Latin.

Margery found all this very stimulating. For God had expressly received her into the Holy Family in a marvellous dream at St Margaret's in Lynn‡ 'Whan sche cam to the tempyl and to the crybbe wher owyr Lord was born', her visions of childbirth, of which she had such extensive experience, were so intense, her 'gret devocyon' and the 'dalyawns in hyr sowle and hy gostly

* Fabri.
† Maundevile.
‡ See p. 22.

comfort' so extravagent, that her companions felt supper would be unendurable, unless strict measures were taken: they forbade her to 'etyn in ther cumpany'. How could one digest with a crazy woman lecturing about herself nonstop?

Besides, they were not through yet. A number of very exciting items remained. The well down which the star of Bethlehem had fallen, for instance. It was said that the pure in heart, on looking into the shaft, could see the actual star, passing over the dark water 'in the same manner wherein stars are wont to cross the vault of heaven'.* Some people doubted the story, though there was a strong party of believers, including 'many doctors of the catholic faith'.* Margery was not a woman to question the powers of heaven, but she doesn't claim to have seen the star.

The cave where the Virgin sheltered before the flight into Egypt was particularly curious. Here, a certain white substance oozed from a stone. This was a drop of the Virgin's milk miraculously flowing for ever. Many churches in Europe had bottles of it. Also in the grotto was a certain 'white earth like unslaked lime',† which, mixed with water and taken at the right time, ensured safe childbirth and plenty of milk. It was drunk by heathens, Jews and Christians alike. Here again, the more educated were inclined to suspect the miraculous ooze. But most pilgrims got out their own bottles and filled them.

Also under the church was a vault where 'were cast many thousand bodies of the Holy Innocents'.* Not only on the island of Murano, at Venice, but throughout Europe, pieces of Innocents, and often entire bodies, were preserved in great numbers. 'Noblemen who go to Jerusalem take a special interest in relics of the Holy Innocents, I know not for what reason.'* They were only for sale in Cairo, however, 'where the Lord Soldan had them in his own keeping'.* It was evidently the most valuable line in the relic trade. Any woman whose child was still-born, or died in its first few weeks, could sell the body to the tourist workshop where it was suitably cut up and embalmed. How many of the

* Fabri.
† Von Harff.

bodies revered in western Christendom were actually little Arabs, Syrians, Greeks or Egyptians, no one presumed to say. 'I do not set much value upon new relics . . . especially those which have been purchased from Saracens, or from Eastern Christians', Fabri remarks cautiously. Margery notes that she obtained 'many gret relykys' in the Holy Land. Some were presented to her by the Franciscans. Others she must have bought.

When every chapel, relic and shrine in and round Bethlehem had been gazed at, prayed before, ticked off their list, the pilgrims re-mounted and took the beautiful road back to Jerusalem. Possibly, Margery's party may have spent a night at Bethlehem, if it was late when they received the last set of plenary indulgences and sang the last mass.

At all events, when supper-time came, the Franciscans were shocked to find Margery eating in a corner by herself. Here was an exemplary pilgrim victimized for her piety in a disgraceful manner. If only everyone were like her, thoughts fixed on holy things without worldly adulteration. They invited her to dine with them. Her conversation, they then observed, was very elevating, her sentiments admirable. She expressed no idea with which they were not in perfect agreement. As for her visions of God, such things happened and the irreligious laity were only too prone to laugh. They had heard of a woman famous in England for her saintliness and familiarity with Christ. This might be she. 'And on of the frerys askyd on of hir felawshep yf that wer' so.

'Whan this cam to hir knowlach', she realized that God's promise to make her famous throughout the world had been fulfilled. 'Dowtyr,' he had said, 'I shal makyn al the werld to wondryn of the.' It was her fate to be despised and mocked at by certain sections of the public, exactly as Jesus himself had experienced. Encouraged in her uncompromising behaviour, she did nothing to conciliate her English companions.

When the time came to make the expedition to Jordan, they refused absolutely to have her in the party. As was her habit, she retired to the nearest chapel to consult 'owyr Lord Ihesu'. She should accompany them he said firmly, 'whethyr thei wold er not'. 'And than sche went forth be the grace of God and askyd hem no leve.' The fact that she had the Franciscans on her side made it easier to follow the divine advice. It was impossible, under these auspices, for them to prevent her trundling along behind on the inevitable donkey. They had to content themselves with either cutting her dead, or insulting her, as circumstances allowed. These 'shamys and reprevys' were a pleasure to endure for 'the lofe of owyr Lord'. She felt it was doing her good and 'was evyr mor strengthyd'. Her companions could only curse their luck.

The road to Jordan was precipitous, wild and dangerous. From the plateau on which Jerusalem stood, at about two thousand four hundred feet, one had to descend over three thousand feet in twenty miles, or so, to the valley of the famous river. The heat in this narrow cleft, a thousand feet below sea level, was tropical and pilgrims often caught fevers as a result of the excursion. No food could be obtained on the way. One had to stock up with hard-boiled eggs, smoked meat and anything else that seemed likely to keep moderately fresh.

At first, the path was familiar: across the Kidron valley, skirting the Mount of Olives to Bethany where 'Mary and Martha dwellyd'. 'Beneath the castle may be seen the sepulchre of Lazarus'* where Christ raised him 'fro deth into lyfe'. Here, 'there was once a great church whose pillars may be seen standing to this day.'* 'One bowshot' from Martha's house 'lower down the hill toward the south, was the Magdalen's house, on whose site stands a ruined church, now made into a goat byre.'*

Once past these melancholy shrines, the pilgrims, accompanied as usual by the galley captains, the Franciscans of Jerusalem and a Saracen guard, trotted as fast as possible over the desert. It was marvellous how the donkeys kept their feet, letting themselves down the steep places more neatly than a horse could ever do. Sometimes they rode during the night, clattering through Jericho, at that date in ruins, before dawn and reaching the banks of Jordan at first light.

These were magic waters, winding, full of mud, between steep banks. Though the distance from the Lake of Galilee to the Dead Sea is only sixty miles in a straight line, the river covers a hundred and eighty three miles, descending lower and lower below the sea. The heat and desolation were indescribable. Lions and wild

* Poloner.

boars could often be seen. Here, where the pilgrims were taking off their clothes, Jesus Himself had stripped and the Holy Ghost had descended on Him.

It had always been a divine river, for Jacob had had to overcome the angel before crossing – though in the middle ages the incident had somehow been transferred to the Bethlehem road. The place retained a peculiar potency connected rather with the pagan god of the Jordan, often shown reclining on a rock in the background in early mosaics, than with the Baptism. Time could be arrested, for instance, for as long as one remained immersed. A bath lasting a day would give an extra day of youth. Bales of cloth thoroughly soaked and afterwards made up into clothes conferred innumerable benefits on the wearer. Small bells, which could be bought in Venice, would, after baptism, avert natural calamities, such as lightning, if rung at the appropriate moment.

The spirit of the river had its sinister aspect as well. Many pilgrims had been drowned trying to swim to the opposite bank because, in the middle, a mysterious paralysis had come over them and they had sunk. For this reason, the Saracens absolutely forbade anyone, however strong a swimmer, to cross to the further side, or to dive under the water. This rule was often disobeyed and the Moors then had to go in on horseback and try to rescue the culprit.

Pilgrims also liked to fill their water bottles in the holy stream, but this too, was strictly prohibited. For it was well known that long calms, or savage storms, could beset the galley carrying Jordan water back to Venice. In any such emergency, the sailors would furiously search passengers' baggage, turning everything upside down, certain that a bottle of the potent water would be found to account for their misfortune.

To these haunted banks came Margery Kempe, perhaps reduced to silence, for 'the wedyr was so hoot that sche wend hir feet schuld a brent for the hete that sche felt'. The lukewarm stream can hardly have been refreshing in the ordinary sense of the word. She must have paddled with the other women among the reeds. One would expect her to have had great visions of herself taking part in the Baptism, holding the towel, or arranging the clothes conveniently on the shore. She records nothing of the sort. Maybe fatigue had dulled her faculties; she was not young.

When the Saracens thought the pilgrims had had enough time for bathing and baptising each other, they ordered them out, employing violence if not immediately obeyed. Everyone, therefore, dressed and got upon his donkey for the ride to Mount Quarantana, on which Christ fasted for forty days and was tempted by the Devil. The path wound through a hilly wilderness where nothing grew except the most ferocious thorn bushes, said to have been cut to make the crown of thorns. They passed Jericho again. The gardens, especially the roses, seemed particularly charming after the desert. Continuing, they came to a spring, called Elisha's Fountain. Here it was usual to rest and have a picnic lunch. The local Arabs came with fruit and other foods for sale.

After this, they broached the mountain proper. It was extremely steep, the rocks dotted with caves in which hermits had lived in the early centuries of the Christian era. It was a dangerous scramble to reach the chapel of the Temptation among the cliffs near the summit. One had to crawl along the face of a precipice. Many pilgrims dared not pass this point, the way was so narrow and crumbling, the abyss so deep.

Margery got stuck and begged her companions 'to helpyn hir up to the Mownt. And thei seyd nay, for thei cowd not wel helpyn hemself.' It seemed a wonderful opportunity to get rid of her, to visit one shrine, at least, without having to endure her tiresomeness, especially since the new and piercing scream had been added to her repertoire. God had taken pity on them at last, in answer to repeated prayers.

Yet, they were deceived in thinking God had lifted this penance from their nerves. As she sat weeping in the scorching sun, a Saracen climbed into view, 'and sche put a grote in hys hand' and made signs indicating that she wished to be dragged up to the chapel. A groat was evidently fair payment: the Saracen immediately seized her by the arm and they reached the top triumphantly, very hot and 'sor athryste'. Here, an infidel demanded an entrance fee.

When they heard her dreadful voice once more pursuing them, even to the top of cliffs, the English party were thoroughly put out. They refused to speak to her, to relieve her thirst, to have her anywhere near them. They must have cursed her in their rage, for the Franciscans were shocked, saying she had better stay with them, for the time being.

The pilgrims stood on the edge where Christ had been invited to throw himself over, and wandered among the many caves. One could see traces of the beds on which the saints had slept, their cooking arrangements and niches for their books. In some places were the remains of frescoes. Other hermitages could not be reached except by goats. It seemed that the monks must have had secret ways of approach, now forgotten. Only wild beasts lay on those beds and admired the view from doorways opening straight on to the void. Here was represented a very different form of Christianity from that the pilgrims knew. This was the golden age, before the Pope became a temporal prince, the bishops civil servants, the priests greedy for tithes. On these hot, bare rocks the saints had sat in rags, with little food, sustained by divine communion and purity of heart. But the world had moved on since then. Hermits still existed; the voice of God was sometimes heard; saints were to be found. Yet, such phenomena were much too rare. There were too many fakes about, bellowing in pretended ecstasy. Too often, the church was a career in this world, rather than a preparation for the next.

Soon, it was time to descend, as best one could, with God's help. It must have been late in a very active day. There was an inn, of sorts, near Jericho. Many pilgrims, having got so far, made a trip to the shores of the Dead Sea, which was reputed full of monsters, some dangerous to humankind. In the distance, the faithful could discern vague shapes in the water: these were the drowned cities of Sodom and Gomorrah. Lot's wife in the form of a pillar of salt still stood at the water's edge. It was a strange, accursed region deep in the earth, twelve hundred or so feet below the sea, torrid, overhung by strong smells, the barren ground either blackened or covered with salt as though it had just been snowing.

Margery does not say she went to this sea, only that on 'comyn down of the Mownt, as God wold, sche went forth to the place wher Seynt Ion Baptyst was born', which was south of Jericho, near the Jordan. In the vision at Lynn, she had assisted at St John's birth, as well as Christ's. Now she stood on the actual spot where the historical St John had begun his earthly career, perhaps really with her help. Who could say? The ways of heaven were different from those of the world. She must have had some inspired moments at the altar of the chapel commemorating the event. It was one more cross for her long-suffering fellowship.

# CHAPTER XX

## *Return to Italy*

'Sche was iij wekys in Ierusalem and in the cuntreys therabowtyn', visiting 'many mo placys than be wretyn'. Twenty years after, when dictating her book, she could not remember all the names, nor all the magnificent visions and holy converse with the Deity she had enjoyed. It had been a marvellous experience, was the nearest she could get to a general description. Hitherto, her imagination had been fed by the Bible and the books of religious life she had absorbed. Now memory could add the background, the authentic setting of Jesus, the Virgin and saints. This must have appealed to the shrewd, realistic side of her character, which was so marked whenever she strayed from improving subjects.

We must admire her stamina. The convulsions and screaming devotions were enough to prostrate anyone, as she herself remarks. These were continuous, in the circumstances, and must be added to traveller's fatigue, heat, bad food, rough accommodation and a programme of sightseeing that it seems hardly possible to compress into three weeks. It was quite usual for pilgrims to die either at Jerusalem, where there was a special cemetery for them, or on the voyage back to Venice. But Margery remained in perfect health.

The Franciscans were sorry to say good-bye to an exemplary pilgrim, one who was never bored by endless relics; who never expressed the slightest incredulity when informed of improbable miracles; found no vigil too long; sought to elevate the mood of less serious companions at every opportunity. They may also have been afraid that her fellowship would subject her to indignities, even dangers. For we must suppose that she had related to these sympathetic hearers previous humiliations and punishments suffered for 'the lofe of God'.

She would have liked to stay longer in the holy city, exploring more widely, but she had paid the return fare and was determined to go on to Rome. It was God's wish and, though the English party had made it plain they didn't care for the idea, they hadn't actually refused to accompany her. The Franciscans, therefore, 'mad hir gret cher' in a warm farewell, presenting relics and 'desiryng that sche schuld a dwellyd stille amongs hem'.

The last day came. Some pilgrims made the trip more than once, but for the majority it was a final good-bye to the most famous part of Christendom. All had seen what mattered of the world and secured a place in paradise when the time came. Future conduct could not alter that. Everything, except their right of entry, had been blotted out of the heavenly registers. On returning home, they would be admired and looked up to as sagacious members of society. They had breathed divine emanations, bathed in magic rivers and some faint essence of the supernatural clung to them. For a few, the experience was the culmination of terrestrial life. Among the donkeys gathered to transport the pilgrims to Joppa were camels with large baskets strapped on their sides. These were for the sick who could not ride.

When they were all marshalled into proper order, the armed guards before and behind, the tickets checked and numbers counted, the cavalcade set out towards Ramleh. They were hardened travellers by this time, passing without a word villages and groups of infidels which, on the outward journey, would have caused them to exclaim, to reach for pens and paper and make a careful note. Some, no doubt, had had enough of travel and holy places and looked forward to ordinary life. Margery wished she could turn back, accepting the Franciscans' invitation, 'for the gret grace and gostly comfort that sche felt' in Jerusalem. However, practical necessity, reinforced by God's direct instructions, obliged her to continue. Go to Rome, the heavenly exhortation ran, 'and so forth hom to Inglond'. Her spiritual merit would not suffer.

Passing the numerous dangerous defiles where robbers congregated, the procession reached Ramleh. The same Moors as on their previous passage appeared with food and drink, carpets, gems, scents, brocades. One feels the pilgrims cannot have been such ready customers by now, except for provisions. They had spent most of their money and seen too many frauds. Besides, they were fully stocked with relics, souvenirs and goods which might be disposed of at a profit in Europe.

When the necessary formalities had been complied with, they trotted through the cotton fields towards the well-remembered ruins of Joppa and St Peter's Caves, from which they saw, with some astonishment, the galleys riding at anchor, exactly as they had been left. It seemed extraordinary to see again a part of the western world, a lodging unconnected with Saracens, their rules, regulations and unpredictable ways. The last formalities took time. The hardships of St Peter's Caves were usually too much for the most seriously ill. The Holy Land was the best place on earth to die in. Yet, it was far from home, friends, relations and anyone who would take a personal interest in one's tomb for memory's sake.

It was a slow business ferrying the passengers and their luggage through the waves breaking on Andromeda's rocks to the ship. Eventually, everyone was aboard, the anchor raised and the discipline of life afloat began. But, at least, one could have a drink without hiding in one's cloak. One might let oneself go in laughter, prayer or rage without the danger of torture and imprisonment in an infidel dungeon, which might last for ever unless one's friends were rich enough to buy one out.

The captain, too, one feels, must have regained his ship with great satisfaction. Here, he was unquestioned master after three arduous weeks of diplomacy, bargaining, tactfulness and incessant physical activity. The tourist business was lucrative, but he earned every penny of his wages.

The homeward voyage was even hotter than the journey to Joppa had been. The cabin stank worse. The stuffiness could hardly be endured. Or, perhaps, it was only that the pilgrims noticed it more in their weakened state. 'Mych of hir felaschep was ryth seke', Margery notes; and it was feared that some would not survive. She prayed to God on their behalf. 'Drede the not, dowtyr,' he replied in his usual encouraging manner, 'ther schal no man deyin in the schip that thu art in.'

The prophecy turned out a true one and they all came 'to Venyce in safte', thanks to her presence on board. Yet, her countrymen were not at all grateful for her good offices. Far from it. When they had got through the customs and re-sold their sheets and pillowcases to the shop near St Mark's, they refused absolutely to escort her to Rome, 'and summe of hem seyden that thei wold not go wyth hir for an hundryd pownd'. With this parting shot, they 'went away fro hir, lvyng hire alone'.

# CHAPTER XXI

## *Richard the Irishman*

This was a situation of which she had had previous experience in Constance. Then, old William Weaver had been divinely appointed her guardian during the wild midwinter of the Alps. It was without surprise, therefore, that she heard God say: 'I shal ordeyn for the ryth wel and bryng the in safte to Rome and hom ageyn into Inglond.' But, added the holy voice, she really must now put on the white outfit he had intended her to wear from the beginning.

She must have had an inclination to do it, one supposes, or else the vision would hardly have contained so irrelevant a clause. On second thoughts, it seemed unwise to draw attention to herself by eccentric dress at this particular point, even though past the dangers of Moslem prejudice. Once the voice had spoken, it was rather awkward to have to argue. However, it was not her way to flinch from difficulties. She suspected this advice, she said firmly, which seemed more likely to lure her to destruction, if followed, than to preserve her life and limb from bandits. But she was ready to make a bargain: 'Yf thu bryng me to Rome in safte, I shal weryn white clothys, thow alle the world schuld wondyr.'

God seemed hurt by her lack of faith. No emanation of the Devil spoke, but 'a trew spiryt wyth cownsel of the chirche'. 'Thu fondist me nevyr deceyvabyl,' he protested. 'I am the spirit of God.' Let her go forth 'in the name of Jhesu ... and I shal flowyn on the in gret plente of grace'. He waived the matter of the white mantle, for the time being.

She rose from her prayers much strengthened. Almost immediately her eye was caught by a humpbacked beggarman sitting on the road. His rags were carefully patched. She judged him to be about fifty. Altogether, there was something promising in his appearance. 'Than sche went to hym and seyde: Gode man, what eyleth yowr bak?'

The omens continued favourable, for he replied in English: 'Damsel, it was brokyn in a sekenes.' In further conversation, it turned out that he was an Irishman named Richard. Margery was now quite convinced that divine intuition had obliged him to take up his position at this particular spot. A certain prophecy, spoken long ago by her friend the holy anchorite in Lynn, came to mind. It fitted her new acquaintance exactly. 'Than sche wyth a glad spirit seyde unto hym: "Good Richard, ledith me to Rome and ye shal be rewarded for yowr labowr."'

Richard was not keen. He knew that her companions had abandoned her. Perhaps he had witnessed the scene. How could it advance a poor man to take up with a woman who had so many enemies? Besides, he pleaded, he was not competent to look after her. Instead of bows and arrows, such as 'thy cuntremen han', he possessed no weapon, except an old patched cloak. It would be impossible for him to guarantee her safety. Most likely, they would both be robbed and she be raped as well.

These were the same gloomy prognostications Margery had listened to from old Mr Weaver of the white beard, as they ascended the Alps. Then, as now, she had been certain 'be revelacyon' that she had found an adequate protector, as, indeed, proved true enough in both cases. She replied: 'Richard, dredith yow not; God shal kepyn us bothen ryth wel and,' she added, coming down to earth, 'I shal geve yow too noblys for yowr labowr.' Thirteen and fourpence was so far beyond Richard's expectations that he closed with the offer at once.

One can only speculate as to what sort of Irishman Richard can have been. A true native of that island in the fifteenth century would have had a Gaelic name and spoken the Irish language. He may have been a Celt from the country round Dublin who had learned English and taken an English name. Or, he may simply have been an Englishman resident in those parts. As to why he should have been reduced to beggary in Venice, again one can merely offer possible explanations. From Margery's later adventures, it appears that he was gradually making his way back to Ireland. Perhaps, therefore, he was a pilgrim who had met with misfortune. He refers obscurely to 'myn enmys' at a certain point in his bargaining with Margery. Whatever his origins, he proved a faithful servant. Neither God, the holy anchorite, nor Margery, had been deceived in their choice of escort.

Having settled the contract, they set out for Rome. It was usual to cross from Venice to Chioggia and take the road southwards through Ravenna and Rimini to Pesaro, then strike inland over the mountains. They were probably mounted, as Margery was in funds. Though fitting into the medieval scene well enough, to us, peering at them from the twentieth century, they are an extra-ordinary sight. Margery was now uninhibited by disapproving companions. As they jogged along, she must have lavished moral advice, improving lectures and exotic demonstrations of piety on her defenceless employee. In spite of his desperate situation, his rags and hump back, he began to wonder whether it was neces-sary to suffer so much, even for thirteen and fourpence. Yet, he did not feel he could abandon her entirely.

Fortunately, they quite soon met a small party who seem to have been Italian pilgrims on their way home from Jerusalem. Margery does not suggest that she was already acquainted with them, though they must have been in the holy city at the same time as herself. They consisted of two Franciscans and a woman 'and sche had wyth hir an asse' which had a chest on its back. Inside this receptacle was a very special 'ymage . . . mad aftyr our Lord'.

Richard seized his opportunity. These were congenial company for his mistress, being extremely religious and also ignorant of English. He spoke of her in high terms, persuading them that it would be an honour, and particularly meritorious, to look after this saintly woman on the road. To Margery he explained that he could not afford to abandon his profession as a beggarman for the wages she paid. It would be much more suitable for her to travel with the Franciscans and the lady. They had better ways of defending her person and property than by waving a patched cloak at attackers. In the morning and evening, before and after business hours, he would visit her to make sure she was all right. His Irish tongue, or else his desperation prevailed: 'sche dede aftyr hys cownsell', though 'non of hem cowde undirstond hir langage' which must have been a deprivation for such an indefatigable talker.

The arrangement worked extremely well. Richard appeared twice a day 'as he had promysed'. Her new friends saw to all practical details, ordered her meals and fixed the night's lodging regularly. She was delighted, and a little surprised, at their regard for her: in general, her comforts were attended to 'rathar bettyr' than theirs. This moved her 'to prey for hem' earnestly, for she did not attribute it to anything Richard might have said, but to their Christian charity and recognition of her excellence. Indeed she had ground for such a view. They seem to have been pious, good-hearted people of moderate education and status. Besides, she usually got on famously with monks. The Franciscans of Jerusalem had always understood her difficulties.

The journey continued at a leisurely pace. 'Whan thei comyn in good citeys', the woman would take 'the ymage owt of hir chist and sett it in worshepful wyfys lappys'. It represented the infant Christ and was probably made of some particularly holy material, such as an olive tree from the Mount of Olives. The worshipful wives cradled it in their arms, as though it were a real child, as, in a supernatural sense, was the case. 'Thei wold puttyn schirtys therupon and kyssyn it' with as much fervour as if their lips touched 'God hymselfe'. Their babies, afterwards dressed in these shirts, would be preserved from all the ills and dangers of childhood. They would be in a generous frame of mind when the two Franciscans handed round the collecting box. For how can we suppose that they threw away such a chance of raising funds for the decoration of a shrine to house the marvellous image?

Margery fitted perfectly into the scheme of things. 'Whan the creatur sey the worshep and the reverens that thei dedyn to the ymage', she was overcome by delicious visions of childbirth and the Holy Family. Screaming and sobbing with celestial joy, she entered on 'hy meditacyons' of various sorts. Her exertions were so tremendous, that the bystanders were quite alarmed for her health. 'Than thei ordeyned a good soft bed and leyd hir therupon and comfortyed hir as mech as thei myth.'

Sometimes 'many neyborwys' would gather in the evening before the house where she lodged, in order to view the foreign holy woman straight from Jerusalem. Since it was not possible to entertain them with descriptions of her travels, or sermons, she would bring out her private collection of relics and souvenirs. At one place, they were especially interested in a set of paternoster beads, made to the exact length and breadth of the Holy Sepulchre. She allowed them to take the measurements, for which they 'thankyd hir hyly'.

By this time, it was late. The day had been long and exhausting, travelling over the dusty roads, accompanied by the image.

Margery 'went to hir chawmbre' which was 'in a good mannys hows' and thoroughly respectable. She always slept with her money hung round her neck. For greater safety, she was accustomed also to take off a certain ring she wore and thread it on to the purse-string. Evidently, she was a good, sound sleeper, unlikely to be woken by creeping footsteps. Besides, she valued this ring far above the metal it was made of. God had commanded her to buy and wear it in a vision 'whil she was at hom in Inglond'. The very words engraved on it, *Ihesus est amor meus*, had been dictated during a revelation. It was a symbol of her chastity and exclusive devotion to God.

What was her horror, therefore, 'in the morwenyng' to discover that the ring had disappeared. After searching everywhere, she 'compleyned to the good wyfe of the hows'. The woman understood what she meant at once and appeared to be taken aback. These seemed to be very suspicious reactions to Margery. They both lit candles and got down on the floor to look under the bed. The good wife rummaged and waved her candle 'and at the last' Margery saw 'the ryng under the bed on the bordys'. Her feeling was that the woman had put it there, especially as she had a contrite air and seemed to be begging her guest's forgiveness.

This is the only unfortunate adventure Margery records of her journey to Rome. One wonders whether it was not all due to misunderstanding. Can the poor hostess really have been so wonderfully light-fingered as to remove the ring from the string round Margery's neck without disturbing her dreams? Even if she had such a gift, how could she hope to get away with the theft, particularly as she was not a convincing liar? It is reasonable to acquit her of the charge and to suppose that Margery dropped her ring without noticing because her mind was wandering in higher spheres and on account of her extreme fatigue. On the other hand, Margery was there to judge the situation and we are not.

Thus, by degrees, they reached Assisi, home town of St Francis and Franciscans. It seems none of her new friends went further than this, for Richard had to make another arrangement for the last part of the road to Rome, as will be related.

In Assisi, Margery met an English resident, a Franciscan, 'and a solempne clerke he was holdyn'. Soon she had related to this patient man her feelings, revelations, holy inspirations, high contemplations and the manner in which God entered her soul. He was extremely impressed. He had never heard anything like it before. He doubted whether anyone living had had such experiences. These things, he said, were God's gift entirely and one should be deeply thankful for them.

Much encouraged by so warm a reception, Margery let herself go. In the church of St Francis, 'sche wept, sche sobbed, sche cryed' with the greatest vehemence. Since the visit to the Holy Land, her visions had an extra intensity and gave her a more complete satisfaction, though the actual subject matter remained unchanged. God still chatted in the same sort of phrases he had always used. No strange new scenes, or understandings, flashed into her mind. Jesus was, above all, her loyal friend, taking her side in little upsets, promising nice things to come, cheering in depressed moments, appearing promptly when required.

The church of St Francis at Assisi was then almost exactly as we see it today. The frescoes by Cimabue with biblical subjects and those in the style of Giotto depicting the saint's life and miracles were, of course, fresher than we know them, having been on the walls only about a hundred years. Margery does not mention them, however. What roused her enthusiasm was the Veil of Our Lady, which was shown during her visit. This venerable relic originally in Jerusalem, had been stolen by a pasha of Damascus, from whom it had been obtained when he was taken prisoner by an Italian prince. He afterwards presented it to the church of St Francis.

At the bottom of the hill on which Assisi stands, near the modern railway station, there was a thirteenth-century church incorporating the chapel used by St Francis, the cell where he died and, adjoining, his garden containing miraculous roses without thorns and a hut he had lived in. Here, on Lammas Day, 1 August 1414, Margery obtained 'grace mercy and forgiveness for hirself, for alle hir frendys, for alle hir enmys' and everyone in purgatory. It was a magnificent gesture towards her perfidious countrymen who had left her to fall among thieves in a strange land.

Richard the Irishman continued faithful to his bargain. The lady with the image was not going any further in Margery's direction. He looked round for another protector. Among the pilgrims arrived to avail themselves of the Lammas Day indulgence was a rich lady 'comyn fro Rome to purchasyn hir pardon'. She was well provided with horses and her party included a number of Knights of Rhodes and 'many gentylwomen'. 'Hir name was Margaret Florentyne' and Margery's is the only mention of her in history, as far as is known. Nothing could be safer than to attach oneself to such a well-defined and high-class party. 'Than Richard the broke bakkyd man went to' this splendid lady, 'preyng hir that this creatur mygth gon wyth hir to Rome and hymself also for to be kept fro perel of thevys.'

Dame Margaret Florentine received him graciously. No, she had no objection to being joined by an Irish beggar and an English candidate for sainthood. The Knights of Rhodes would escort them all impartially back to Rome. These were splendid arrangements. Margery must have been more than ever convinced that God had directed her attention to Richard in Venice.

# CHAPTER XXII

## The Holy Father

Margery does not say exactly when she started for Rome, but since the Lady Margaret Florentine had travelled to Assisi especially for the indulgence given on Ausust 1st, one would expect her to return shortly afterwards. It would not take long to visit all the other shrines of the town, and lodging for the many gentlewomen, knights, servants, horses and so on must have been expensive. From pictures of the period, we can visualize the brilliant cavalcade, passing over the hills and through the woods of the Italian landscape. It is almost always warm and sunny in these paintings. In the distance is a small walled city, such as Assisi, perched on a steep little mountain; in the foreground, most usually, the Three Kings, their lords, ladies, and attendants, handsomely arrayed and mounted on good, stout horses.

The ecclesiastical picture was less charming. By the summer of 1414 the papacy, long ailing as an institution, had become perfectly ludicrous, considered from any religious point of view. In 1378, the great schism began with one pope at Avignon and another in Rome. This situation was the result of quarrels between the French and Italian parties among the cardinals. There was a general state of unrest as each pope tried to buy up, or conquer, the Papal States. The holy fathers were poor, what with extra expenses for campaigns and shrunken revenue from a divided obedience. They would sell a licence for anything in their power as keepers of the keys of heaven in succession to St Peter. A priest had only to pay in order to enjoy concubines without jeopardizing his chances in the next world. Pardon could be bought for any layman's sin.

Although a convenient state of affairs, this was also found shocking. It was so much at variance with the whole theory of a Holy Father, reigning under direct mandate from God. For people did not, in general, dispute the reality of sin, or heaven, or hell, or even the sanctity of the Pope's office. It was just that the Devil and all his works had obtained a strong foothold in the fortress of Christendom. Politics of a particularly worldly kind were a constant preoccupation in the sacred college. Should they vote to please the King of France, or Naples, or the Holy Roman Emperor in Germany? Would it be better to bribe the Lord of Milan, or the Doge of Venice? Which of the various mercenary captains would be cheapest and best for a war against the other popes and cardinals who were usurping their titles in the most barefaced manner? How to raise money? What conspiracy to join? Machiavelli's *Prince* merely reflected a state of affairs that had existed longer than anyone could remember.

Under these conditions, continually subject to depredations by one side or another, the Papal States became poor and degraded, the Roman mob terrifying in its unpredictable violence. The popes had failed both as spiritual and temporal masters. This was especially painful to persons of a religious turn of mind. St Catherine of Siena and St Bridget of Sweden never tired of giving the Pope good advice. But it did not avail. The Holy Father was too weak politically and temperamentally to be saved by the example of saints. He had been elected, very often, simply on account of his ineffectiveness, and his consequent inoffensiveness, to the various irreconcilable parties whom the cardinals hoped both to appease and make use of.

It is no wonder that people like Wyclif in England and Hus in Bohemia began to have numerous followers, to assume the proportions of mass movements and to frighten lay as well as ecclesiastical authority by subversive ideas smacking of protestantism and democracy, though no one had coined these words, as yet. Even persons of the most subservient orthodoxy were infected by the spirit of the times. Margery always showed the greatest respect for the office of priest. But her whole system turned on direct communication with God. She required no intermediary. Had there been no organized religion at all, no hierarchy, no superstructure of courts, princes, monks, taxes, palaces, wars, it would not have affected her prayers in the slightest. She required only a sacred place on which to kneel- Her own mind supplied the rest.

In 1414, there were three popes, the one most generally accepted being John XXIII. As Baldassare Cossa, he had started life as a Neapolitan pirate, though of quite respectable family. Finding this career did not offer sufficient prospects, he determined to enter the church where he felt, as proved true, that his gifts would bring rapid promotion. After studying at Bologna University, he became chamberlain to the then pope, who made him a cardinal in 1402. In this capacity, he ruled Bologna in the manner of an independent prince. His administration was efficient, from a governor's point of view. He could lead an army to victory, should it prove necessary. He was uninterested in chastity as a way of life.

Clearly, such a man was not going to put his heart into a serious programme of reform. The two other popes, though recently deposed at the Council of Pisa, still clung to their titles and had friends who asserted their rights. The Holy Roman Emperor, Sigismund, newly elected, resolved to end the schism. He would immortalize himself as the saviour of Christendom. A council should be called at Constance, in his dominions. Delegates would come from all over Europe and from the eastern church also. They would continue the debate until one pope had been accepted indisputably, the heretics been worsted and the reforms initiated which everyone knew to be essential.

Pope John prevaricated. He was doing quite well under existing arrangements. He devalued the coinage, extorted loans and raised the price of corn to astonishing heights in an effort to fill the treasury. As for the heretics, he ceremoniously burnt Wyclif's writings on the top of the steps in front of St Peter's in 1413. But the omens were bad. While he was singing *Veni Creator Spiritus* at vespers, a screech owl flew down from the vault and perched on his head. Everyone was much struck by this devilish apparition.

Sure enough, the King of Naples attacked the city soon after and John became a refugee, unable any longer to resist Sigismund's plan for the church's salvation. The Council of Constance opened in November 1414. When Margery passed through the city in the first months of the year on her way to Jerusalem preparations must have begun for the reception of delegates and their suites. Besides lodgings and provisions for princes, lords, servants, horses, huge numbers of people connected with the entertainment business arrived: 1,500 prostitutes, for instance, and 1,400 flute players. It was calculated that during the conference, 500 men, overcome by excesses of one sort and another, fell into

Lake Constance and were drowned.

These momentous events were in the immediate future as the Lady Margaret Florentine's magnificent cavalcade entered Rome at about the end of August, or beginning of September, 1414, as far as one can judge. For, the King of Naples died on August 6th, whereupon the Romans immediately rebelled against his governor. One would expect Lady Margaret to defer her arrival until the fighting was over.

# CHAPTER XXIII

## *Arrival in Rome*

Owing to the disastrous position to which the popes had sunk, Rome was a decayed city in the fifteenth century and only half inhabited. Continually besieged by one side or another, the government having more or less broken down, most of the citizens had left. The town consisted of a network of narrow, dark and insalubrious alleyways, broken occasionally by squares, on the flat tongue of land in the bend of the Tiber between the Vatican and the suburb of Trastevere. The larger houses were of the type still to be seen in San Gimignano in Tuscany: a stout, forbidding exterior with defensive tower and, inside, well protected, a courtyard and small garden. The poorer houses were extremely squalid and so encrusted with outside staircases and balconies that they almost met across the roadway. Some streets were arcaded, the pillars being classical columns cut down to size.

As one went away from the river, towards the famous seven hills of ancient Rome, one found oneself passing into the country. Sheep and goats grazed among fallen columns and blocks from massive walls. Vineyards and orchards lined the famous streets which every educated person had heard of from the Latin authors. The Forum made a convenient enclosure for oxen and pigs. The walk to the Lateran was especially recommended as a peaceful, rural interlude where one could compose one's thoughts and consider holy things, uninterrupted, except by birds.

Sometimes, one came on clusters of houses, like villages in the fields. These had mostly been built with stone from a handy ruin, such as the Colosseum, the temples of Jupiter, or Mercury. The many churches and monasteries, at this date themselves dilapidated, had been entirely constructed of ancient materials. One can see today how, if a column was too short, they shoved a block of stone under it: if too long, they cut the end off. This was shocking enough to contemporaries, imbued with the new Renaissance dreams. But the lime kilns were far worse. The manufacture of lime was one of Rome's industries. The furnaces were ubiquitous and into them went every bit of marble the workmen could conveniently lay hands on. Nothing could stop them. What were

Travellers. (From a collection of stories, verses and ballads by the poetess Christine of Pisa. Early 15th century, French. Harley 4431.)

The Market at Constance. (From the *Chronik des Ulrich Richental.* Circa 1460.)

pagan ruins, after all? From the time of Constantine, they had been pillaged for Christian use. It was a tradition. Besides, one had to make one's living.

Rome's other speciality was, of course, the tourist business. The city was second only to Jerusalem in holiness. Here were enshrined the memories and relics of the apostles and of innumerable martyrs who had endured horrible ends at pagan hands, by torture, execution, lynching, or being thrown as living fodder to the wild animals of the arena. At every turn were places where saints had been roasted, boiled or screwed to death. The details were all recounted to the accompaniment of pious screams of grief from the devout. Hostels were maintained for every nation. Careful guide books had been written, giving lists of churches, relics and the bloodthirsty martyr biographies.

In some ways, Rome must have been more interesting than Jerusalem. There was a far greater variety of saints, all with unhappy histories. Persons who enjoyed wallowing in the horrors had almost unlimited scope. For us, the Roman guide books are rather specialist. The perils to be averted were hardly less than those encountered in Moslem lands, but they were well known and common to all Europe at that date. The pilgrim needed no particular warnings, or rules of conduct, to help him. He knew how to obtain food and lodging; and how to comport himself without giving offence to such an extent that his life was in danger.

To this degraded city, half classical rubbish heap, half slum, came the Lady Margaret Florentine's splendid train. Margery. and Richard took a cordial leave of her now, making their way to 'the Hospital of Seynt Thomas of Cawntyrbery' almost on the Tiber banks. This was the hostel for English pilgrims.

When her fellowship saw her coming through the door, they were dumbfounded. They had arrived some time previously and perhaps had had adventures during the city's revolt from the King of Naples' government in August. It seemed to them impossible that she should have passed alone through all the robbers, all the mercenary bands 'in safte', escorted by an unarmed beggarman from Ireland. Those who had declared in Venice that they would pay a hundred pounds to be rid of her must have put it down to the Devil. The weaker party, always inclined to be secretly impressed by her claims to divine guidance, thought it more like a miracle.

Margery had no doubt that God had engineered everything, from first to last. She had promised to wear white if he conducted her to Rome. Now she hastened to fulfil her side of the bargain: 'sche went and ordeynd hir white clothys' and put them on as soon as they were ready. It was a time of triumph. The monks in charge of the hospital of St Thomas encouraged her. Her old travelling companions had to bear with their luck. At least, they were not obliged to take their outings in her company, which had been their worst trial in the Holy Land. In Rome, one could come and go as one pleased, sampling new wonders every day as one felt inclined.

It was possible to be sated, for the time being, with 'grete pileres of brass hol ful of seyntes bones',* 'the ymage of our lady'* carved by St Luke, 'the arme o seynt mathew the evangelist',* especially when one had seen some pieces better during one's previous travels – St Zaccharias' head, for instance, which one had fully admired in Venice. 'The cradill that crist was layd in'* had more impact when first seen in Bethlehem. As for 'the mylk of our lady',* one had a bottle of that in one's luggage, laboriously collected from the oozing stone in the cave where she had fed the infant Jesus. It was not that one disbelieved in any of these things, but relics of the Caesars made a nice change.

For this the guides were ready. There was not much left above ground, but they knew how to embellish tumbled columns and broken pavements. The Circus Maximus, they said 'was of marvellous beauty . . . At the top were arches all around, ceiled with glass and shining gold.'† 'And in the Capitol,' they cried, standing in the rough grass among the debris, 'were molten images of all the Trojan kings,'† and inside 'was a palace all adorned with marvellous works in gold and silver and brass and costly stones'.†

Sometimes imperial glory and Christian legend became confused. The vaults under the ruins on the Palatine marked the spot where hell had once burst forth 'and brought great mischief

---

* Capgrave, *Ye Solace of Pilgrimes, c.* 1450. British and American Archaeological Society of Rome, 1911. Capgrave was a younger contemporary and fellow citizen of Margery's, being Prior of the Augustinians at Lynn.

† *Mirabilia Urbis Romanae*, ed. & tr. by F. M. Nichols, 1889.

upon Rome'* until a certain knight cast himself into the orifice as a sacrifice to the demons. This satisfied the infernal powers, the guides recounted: 'The earth closed, so the city was delivered.'* Under the temple of Vesta crouched a dragon, immobilized for ever by an early saint.

Occasionally, the eye had something more substantial to feed on. The Pantheon had been turned into a church dedicated to the Virgin. It had been necessary to do this, the guides explained, because of the evil spirits that lived there, during its pagan days. Christians had often had seizures when passing. 'In the top,' they added to attentive pilgrims '. . . stood the golden pine-cone that is now before the door of St Peter; and the church was all covered with gilded brass, insomuch that from afar it seemed as it were a mountain of gold.'*

Those times were rich and fabulous. Great emperors lived then in enormous palaces built of rare stones, embellished with gems and precious metals. Though one and all were heathens, now denizens of hell, one could not help an envious sigh for vanished splendours. This path between the fields marked a street where Virgil once had walked. He was a great magician of that enchanted age. If in a difficulty, he could fly through the air, invisible to mortal eyes. His spells were formidable. He had carved the marble mask, known as the Bocca della Verità.‡ Anyone putting a finger into the mouth and swearing a false oath was immediately bitten. It was considered, so the legend ran, practically the only way of telling whether or not a woman was a deceiver.

Wherever one turned, glorious temples rose in the imagination from heaps of rubble and the waste from lime works. All had been furnished with golden images, precious stones, magnificent paintings and carvings of famous events. Extraordinary ceremonies went on in them with the emperor in full regalia on his throne, surrounded by priests going through devilish rituals. Everything was beautiful beyond the power of words to express. In many places were oracles, speaking strangely of the future to those Romans whose business in the world was to 'govern the earth'.*

* *Mirabilia Urbis Romanae.*

‡ Now built into the wall of Sta Maria in Cosmedin. It is of classical date.

# CHAPTER XXIV

## *Expelled from the Hostel*

Margery had no use for classical antiquity. God was far too exciting a friend and mentor to require profane relief. He could come to her in any of these innumerable Roman churches which she could visit as she pleased. For now she had opportunity to relax with her thoughts, if her energetic visions may be so described. She was not being driven by infidels from place to place to a strict timetable. She could spend hours flat on the ground in a chapel while Jesus conversed, assuring her of his continued regard, promising to stand by her in troubles and predicting the ignominious defeat of all enemies.

She had need of comfort, for the English pilgrims were not able to endure the prospect of her company at the hostel. Her worst enemy was a certain 'preste that was holdyn an holy man in the Hospital and also in other placys of Rome'. He was one of the original English party. Long observation of her habits from Yarmouth, across Germany, in Venice, on shipboard and in the Holy Land had convinced him that she was possessed by the Devil. All her visions were, in his view, infernal deceits. It was not just that she was a colossal bore, as the others complained, but it was actually unsafe to have anything to do with her. One would be dragged down into the flames of hell by her devil friends with their pitchforks and instruments of torture.

His vehemence so impressed the master of the hospital and his brother monks, that they began to be afraid of having encouraged her. It was not disputed that she had supernatural gifts, but what if these were malevolent, as the priest declared? The white outfit was disturbing. She had no licence to do such a thing. The great council at Constance which was to set the whole Church to rights for ever, had the question of heretics on the agenda. They dared not risk it. 'Sche was put owte of the Hospital.'

Richard remained faithful, so it was not difficult to arrange new lodgings. But she had now no priest to absolve her and administer the sacraments. This distressed her very much. She had learned a few phrases of basic Italian during her travels, but these were not nearly enough for confession. 'Sche was ful hevy.' Richard knew of no one suitable.

'Than preyde sche owyr Lord ... wyth gret plente of teerys', but he was not able to offer any practical advice. The matter seems to have been urgent. Perhaps it was Saturday evening. They could not think of anything better than that Richard should go across the road from the hostel to Sta Maria in Caterina 'and enformyn the person of the chyrche' of her needs. Like all members of his profession, Richard possessed a ready tongue. He had had no difficulty in describing his employer in such terms that the lady with the image and Dame Margaret Florentine had been delighted to take her on. He was equally successful with the priest of Sta Maria.

It is not reported that his persuasions went beyond a plain description of Margery's 'contricyon and compunccyon', her devotion and nearness to God. One cannot say whether or not he represented her as a saint, miracle worker, dramatic visionary, prophetess, seer and free with her money. One, moreover, who had travelled alone through dangerous country, except for the inadequate protection he could provide. Yet, both her virtue and gold remained intact. Could anything prove more conclusively that God was on her side? As for her being thrown out of the hostel, that could be explained as the Devil's work.

Whatever his exact words, the priest was won over, declaring himself 'ryth glad' to receive this estimable woman at his altar. As 'he cowde not undyrstond non Englysch', confession was not possible. It didn't matter. He would administer the sacraments 'hys owyn self'.

The problem of a confessor was easier to solve. Other holy women in a similar fix had summoned St John to appear in their visions and listen to the tale of their sins. It was one of his recognized duties. She appealed to him, therefore, 'wyth many swemful teerys' and he listened 'ful mekely and benyngly', standing before her so plainly that 'she saw hym and herd hym in hire gostly undirstondyng' just as if he were a real person, perceived by her 'bodily wittys'.

She does not describe what sins the apparition was asked to consider, but they included, perhaps, hard words and worse thoughts towards her fellowship during the recent fight. When the saint had heard her out, he forgave her, in the name of God, made a short, improving address and vanished. She could now take the sacraments from the Italian in Sta Maria.

Though all was in order, and there were good precedents, Margery was still upset. She might converse with God directly for hours at a time, but that did not mean she questioned the church's place in the scheme of things. Her orthodox soul required a proper priest and confessor, the whole hierarchy of ecclesiastical authority. These arrangements had divine sanction. God had delegated certain of his powers on earth to the Pope and his subordinates. If Jesus thought fit to speak to Margery Kempe, Bridget of Sweden, Julian of Norwich and Catherine of Siena, it did not mean that they could dispense with his representatives.

Even if Pope, cardinals, bishops and monks were, in some cases, unworthy of their positions, that did not mean that they should be abolished, as heretics averred. The incumbent could not taint the spiritual aspect of his office as such. It was necessary only for men of goodwill to convene a great council at Constance for the whole church to be reformed, the accumulated evil of centuries to be expunged and the pristine glory of Christ's kingdom on earth restored.

For, as Margery's career shows, devotion in the fifteenth century was widespread, sincere and powerful. The upper reaches might have passed into a secular atmosphere, but the mass of Christendom, whether heretic or orthodox, accepted the reality of God and the necessity of proper relations with him. Margery was not at all happy to have to confess to St John, though to be served by him was an honour reserved for saintly characters. Jesus had to come and comfort her afterwards, promising to stand by her always and never to abate his love for her, no matter what happened. She did not know what to do, as all the English priests in Rome had been turned against her by the machinations of her enemies.

In the many churches, she prayed for help, certain that it would come. Someone suitable would be divinely indicated and her problem would be solved. It had happened at Constance where William Weaver had been provided for her material protection. In Venice she had not been failed. How much more now should she have confidence when her need was for spiritual assistance and not merely for such earthly services as Richard could provide?

The revelation came in the Lateran, a place full of magic, founded by the Emperor Constantine, after his conversion. It was, says Capgrave, writing in 1450, or so, 'the first that evyr was bilid in cristendam'. Erected in the grounds of the imperial palace, 'it was nevyr made with mannes hand but sodeynly thus it appered.' At the consecration, the face of Christ became visible on the wall, as if painted. Here the early popes lived until obliged to move across the Tiber to St Peter's for political reasons. Here, they were still crowned in the ancient basilica, supported by classical columns.*

Before the door was the famous equestrian statue of Marcus Aurelius, then thought to represent Constantine. Inside, the most splendid collection of relics were displayed at appropriate feasts. The week before Easter, one could see St Peter's head, which had 'a brood face with mech her on his berd and that is of grey colour'.† St Paul's head, on the contrary had, 'a long face balled with red her both berd and hed'.† There were the Ark of the Covenant, the Tables of the Law and Aaron's Rod. The heads, shoulders, bones and possessions of many lesser saints could be admired. Also the loaves and fishes and part of the maundy dish. One could kiss a certain stone, especially mounted to make it easy to get at, where 'stood seynt jon the evangelist and prechid ... to domician emperour and to the puple of rome'.†

This concentration of divine influences made miracles likely to happen. St Bridget of Sweden, who had lived in Rome at the end of her life, was seen to levitate before one of the altars. High up near the ceiling was a crucifix, originally at ground level, where a saint had been condemned to die. People had kissed it, with great advantage, until a certain 'gentil woman cam'† who thought to wipe the cross because the previous worshipper had looked particularly unappetizing. The crucifix, or perhaps the saint's ghost, was, however, imbued with democratic feelings. Everyone was equal before God. The first shall be last and the last shall be first. 'Al sodeynly it fled fro that place up to a wal and mor than four fadom hy.'†

In these surroundings knelt Margery Kempe, very worried

* The present baroque interior dates from the seventeenth century.
† Capgrave.

135

because she could not find a decent confessor who knew English. The priest officiating, she noticed 'semyd a good man and devowte'. As she watched, a feeling of certainty overcame her. This was the right person. 'Sche was sor mevyd in spiryt to speke wyth hym.' After the service, the obliging Richard informed the priest that a remarkable woman wished to speak to him. Though 'a good man', a German, 'a good clerke and a wel lernyd man, hily belovyd, wel cherschyd and myche trostyd in Rome', the priest unfortunately was entirely ignorant of English, 'and therfor thei spokyn be an jnterpretowr'.

The conversation convinced Margery that God intended this man to serve her. His attitude was so sympathetic. It was only necessary, she declared, to address himself to the 'blysful Trinite, to owir Lady and to alle the blissed syntys in Hevyn', his friends praying also, as vehemently as they could. The gift of the English language would then fall on him. Quite carried away by her earnestness and 'desyryng to plese God, he folwyd the cownsel of this creature'. Prayers continued strenuously for thirteen days while God imparted the desired knowledge. It is not stated that he took any other kind of lessons. On the fourteenth day, 'he undirstod what sche seyd ... and sche undirstod what that he seyd', though English spoken by anyone else was as incomprehensible as ever.

One can regard this as a plain miracle. Or, he had a vague smattering of English and took practical steps to improve it. Or, he did not, in fact, understand anything she said, but made agreeable noises and gestures during the breaks in her monologue. For what she required was a listener and supporter in this strange city where her countrymen had cast her out. She had never had much use for advice. God looked after that side of things. On the whole, it seems that, in time, the priest came to grasp pretty well what she meant.

Assured of his comprehension, Margery at once settled down to an exhaustive confession. She cannot have had the opportunity since leaving the hospital of St Thomas. She had been muzzled for weeks, perhaps more. Now she related every sin 'fro hir childhode unto that owre', adding a resumé of her prophecies, revelations and 'hey contemplacyons'. In relating her visions, she swayed with emotion, made wild movements and almost fell flat on the ground. At other passages, tears cascaded over her cheeks and violent sobs shook her from head to foot. The discourse was punctuated by her screaming 'ful lowde and horybly'.

This was, after all, only an emphatic form of accepted pious behaviour and 'the preste had gret trost that it was the werk of God'. Later, he began to doubt. Was there not something a little too shrill about it? Where did humility come in? She was always right. Jesus invariably addressed her with the greatest cordiality, even admiration. If she abased herself for a moment before him, he hastened to raise her up uttering strings of platitudes and promises of the best seat in paradise. Yet, no sooner had the poor man expressed misgivings, than she told him disgraceful things concerning his private life that he thought she could not have learned, except 'be revelacyon'. He was obliged to believe, even more fervently. He treated her thereafter 'ful mekely and reverently' as if she had been 'hys modyr' or, at any rate, 'hys syster'.

He promised to support her through thick and thin. In a way, he did. But sometimes he weakened slightly. Though overwhelmingly sincere, she had a bogus tinge which worried him. He could not help feeling that her detractors were not altogether unreasonable. The feud with her fellowship was now of extraordinary bitterness. They pursued her from shrine to shrine, jeering at her pretensions and making insulting remarks. Above all, they refused to believe that she could not refrain from tears and screams if she wished. In this they did her an injustice. Her state of mind was such, especially since the visit to Jerusalem, that a holy object, or even thought, threw her into uncontrollable hysterics. Besides, why should she make any attempt to suppress convulsions and bellowings when she was absolutely certain that these were a mark of heavenly grace? Many respected persons agreed with her.

Others did not. Following the lamentable example of her countrymen, they scoffed, saying her antics were a 'symulacyon and ypocrisy falsly feyned of hir owyn self'. The more charitable put it down to 'a sodeyn sekenes' of an epileptic nature. The superstitious were 'aferd and gretly astoyned, demyng sche had ben vexyd wyth sum evyl spiryt'.

Margery was used to this from the old days in England and did not mind very much, particularly as it brought sainthood closer.

But the priest became upset. She was noisiest on Sundays at communion. He resolved to test her by administering the sacraments privately, instead of among the congregation. If she bellowed then, it could not be in order to impress an audience. To his relief, since he had staked his reputation on the genuineness of her claims, she passed with flying colours: 'for it semyd to hys heryng that sche cryed nevyr so lowde befor that tyme'. She was undoubtedly filled with 'the Holy Gost'. He was glad to suffer obloquy on her behalf. It was the way to heaven. 'Meche pepyl in Rome that wer disposyd to vertu' admired him for this stand. A band of supporters rallied round them both. Margery's prayers were asked for by those in difficulty. She received invitations to dine and other flattering attentions.

# CHAPTER XXV

## St Bridget's Example

In the fifteenth century, St Bridget of Sweden was one of the best known and most revered saints in northern Europe. Her *Revelations* circulated widely and Margery was acquainted with them. It was her ambition to surpass this famous woman in holiness and fame. God frequently assures her that he loves her just as well as, or better than, St Bridget. Sometimes, he remarks, her visions are superior to the saint's. He never adjures his faithful Margery to emulate Bridget, but, full of envy and admiration, she cannot help doing so.

There was a certain similarity in their lives on earth. Bridget, born about 1303, married at an early age, came greatly to enjoy sex and had eight children. Gradually, she began to have an aversion for physical relations and to urge on her husband the moral advantages of a vow of chastity. She said it was the divine will that they should live as brother and sister. Vague and terrifying supernatural punishments would fall on him if he persisted in what had become a sin.

As they were returning from a pilgrimage to Compostela in Spain, he caught a severe illness and thought he might die. At this point, he consented to take a formal vow. He never fully recovered his health, however, and died shortly afterwards in Sweden in 1344. Bridget was now free and she had money. God wanted her to go to Rome and Jerusalem. In 1349 she left Sweden to spend most of the rest of her life in Rome. She died in 1373 and was canonized in 1391.

Some of her meetings with divinity resembled Margery's. God and the Virgin conversed with her affably and promised the joys of heaven. When at Jerusalem, on the Mount of Calvary, she had a most grisly vision not only of Christ on the cross in the agony of death, covered with wounds all pouring blood, but also of the early preparations: how a scaffolding was put up with special stairs to enable workmen to fix him to the cross securely; how they stretched him out and nailed him; his various movements as he hung there. The whole scene was as real to her as if happening at that very moment. Intense grief filled her and she wept unrestrainedly. On leaving the place she at once dictated a full account to her confessor.

At Bethlehem, in the church of the Nativity, she saw the actual birth of Christ, the Virgin kneeling and praying meanwhile. Here, too, the detail was vivid. Like Margery, she had a thorough knowledge of the subject. Her attitude, however, was quite different from that of a self-assertive mayor's daughter. She remained a humble spectator, worshipping unobtrusively, making no move to snatch up the holy child, as Margery did later, and act as its nurse. She always approached God with a fitting respect and never represented him as standing by in the manner one associates more with a loyal servant of moderate intelligence than a supernatural being. She did not ask him for fulsome addresses in praise of herself. Though appreciative and ready to take her side, Christ retains a kingly dignity.

For Bridget was a lady, accustomed to the best circles in Sweden. Sometimes God appeared to her as a monarch, sitting on his throne, a crown on his head, surrounded by his court of saints and angels. The earthly counterpart of this scene was familiar to her. She had, in her day, acted as a sort of governess to the young king and queen of Sweden, guiding them as far as possible, towards the medieval romantic ideals of perfect Christian virtue: justice, mercy and loving care towards inferiors. St Louis of France, that last forlorn crusader, made the nearest, and most famous, approach to these standards in the thirteenth century.

Whereas Margery had no particular mission, except to prove herself a saint, Bridget, like her younger contemporary Catherine of Siena, had the greatest desire to reform the church. Priests and monks had mistresses openly, she observed. Even more disgraceful was the pride they took in their children, shamelessly boasting of how clever, well-grown and handsome they were. One had only to keep watch on a nunnery at night to see the lovers slinking in and out. She founded the Bridgettine order as an answer to this.

For the rest, she realized that reform must come from the top. A pure church could not exist under a corrupt head. She sent exhortatory letters to kings, popes, dukes and others in authority. Many remained unanswered, though they were eloquent epistles, written as from God. Divine vengeance was promised to unappreciative recipients. Above all, the Pope must come back to Rome, conducting himself with suitable humility. These were the views of all serious people, but, in this world, there are practical politics and there is human nature; the two together proved insuperable obstacles to the advent of the millenium.

While conducting this correspondence, Bridget lived mainly in Rome, visiting shrines, foretelling the future, healing the sick and spending long periods in meditation. She was accompanied by a daughter, herself to become a saint in due course. None of Margery's daughters showed any inclination for the holy life, as far as we know. Certainly, they did not take the opportunity of seeing Jerusalem with their mother. Indeed, we have no information as to how Margery's family were doing during an absence which had now lasted about nine months. She never mentions any of them in her narrative.

As a feeling woman, she must sometimes have remembered them in her prayers. But they cannot have been much in her thoughts, or God would have spoken on the subject, enumerating blessings he would give, or punishments deal out, according to their deserts. Though often alarmed by being cast among strangers to fend for herself, Margery never expresses a longing for the old days at Lynn with her house, her sons and daughters and the faithful John Kempe standing by obediently. She was a born traveller, resourceful, indomitable, indifferent to hardship. As her fellowship had learned, nothing turned her back; there was no way, short of murder, of preventing her from following a programme on which she had determined with divine approbation.

There were still people in Rome who had known St Bridget personally. Margery's landlord was one of these. It was a great surprise to him, he said, to learn 'that sche had ben so holy a woman as sche was'. Her geniality and readiness to converse in an ordinary manner were not in accordance with his ideas on sainthood. 'Aftyrward this creatur spak wyth Seynt Brydys mayden in Rome, but sche cowde not undyrstondyn what sche seyd.' A man was found to act as interpreter. The lady wanted to know, he said, what St Bridget was like to meet. The maid confirmed the landlord's opinion. Her late mistress, she replied, was entirely unpretentious, polite to everyone and had a very cheerful expression.

Margery records both testaments without comment. They must have been as unexpected to her as the saint's demeanour had been to the landlord. Her whole life was given over to the extravagant expression of grief and to lecturing her acquaintance on their moral shortcomings. All her many difficulties were due to this. She had suffered violence, and even the possibility of death, gladly in the belief that she would be rewarded with the title, St Margery. Now it appeared that Bridget had been accepted by heaven in spite of having lived always in the secular world, borne eight children and openly enjoyed the society of her friends. Repentance and penance for the past had evidently been kept strictly private.

It was, however, impossible for Margery to emulate her heroine in this respect. The habits of many years were too ingrained. Temperament made her incapable of facing the world with equanimity. Except in the most crude sense, modesty was alien to her. Besides, why should she worry? God approved of everything she did. He had told her so himself. He had even sometimes suggested that her visions were superior to those of St Bridget. In the end, perhaps, she would rank as a senior saint. Other qualities counted with God as well as the ability to found religious orders and write letters to popes.

It was now October, 1414, as near as one can judge. The feast of St Bridget was on the seventh of the month. The house where she had lived was carefully preserved, the main chapel being the room in which she died. In these sacred precincts, Margery listened to a sermon treating of the saint's 'revelacyons and of hir maner of levyng'. Either the discourse was given in English, or else the gist of it was explained to her afterwards by a friend. She knelt devoutly on a stone 'on the whech owr Lord aperyd to Seynt Brigypte and telde hir what day sche shuld deyn on'.

The Romans, in general, did not think much of the saint. Her feast was not kept very seriously. Was it surprising, then, that the day was marked by the most frightful storm? The wind and rain were extraordinary and people scampered for shelter to escape being struck dead by lightning. Plainer proof of divine displeasure could hardly be required. Nor was this the only indication given to a sinful city. She was subsequently warned in a dream to stay indoors next day. Informed of the prophecy, the little band of followers she now had remained under cover waiting for God's wrath to fall. The wind, rain, thunder and atmospheric effects developing were so violent that 'ryth elde men' declared they had never experienced anything like it. The lightning was so brilliant and frequent that her friends were afraid their houses would be burnt down 'wyth contentys'. 'Than cryed thei upon the forseyd creatur to prey for hem.' She did and the storm died away, in due course.

# CHAPTER XXVI

## Married to God

Margery's peregrinations through the city of Rome became more and more exciting. These streets had been walked by hundreds of martyrs. Bridget was only one of many saints who levitated, saw bright visions, smelt heavenly scents and heard the sounds of heaven echoing between these walls. Her 'contemplacyons' became more intense. Continual fasting, prayer and penance, she now perceived, were strictly for 'yong begynnars'. She had advanced to a stage of meditation where she lived in a perpetual dramatic dream, hardly connected with reality at all.

On meeting a woman carrying a baby in her arms, she would begin 'cryin, roryn and wepyn' to the great astonishment of spectators who could not know that, in imagination, she saw the Virgin and Child. She longed to snatch the infant and cover him with kisses, but prudence fortunately prevailed. Similarly, on passing any handsome man she was 'meche affectyd'. He seemed a personification of Christ.

The various stages of spiritual advancement were fully described in the popular handbooks written by hermits and recluses with which she had become familiar in England. Women who took a vow of chastity whether on becoming a nun, a widow, or for other reasons, became the bride of Christ in a preliminary sense. They wore a ring to symbolize the event. This was not, of course, the union with the Godhead which marked the acme of the meditative life and could be attained by few, after many years of discipline and subtle temptations overcome.

The supreme happiness brought about by this mysterious and invisible union with divinity was impossible to describe in words. Language had been invented for practical use in everyday things and the extra meaning could not readily be conveyed. To say that it resembled the greatest harmony and ecstasy obtainable between two lovers was a travesty of the truth, but was the best writers could do. The description was intended as an indication of the superlative joy and freedom to be found at the end of a long discipline. It was read in an allegorical sense by those capable of understanding. But humbler followers of the mystical fashion could not be expected to grasp such elusive concepts. To them, union with God was a lovely dream of marriage, the details most vividly imagined, the satisfaction perfect. In many paintings of the mystical marriage of St Catherine, the saint is shown as a bride, kneeling to receive the wedding ring Christ holds towards her. Usually the infant Jesus is depicted, in order to discourage the feeling, so prevalent among congregations, that an ordinary wedding is intended.

Margery felt she had now reached this final stage of the contemplative life. After her extended pilgrimage, the many dangers miraculously surmounted, the prophecies fulfilled, the enemies discomforted, surely she had qualified for this sacred marriage. What saint had been accorded more grace, or better visions, than Margery Kempe? The scream bestowed on her in the Holy Sepulchre at Jerusalem caused consternation in all hearers. Her prayers were answered promptly. God backed her up in everything she did.

It is hardly surprising, to us at least, that, kneeling in the church of the Holy Apostles on the 9th November 1414, God the Father 'seyd to this creatur: Dowtyr, I wil han ye weddyd to my God hede.'

The dream continues with an imaginary wedding, the saints and the Holy Family standing by. It resembles any marriage between two very respectable people. Nothing could illustrate more clearly Margery's total incomprehension of the meditative life. Here is no strange union with the source of being; no ecstatic merging of the self into the absolute. Her soul is not liberated by the annihilation of its individuality.

The atmosphere is thoroughly terrestrial. In the background are 'alle the xij apostelys', Saints Margaret and Catherine 'and many other seyntys and holy virgynes wyth gret multitude of awngelys'. 'I take the Margery,' said the Godhead before the assembled crowd, 'for my weddyd wyfe, for fayrar, for fowelar, for richar, for powerar.'

One feels that innumerable pious women of the fifteenth century must have enjoyed this sad imitation of a vision. The mystical way was fashionable and the various books on the subject had been written because there was a demand for them. Women could often read and many were inspired by a desire for self-improvement.

As a result of the new closeness to God, Margery received many of the signs of divine favour described by holy men and women. 'Sum tyme sche felt swet smellys wyth hir nose' which could not be compared with any perfumes to be found on this earth. She tried to describe them, thinking it might do her listeners good, but never could, except in the most inadequate way.

Frequently, 'hir bodily erys' were so full of heavenly music that she could not hear what people said, unless they shouted. Other supernatural noises were more original. There was 'the sownd of the Holy Gost,' for instance, which resembled 'a peyr of belwys blowyng in hir ere'. But this was, perhaps, too homely. 'Owyr Lord' changed 'it into the voys of a dowe'. One would expect both God and Margery to be satisfied with such an appropriate manifestation. Yet, they were not. Whether she had a sudden sharp remembrance of England in November; or whether it was merely the inscrutable workings of a celestial mind, we do not know; it is simply recorded that the dove became a robin 'that song ful merily oftyntymes in hir ryth ere'.

As a person well advanced in the spiritual life, she was now qualified to experience the celebrated fire of divine love, as described by saints of all religions. Certain Indian mystics have become the most famous examples of this strange concomitant of the meditative life, mainly because their ideas of decency and their habitat permitted them to sit naked in the snow. As no occidental holy man could possibly undress in public and hope to be respected, he had to endure God's gift as best he might. In Margery's case, however, the effects were not disagreeable. It was 'wondir hoot and delectabyl', she says 'and ryth comfortabyl', though she was a little alarmed at first. God reassured her. She need not fear illness. It was a veritable sign that all her sins were being burnt away. Thereafter, for 'abowtyn xvj yer' she enjoyed a cosy feeling, 'thow the wedyr wer nevyr so colde'.

Her sense of sight was also graced. She had 'white thyngys' before the eyes, flying thickly 'al abowte hir on every syde', dancing up and down like dust in a sunbeam. On fine days, in a bright light, she saw them especially clearly. The appearances were not confined to what might seem to be suitable occasions. They came in church and at her prayers, certainly, but also at unusual times: 'at hir mete', for instance; or as she walked about 'in felde and in towne, bothyn goyng and syttyng'. It worried her a little that they should be so ubiquitous. Suppose it were really a deception of the Devil?

When she began seeing them in the middle of the night as well, 'sche was aferde what thei myth be'. Darkness belonged to Satan. One had to keep continual watch against his subtle machinations. Suppose they represented an army from hell instead of the crowd of angels she had taken them to be? God was mercifully reassuring. He was always accompanied, he said, by a great retinue of angels. It was these that she saw. Moreover, they had a duty to protect her from all evil influences, whether natural, or supernatural. 'Fro that tyme forwarde sche' was much comforted and 'usyd to seyn whan sche saw hem comyn: Benedictus qui venit in nomine domini.'

# CHAPTER XXVII

## *The Affair of the White Clothes*

She needed something to sustain her, wandering the streets of Rome. Life, in the ordinary everyday sense, became increasingly difficult as the months went by. 'Evyr hir owyn cuntremen wer obstynat and specyaly' the priest who had been the principal cause of her expulsion from the English hostel. He particularly objected to the white outfit she now wore as an outward mark of dedication to God. He also had claims to holiness and, in his opinion, she had sold herself to the Devil. The authorities at the hospital had quailed before the sincerity of his conviction. So now, Margery's German confessor and friend, whose miraculous understanding of English has been recorded, began to have doubts.

He had been deeply impressed by her revelations and frightened by her powers as a seer. Previous tests had always proved her right. Yet, this English colleague disturbed him. Was he merely envious of God's favour towards Margery; or was she a contumacious woman, disobedient to the church, full of devils and heresy? He felt obliged to try her. Would she obey whatever spiritual directions he might give, he asked, the next time they met? 'Ya, syr,' she answered unsuspectingly. 'Wyl ye don than as I schal byd yow don?' he pressed her further. 'Wyth ryth good wyl, sire, sade she.' It must have been a disagreeable shock to hear him say: 'I charge yow that ye leve yowr white clothys and weryth ageyn yowr blak cloths.' However, there was nothing for it but to change her dress at once. She had given her word and felt it impossible to extricate herself. Obedience to representatives of God's kingdom on earth was one of her cardinal principles. She had no sympathy with heretics. Her ambitions lay entirely within the church as constituted. This must be a trial laid on her because of her sins.

It turned out a severe penance. The 'wyfys of Rome', for instance, were very sarcastic. She had, perhaps, been waylaid by highwaymen, they inquired with false solicitude? It could not be that she had voluntarily put off a costume which had, they understood, been expressly ordained by God as a sign that she

148

was a cut above the usual. 'Nay, madame,' she had modestly to reply.

Even worse, 'it happyd hir to metyn with the preste that was hir enmye'. He was delighted to see that she had submitted to the will of the church, and therefore of God. 'I am glad that ye gon in blak clothyng as ye wer wont to do,' he cried. She could not refrain from saying, mildly and politely, that, in point of fact, God really preferred her in white. 'Now I wot wel,' replied he in a rage, 'that thu hast a devyl wythinne the, for I her hym spekyn in the to me.' Pray for me then, she said in a saintly manner. Her only object was to please the heavenly powers.

Suddenly, he was overcome by the extent of his sufferings at her hands. All the way to Jerusalem he had endured her and all the way back as far as Venice. She was a devil sent to torment him. It must be so. No natural woman could possibly defy a man in his position as she had done, day in, day out. No mortal could have escaped the dangers she had been obliged to face. Beside himself, he cursed her with all the authority of his office.

She continued calm and sweet, pointing out that if possessed of a devil, she would now be very angry with him. As he could see, this was not the case. On the contrary, such was the strength of divinity in her that she could not 'be wroth wyth yow for no-thyng that ye can don on to me'.

Perceiving that the forces of evil were too much for him, the priest left her in possession of the field 'wyth hevy cher'. We don't know whether there were any spectators of his defeat, but as the scene appears to have happened at some shrine which was the object of pilgrimage, one would expect at least a small crowd. Even those who did not know English would realize that he had been worsted.

Though triumphant, Margery was shaken. It was no light matter to be cursed by a priest, however undeservedly. 'And than owyr Lord spak to this creatur in hir sowle and seyd, Dowtyr, drede the not what that evyr he sey unto the.' It was a sign of wickedness in a man to disparage Margery. Even an annual trip to Jerusalem could not expiate this sin, for it amounted to a slander of God himself, such was the closeness of their mutual relationship. 'This prest that is thyn enmy,' God concluded roundly, 'he is but an ypocryte.'

Her German confessor, however, thought it not a moment for self-assertion. It was safer to be humble in the face of danger. She had no friends to look after her interests except himself and Richard the beggarman. Her funds were getting low. Only well-off people could afford to court trouble. As a further exercise in obedience, and as a penance, he set her to serve an old pauper woman.

Always ready for any spectacular abasement, Margery entered on her duties with enthusiasm. 'Sche served hir as sche wold a don owyr Lady.' Had not Mary been poor and persecuted, obliged first to give birth in a stable and then flee to Egypt on a donkey? She felt a great glow of virtue suffuse her as she drank the poor woman's sour wine, pouring from her own good bottle for her charge. She lived in the old woman's hovel as a servant, having no bed and only her cloak to cover her as she lay on the floor. The dirt was frightful. She became full of vermin 'and suffyrd gret peyn therwyth'. She would go out and fetch water and collect sticks so that they might have a small fire to keep out the damp. There was no money for food most days and Margery would set off 'and beggyd mete and wyn bothyn for hir'.

How could God fail to recognize and reward such efforts? She was his recent bride. Hosts of angels appeared at all hours of the day and night. She could hardly hear herself speak for heavenly music and the Holy Ghost breathing in her right ear. Her confessor must have been very impressed by the wholehearted way in which she shouldered the burden he had imposed. The daughter of a rich merchant and mayor in an important English town became, at his word, uncomplaining servant to the lowest of the low. It was her enemies who were hypocrites, as she had said. Her account of her mystical marriage and subsequent signs of grace completed the conquest of his doubts. When she announced that God wished her to resume white clothes 'he durst not onys sey nay'. She wore them 'evyr aftyr' with proper ecclesiastical licence.

It was now almost Christmas, 1414. The celebrations in Rome could not have their full magnificence, for Pope John XXIII was at Constance, the centre of Christendom at this moment. There, he was to conduct mass on Christmas morning, The Emperor Sigismund acting as deacon, the congregation sprinkled with potentates from all over Europe. He had, as yet, no suspicion that many of his audience thought it impossible to reform the church unless he were first deposed and a fresh start made with someone of a character more in keeping with the Christian virtues, as generally understood.

It is not quite clear where in Rome Margery spent Christmas Day, as she is slightly ambiguous on the subject. After the triumph over the white outfit, she was divinely informed that it was time to end her penance and return to the English hostel, despite all enemies. When the poor woman was told of this, she 'was ryth sory and mad gret mone'. Never in a poverty-stricken life had she had such a wonderful holiday as during the last six weeks, waited on hand and foot, her every want attended to, good quality wine poured into her cup. It was like a miracle. She did not subscribe to the view that Margery was a woman to be got rid of at all costs. What did it matter if she talked too much and was rather queer? The pleasures of a free personal maid far outweighed everything.

Margery replied to her entreaties that it was 'the wil of God that it schuld be so'. Plainly the foretaste of heaven had come to an end. God's ways were not the ways of this world. After some such reflections and perceiving also that Margery was not to be dissuaded, 'sche toke it the mor esily'.

It is doubtful, however, whether Margery was able to move back into the hostel quite yet. The narrative of her stay in Rome, though full of detail, is not altogether consecutive. One has to arrange the events described in the order which best makes sense. It seems more likely that the victory over her fellowship, led by the English priest, happened a little later when she had found more important friends than a German confessor, his admirers, the pauper woman and an unfortunate Irishman.

# CHAPTER XXVIII

*Beggared in Rome*

During the Christmas season, Margery evidently felt some sort of a grand gesture was required. She had suffered considerably in the old woman's employment; but it had only been a pretence of poverty and humbleness. She remained the mayor's daughter, doing a bit of slumming for moral reasons. It occurred to her now, and God supported the view, that she ought to give away everything for the love of Christ and live in apostolic simplicity. Holy people never had money in their pockets. All the well-known hermits, recluses, saints, prophets, lived on alms from patrons and admirers.

She acted on the idea immediately. She had not much cash left by this time. Fortunately she had borrowed a certain sum from Richard. It was enough. She distributed the lot to deserving persons. Perhaps the old woman got a last bonus. With a fine glow of satisfaction, she became as poor as any saint had ever been.

When Richard heard she had given away even the money he had lent, 'he was gretly mevyd and evyl plesyd' and said so rather forcibly. His experience of life convinced him that nothing could be more foolish, or indeed wicked, than to throw away one's means of support. Had he begged night and day for this? How would she repay him? He had been her loyal friend for many months, taking her side in numerous fights. He had stood a lot because he liked her, or pitied her, or half believed in her claims – we do not know the exact reason. Anyway, this was the end. He would have nothing more to do with her. He 'spak ryth scharply to hir'.

'Richard,' she said, in an effort to soothe him, 'be the grace of God we shal comyn hom into Inglond ryth wel.' There, she could collect money, for the faithful John Kempe was looking after her affairs. At Whitsun, 1417, she calculated, she would be in Bristol, waiting to embark on a pilgrimage she had determined to make to Compostela in Spain. Let him come to her then. It was a convenient port for Ireland. 'And ther shal I pay yow ryth wel and trewly be the grace of God.' He had no option but to agree to this distant appointment 'and so he dede'. He was far from mollified. His hard-earned gold had been thrown away in a fit of dramatics. He could not forgive her. We do not hear of him again until he turns up at Bristol, two years later, demanding settlement.

Being misunderstood was a fate to which Margery was perfectly accustomed. She did not much mind. Every false accusation suffered, brought her closer to the niche of sainthood. We may be sure that she received Richard's reproaches with a sweet humility and begged him to remember her in his prayers. The heavenly music, perhaps, was louder and more continuous, the smells more intoxicating, the fire of love and the phantom robin more comforting than ever.

Unfortunately, she had misjudged her reputation. Her followers proved too few and too poor to depend on for alms. The day came when she lay flat on the ground in S. Marcello, wondering what on earth to do. She 'had neyther peny ne halfpeny to helpyn hirself wyth'. St Marcellus himself might intercede for her. He had known what it was to tumble from a comfortable station in life to destitution. A Roman living at the turn of the third and fourth centuries, he was converted, rose to the pontificate and was expelled from the city for his activities. Later he returned, was arrested and died as a workman in the public stables. It seems a tame history beside the torments endured by humbler martyres. But the degradation was the worse for him since he had been Pope.

His church was founded in the fifth century and his body brought from the catacombs and put in it, along with the heads of Sts Cosmas and Damian and parts of St Phocas. It was a place where sacred influences were strong. Indulgences were given to pilgrims. It was listed in the guide books and was easy to find, being near 'a grete memorial of rome'* the column of Marcus Aurelius, on which were depicted 'all the stories of the batail of troye'.* We cannot admire today what Margery saw as she lay on the pavement because it was thoroughly done up and modernized about a hundred years later.

She was able to get through to God in these auspicious surroundings, but, at first, he was rather unsympathetic. 'Thu art not yet so powr as I was whan I heng nakyd on the Cros,' he pointed

* Capgrave.

out. She owned a decent set of clothes, at least. Further, he remarked: 'Thow hast cownseld other men to ben powr for my sake and therfor thu must folwyn thyn owyn cownsel.'

After these preliminaries, he relented, however, saying that gold would come to her in the near future. She ought not to despair. He would not desert her. 'I have frendys in every cuntre,' he reminded her, 'and shal make my frendys to comfort the.'

Feeling much less homesick and abandoned, she went out into the street with renewed courage. Something would turn up. Her luck had never failed, by the grace of God. Sure enough, as she went along she 'met casualy wyth a good man' who spoke English and perhaps was a pilgrim from England. 'They fellyn in good comunicacyon as thei went togedir be the wey.' The conversation seems, on the whole, to have been one-sided, consisting of 'many good talys' and pious 'exhortacyons' by Margery 'tyl God visited hym wyth terys of devocyon and of compunccyon to hys hey comfort and consolacyon'.

She was able to confide her difficulties to this understanding man. Evidently feeling, in the emotional atmosphere, that his life had been enriched and heaven brought within his grasp, he responded generously. 'He gaf hir mony be the whech sche was wel relevyd.' They parted on an auspicious note, but do not seem to have met again. Either he left Rome; or else, being an impressionable man, he listened to her enemies at the hostel and felt he had been taken in.

In due course, Margery found herself once more faced with starvation and eviction from her lodgings. She may have had audiences, but they did not contribute. Her staunchest admirers were among the poor Italian women who did not know a word of English and, in any case, had no money. They would sometimes invite her in to warm herself by their meagre fires and she, full of holy thoughts, would weep uncontrollably, especially if there was a small boy in the family; for the poor mother 'syttyng ful of sorwe and sadnes' seemed an incarnation of the Virgin. Her tears were so distressing that the woman would try to comfort her 'not knowyng why sche wept' precisely, but seeing her poverty and thinking that reason enough. The Roman populace, as Margery noted, were very wretched at this date, what with taxes, wars, papal rapacity, lack of trade and insalubrious situation; for the marshes were not properly drained any more. It was different in Lynn.

Something had to be done. She could not earn her living as a holy woman only. It was necessary to have a supplementary job. Richard had made a success of begging. The idea had been at the back of her mind as a last resort since she first got into financial difficulties. What other profession was open to an outcast in Rome, except that of prostitute?

She began, therefore, to frequent the richer quarters of the town, joining the indigent crowd near palaces in the hope that a gentleman would throw her a coin. She had a taste for humiliation in the form of penance and mockery from her fellow pilgrims, but this was another matter. Now she was fighting to keep body and soul together. The little inconveniences she had suffered in order to atone for vanity, or on account of self-assertion, must have seemed a perfect paradise in retrospect. They had been so short, for one thing. Only six weeks with the verminous old woman; about the same period wearing black instead of the ordained white. Was it possible to see an end to her present degradation? How would she ever get home without even the resourceful Richard? One could simply trust in God, reflecting that Jesus had been reduced to worse straits during his life on earth.

It must have been a great moment when she saw Dame Margaret Florentine passing by. This was the very lady whose party, conducted by the Knights of Rhodes, she had joined at Assisi. Dame Margaret was shocked on recognizing Margery, for whom she had conceived an affectionate regard. Conversation was difficult: 'neithyr of hem cowd wel undirstond other but be syngnys er tokenys and in fewe comown wordys.' 'Margery in poverte?' the lady stammered. 'Ya, grawnt poverte, madam,' replied she sadly.

'Than the lady comawndyd hir to etyn wyth hir every Sonday.' These dinner parties turned out a success. The language barrier prevented Margery from launching into her monologue. The company saw only a pious woman, rather demonstrative perhaps, but grateful, honest and with sufficient idea of how to behave politely at table. Dame Margaret became quite a disciple, putting

Margery in the place of honour and helping 'hir mete wyth hir owyn handys'. As we hear nothing of any husband, it seems likely that she was a rich, elderly widow who had turned to religion as a consolation in her loneliness.

She had met Margery on pilgrimage and would naturally incline to a woman who had travelled far and dangerously for the love of Christ; who had been affected by the divine influences emanating from the holy city of Jerusalem; who seemed close to God, as far as one could judge from outward signs. After the meal, she would give her protégée 'an hamper' containing enough for two days, 'and filled hir botel wyth good wyn'. Sometimes she would give her money as well.

The whole atmosphere of Dame Margaret's house was congenial. Her friends were serious and respectable, united in esteem for the curious English castaway. It may be that they put many of her peculiarities down to her being a foreigner, native of an island far off in the northern fogs. Being protected, to some extent, from her ruthless egoism, they could more easily accept her claims to grace. It became quite the fashion to entertain her. A man called 'Marcelle bad hir to mete ij days in the woke'. His wife was pregnant and he wanted Margery to be godmother to the baby, but unfortunately she left Rome before it was born.

'Also ther was an holy mayden gaf this creatur hir mete on the Wednysday.' That left only once a week entirely unprovided for, when 'sche beggyd hir mete fro dor to dore'. Perhaps even this day was filled up later on: for she made the acquaintance of 'a gret jentylwoman in Rome' who wished her 'to be godmodyr of hir childe'. It was a little girl and they named her Bridget after the saint, whom they had known in her old age.

'Whan the Maystyr and Brothyr of the Hospital of Seynt Thomas' heard what grand friends she now had, they began to doubt that she was possessed by a devil, as the English priest had said. To take the side against someone who was godmother to a great gentlewoman's daughter was obviously bad policy. They had to live permanently in Rome. What could a passing company of English pilgrims offer which was more advantageous than the favour of Dame Margaret Florentine?

They sent a message declaring 'thei weryn ryth sory' to have put her out. If she would consent to come back, 'sche shulde be wolcomear than evyr sche was beforn'. As she had no money, they must have offered to accommodate her free of charge. She thanked them for their charitable thoughts and moved in forthwith. 'Thei madyn hir ryth good cher and weryn rith glad of hir comyng.' What her fellowship said when they found she had caught up with them again is not recorded. One can be sure she forgave all the wrongs she had suffered, elaborately, meekly and infuriatingly. She must also have regaled them with the improving monologue they had come to hate so long ago; for she found it impossible to curb her nature in the interests of peace.

# CHAPTER XXIX

*Last Roman Victories*

The worst was over. She had won almost the final round in the running fight with her fellowship. Reconciliation was not to be hoped for: their mood was too bitter, their sense of an unjust fate too strong. However, on account of Dame Margaret Florentine, Marcelle, the holy maiden and the great gentlewoman, they were obliged to endure her triumph. The authorities at the hospital were now her devoted admirers. The company could only bide their time and wait for an opportunity to discredit her, if they could.

Ever since the first parting at Constance, Margery's perfidious servant girl had remained in their employment, steadfastly refusing to return to her lawful mistress. She did not care that her behaviour caused gossip. The fellowship were much more amusing to work for than a demented woman who thought laughter a sin. She was a gay young person, well suited by her present position of general housekeeper and barmaid at the hostel. This was a lucrative job. Margery found her 'in meche welth and prosperyte', less inclined than ever to listen to suggestions of returning to her duty.

Sometimes, as an exercise in humility, Margery would apply to the girl on the days when she had to beg a dinner for lack of cash. 'And the mayden' dished her up a plateful 'wyth good wyl' occasionally adding 'a grote therto'. But no entreaties, threats, visions, prophecies, reported apparitions or messages dictated by the Almighty could induce her to seek salvation in Margery's service.

This defeat, however, was entirely overshadowed by the arrival of a new party from England. Among them was an earnest priest who had met friends of hers in England. Convinced by her claims to sainthood, he enquired at the hostel and 'cam into the place wher that sche was and ful humbely and mekely' he addressed her as mother. He wished to be accepted as her disciple, he said. He had also brought money in case she should be in need of it.

Margery was extremely glad to hear that God's promise of

financial relief was now to be fulfilled. There was enough to get her home, if she was careful. 'Sche seyd that he was wolcom' and began to sound him, a little cautiously at first, for it seemed too good to be true. She related 'sumwhat of hir maner of levyng' inspirations, contemplations and other matters. This man was bound to meet her enemies and who could tell exactly what turn his opinions would then take?

Even an abbreviated account of her spiritual adventures must, one feels, have taken time. She had never found it easy to stop, once well started. As he listened his enthusiasm rose. Everything he had heard in England which had so impressed him was a mere fraction of the truth. She was a saint, a mystic, a seer. 'Than wolde he no lengar suffyr hir to beggyn hir mete fro dore to dore.' She must dine with his fellowship whenever an invitation failed. He would like it better still if she refused others and gave him the benefit of 'gostly comfort' and uplifting discourse every day.

Margery's enemies were much displeased by the new arrangements. The dining hall again re-echoed to her platitudes. Their jokes and laughter brought on a horrible atmosphere of disapproval and forgiving sorrow. Something must be done. They 'seyd that sche was shrevyn at a preste whech cowde not undirstondyn hir langwage ne hir confessyown'.

The new friend was upset by the alleged irregularity. No doubt many other stories were poured out to him, but this seemed to him so serious that he had to ask her about it. Perhaps he had been introduced to the man and found his English inadequate.

Margery was not alarmed. She would win this round too. 'Good sone,' she said in reply to his questions, 'I beseche yow, preyth hym to dyne.' Then they would soon discover whether, or not, he had a miraculous power of understanding her remarks, as she averred.

It was done. 'Hyr confessowr was preyd to mete.' He accepted. He could not do anything else. It was a trial such as the medieval mind adored: simple, dramatic and with inescapable consequences on failure. He sat down in the middle of Margery's new fellowship. 'The good preste of Inglonde' conversed affably with Margery, while the German 'satt al stille in a maner of hevynes', giving the company to understand that he could not follow their pious flights 'les than thei spokyn Latyn'.

Eventually, Margery from pity for his obvious boredom and also 'mech more to prevyn the werk of God' began to relate 'in Englysch a story of Holy Writte'. She would not speak 'of no vanyte ne of no fantasijs' at a moment like this, she records. That would have been to cast a frivolous air over an important occasion.

This was the highlight of the evening. For this they had been convened. Everyone listened carefully, including the German. We do not know what story it was, nor how long Margery took to tell it. But brevity was not one of her virtues. At last she finished. 'Than thei askyd hir confessowr yf he undirstod that sche had seyd.'

They must have awaited his response with considerable excitement; for none doubted that the trial would prove whether, or not, a miracle had been worked especially to rescue Margery and confound the machinations of her enemies.

'He anon in Latyn telde hem the same words that sche seyd beforn in Englisch.' It was not exactly a surprise as they believed in Margery and expected her to triumph. It was a splendid demonstration of her heavenly powers, a vindication of everything she had ever done. Nobody suggested that he might have caught the names in the story and guessed which one it was. None said that he had only pretended ignorance of the previous conversation. Far from it. 'Thei had gret mervayle' and praised God that he had 'mad an alyon to undirstondyn hir' when all her fellow countrymen had cast her out.

Now she could let herself go. Her supporters inside and outside the hostel were numerous and influential enough. No one dared to shut her up, or openly to accuse her of deviations from the orthodox. She was able to enjoy dramatic scenes in churches without having to endure the mockery of her enemies. She had sufficient money to ensure a passage home. Christ himself interpreted when she could not understand the sermons, owing to their being delivered in a foreign language.

What wonder that she became excited, staggering 'as a drunkyn man' while Jesus' 'melydiows voys' was 'softly sowndyng in hir sowle'. Sometimes the fire of love burnt so hotly within her that she writhed on the ground, screaming, crying and with terrible

Pilgrims arrive at Joppa. (From a book of 28 miniatures, without text, illustrating chapters 1–5 of Maundevile's *Travels*. Early 15th century. Additional 24189.)

Jerusalem. (From a Book of Hours belonging to René of Anjou, titular King of Naples [died 1480]. Egerton 1070.)

sobs. The congregation were amazed at such evident suffering and asked what was the matter. 'To whom sche' with a mad screech shouted, 'The Passyon of Crist sleth me!'

The women of the audience were greatly impressed even though they did not know a word of English. They could see that she was possessed by the supernatural and must have supposed it to be the Holy Ghost, or the saint at whose altar the scene took place. When she returned to her normal senses, they insisted on taking her home. It seemed to them that their affairs were bound to prosper if a sainted pilgrim drank a cup of wine beside their fire. In this way, she much increased her following among the humble of Rome.

Priests also rallied to her side. If the Master of the Hospital, Dame Margaret Florentine and other notabilities said she was all right, who were they to disagree? They made a point of saying to the English pilgrims admiringly: 'This woman hath sowyn meche good seed in Rome sithyn sche cam hydir.' Her enemies were obliged to admit total defeat.

'Blissed art thow, dowtyr,' cried St Jerome to her in Sta Maria Maggiore where he lay miraculously translated from his tomb in Bethlehem, 'where he was first buried, after which he was carried to Constantinople. How he then came to Rome, I leave to the learned to decide.'* She should encourage her tears, the saint continued, 'for many shal be savyd therby'.

This was a particularly auspicious place for a vision. The holy influences were strong. St Matthew lay above the high altar† and there was a portrait of the Virgin executed by St Luke. A third part of one's sins were automatically forgiven on stepping into the church in a proper frame of mind. Margery was deeply grateful for St Jerome's 'gostly comfortys'. Without them, she records, she would have found it difficult, if not impossible, to have 'boryn the schamys and wonderyngs the whech sche suffyrd pacyently and mekely' and, at the last, had vanquished.

The long visit to Rome was now coming to an end. Shortly after Easter, 1415, she would begin the journey home in the company of her new friends who, it appears, were not extending their pilgrimage further. She had worshipped every relic and

* Von Harff.
† Von Harff found him also in Padua.

obtained every indulgence the city had to offer, except the Pope's blessing: John XXIII remained throughout at Constance, fighting for his title against those members of the council who had decided that he would not do as head of a reformed Christendom. The Easter ceremonies had to be performed by deputies. Some, no doubt, had to be omitted, as only St Peter's personal representative on earth could properly conduct them.

Margery does not mention the Pope at all, nor even St Peter's with its seven principal, and ninety-three subsidiary, altars, its magnificent spread of the most precious relics; especially the Veronica, or handkerchief, on which Christ had imprinted his anguished face during the last hours of his life. There was also the rope used by Judas Iscariot to hang himself, the stone on which St Peter had cried after denying Jesus and a great variety of parts of saints.

Since the Passion was the centrepiece of Margery's religious system, Easter in Rome must have been an exciting experience. She could now indulge in her excesses unchecked. One can imagine her writhing and staggering in the processions round the innumerable churches; screaming and throwing out her arms like a cross as she watched the passion play at the Colosseum; applauded admiringly by friends and supporters; watched with some trepidation by others. Neither the rigours of piety, travel nor destitution undermined her health to any appreciable extent. She was always ready for another vision, another fit, a go of fasting, or a strenuous penance – though what sins can have remained unaccounted for is a mystery: practically every church in Rome bestowed indulgences and forgivenesses of all kinds, not to speak of the eternal benefits deriving from a visit to the Holy Land and God's monotonous assurances of a good seat in paradise.

But the medieval mind never tired of the underside of religion. Sin, death, blood and hell were perpetually dwelt on. The happy relaxation to be found in heaven is hardly described. The holy saints and martyrs lived there with God; how they passed the time is not particularly considered. Their torments on earth, on the other hand, so much resembling the pains of hell, were fervently studied. Everyone knew their gruesome legends. The mystery plays abounded in elaborate stage effects, such as bags of blood to be emptied at the appropriate moment and hellmouths full of smoke and capacious enough for the damned to be fitfully seen, contorting themselves in agony. One can easily imagine how so violent and gloomy a creed produced such devotees as Margery Kempe.

# CHAPTER XXX

### Return to England

The Easter celebrations being past, the time had come to start the arduous journey home. Many thieves and desperate persons were reported on the road. One would be lucky, the jeremiahs said, to get through alive, let alone with one's belongings intact. Others must have given a rosier picture, for the company decided to start. It was April 1415, as far as can be judged. The weather was not yet so hot as to make travelling uncomfortable, though spring can be very wet in Italy. By the time they reached the Alps, the snows would not be deep. Financial considerations must also have entered into their discussions: one had to keep enough money to see one safely to one's 'owyn natyf lond'.

Margery prayed earnestly for divine assistance, reminding God 'wyth many a bittyr teer of hir eye' of all the dangers she had safely avoided under his aegis. Surely he would not fail in his protection? Brigands were no threat to the soul; she was not worried about that; it was their lives and their goods that she wished him to preserve, 'Lord, yf it plese the. As thu wilt, so mot it be.'

'Drede the not dowtyr,' replied God in his usual kind manner, 'for thu and alle that ben in thy cumpany shal gon as safe as yf thei were in Seynt Petrys cherch.'

Everyone was much cheered by this assurance. Preparations for departure were completed. Farewells were said. It must have taken Margery some days to get round her large circle of friends, bidding each an emotional good-bye and looking forward to an eventual reunion in heaven 'whan thei were passyd this wretchyd wordelys exile'. It seemed most unlikely that they would meet again sooner.

The parting with her German confessor was particularly affecting. They had been through so much together. Their connection was sealed by what seemed to be a miracle as genuine as any recorded of St Bridget. 'Sche fallyng on hyr knes receyved the benefys of hys blyssyng', the inevitable tears meanwhile 'rennyng down be her chekys'.

All her acquaintance, from Dame Margaret Florentine down

to the women she had known in her poverty, must have been sorry to see her go. They believed in her sainthood. The advantages to be derived from direct commerce with holiness were at an end. Who knew what good fortune might have come their way, if she had stayed?

At length, they were ready. All suitable saints had been prayed to, all possible blessings obtained. They had packed up securely their relics, money and food. A guide was not required, for the road was well known. They had sufficient Italian to ask the way, if lost. Thus 'sche and hir felaschep passyd forth into Inglond-ward.' It was more than a year since Margery had seen her husband and family. She had had adventures that remained in her memory for the rest of her life. The special status accorded to one who had endured the long hardship of travel to the Holy Land and obtained the ineffable benefits there dispensed was hers, should she live through present dangers.

'Whan thei were a lityl wey owte of Rome', they saw signs, or heard rumours, of the dreaded bandits. 'Modyr,' quavered the priest, on whose friendship and money she now depended, 'I drede me to be deed and slayn wyth enmyis.'

'Nay, sone,' she replied with her invariable courage, 'ye schal far ryth wel and gon saf, be the grace of God.' He was satisfied with this, believing that she spoke from supernatural knowledge. His confidence was not misplaced. No one molested them. It was certain that she must be divinely protected. Her invulnerability would perhaps extend to him, were he close enough to her affections. He became as attentive to her needs 'as yf he had ben hir owyn sone, born of hir body'. More so indeed.

Thus companionably, they travelled northward many days. We do not know exactly what was their route, but as they arrived at last in Zealand, it seems likely that, after crossing the Alps, they followed the Rhine valley road. They would, in that case, have passed through Constance, where the great international conference had entered a dramatic phase, the consequences of which affected Margery strongly after her return to England.

The council had been called ostensibly by Pope John XXIII as head of the church with the object of eliminating the multitudinous corruptions that had affected religious life in the course of centuries. John, himself, was quite happy to continue the sale of offices, indulgences, licences to priests to do anything they fancied, and the imposition of ingenious new taxes, as well as the strenuous collection of old ones. It suited his character as an ex-pirate and successful general in the field. He required mistresses and money in order to enjoy life to the full. One need not assume that he disbelieved in God. It was just that his whole turn of mind was secular.

He was, however, obliged to convene the council and lay before it a tremendous programme of reform because all serious persons, lay and ecclesiastical, could no longer stand the scandal caused by the papal system. Also, they dared not procrastinate in case the church should disappear in a sea of heresy. This would mean the coming of Antichrist and the end of the world. Pope John brought with him to Constance a strong contingent of Italian bishops and cardinals, with whom he hoped to control the voting.

The principal heretics in the winter of 1414 were the followers of John Hus in Bohemia. There had been a connection between England and Bohemia in the late fourteenth century, for Richard II had married a princess of that country. It was about the time when Wyclif's ideas and writings were being eagerly discussed at Oxford. The University of Prague read the new books with great interest, for the ideas expressed therein were similar to their own. Both the Husites and the Lollards represented the latest movements in a heresy which had always existed since the church became rich, organized, bureaucratic and far removed from those ideals of simplicity and solitude to be found, for instance, in the Celtic church.

Hus was a priest of humble birth and forceful character. He possessed eloquence and no one could doubt the purity of his life or the sincerity of his ideals. He preached powerful sermons in the vernacular and people who disliked the German influence in Bohemian national affairs, were attracted. He was well received, as time went on, by persons of substance in Prague, even becom-ing confessor to the queen.

When he denounced clerical abuses, the orthodox party was with him. The denial of transubstantiation, however, could not be accepted by upholders of the Roman faith. The doctrine that a priest was not a priest, nor could a pope be a pope, unless his moral character were acceptable to God, was seen to have political dangers. If it were granted that every individual, by a study of the scriptures, was qualified to decide whether those in authority had a right to their positions, complete anarchy would result. The system could be applied to secular princes as well. In Bohemia, they wished to turn out the Germans, particularly from their dominant position in the University of Prague. In England, Sir John Oldcastle, the best-known Lollard in the country, had raised a rebellion. But the Lollards were not nearly so numerous and powerful as the Husites of Bohemia.

The Council of Constance, therefore, set itself to obtain the reformation of the papacy and the forcible repression of the extreme party who wanted to make a clean sweep of everything, leaving no intermediary between man and God. Pope John and his two rivals, Popes Benedict and Gregory, must be brought to abdicate and a new pontiff, acceptable to all, be elected. Hus must be persuaded to abjure, or, if he would not, burnt.

Hus was summoned to give an account of himself. He came under the guarantee of a safe conduct, from the Emperor Sigismund, chief lay potentate of the council. It was his intention to be remembered as the most famous emperor of all time: the man who had ended the schism, using his great position to further God's aims. In this way, the world below would become extremely agreeable for him, almost like heaven; and his passage to the world above be secured.

The council set to work with enthusiasm. With regard to Hus, it was decided that one could not give a valid promise to a heretic. That would be as if one pledged one's word to the Devil. His safe conduct being, therefore, valueless, Hus was imprisoned. Sigismund would have liked to counter these arguments, feeling that they showed him in a poor light, whatever the correct theological interpretation. But he could not.

In the case of John XXIII, it was said that though he had supreme power in the church, the council, representing the whole of Christendom, had a mandate of its own superior to his. In this context, the pope became merely a member of the church. John was very uneasy when he heard the new theory propounded, especially on finding that even his own Italian party was not fully behind him. He was resolved not to abdicate, come what might. It must have been a great pleasure to re-canonize St Bridget in February 1415 with suitable pomp at Constance. She had, of course, been canonized already, but her supporters were afraid it was not properly done because that pope had subsequeltly been declared schismatic. As he conducted the necessary ritual, John could reflect that in this case, at least, his authority was recognized.

The evil day, however, was not to be postponed indefinitely. At the end of May 1415, he was formally deposed after humiliating adventures, imprisonment and the presentation to the council of a most degrading list of accusations concerning his private life.

It took longer to dispose of Hus. Arguments continued for months in an effort to make him see the error of his ways. They failed, for he was convinced that his ideas were pleasing to God. He could not, with honesty, abjure. It was not until June 1415 that they gave up the struggle and burnt him. By then, Margery was home. She does not mention the council past which she journeyed, screaming horribly, taken with fits, receiving God's compliments, greatly admired by her new disciple; though there is a suggestion that others of the fellowship were unable to appreciate her virtues with quite such intensity.

Perhaps there is something to be said for her indifference. The council, and others which followed it at intervals, were only superficially successful. In 1418, after four years deliberations, it had burnt two heretics, got rid of three popes and elected one supreme pontiff, accepted by all. Yet the ecclesiastical system which was the cause of the trouble remained essentially untouched. By the last decade of the century, a Borgia was pope and the protestant movement had grown to overwhelming size.

Skirting danger as best they could, the pilgrims had an uneventful journey to Middleburgh in Zealand. They ran into nothing worse than bad storms, which Margery found alarming enough. She had a particular horror of lightning and also of being washed away by torrential rain. Though she knew her fears were silly – God had told her so – she could not help being nervous at such times. She was as safe as if in 'the strengest chirche in alle this worlde' no matter what the weather. A special revelation had assured her of it. Yet, thunder still made her tremble.

On reaching Middleburgh, so close to home, the pilgrims were, naturally, anxious to cross the sea at the first opportunity. It happened that the next boat sailed on a Sunday. 'Modyr,' said her disciple, the priest, torn between longing to embark and a feeling that one oughtn't to spend Sunday listening to sailors swearing, 'wyl ye gon wyth yowr felaschep er not on this good day?' 'Nay, sone,' she replied firmly, 'it is not my Lordys wille.'

The more devout among the party were, therefore, obliged to stay. The rest set off with a fair wind, rejoicing at the end of their travels and, no doubt, glad to be relieved of an oppressive companion. It is not recorded that they suffered any misfortune because of their impiety. On the contrary, it was those adhering to Margery who were incommoded: a week passed before another boat could leave. The hostel filled up and the pilgrims, in their boredom, began fighting, cursing, drinking and generally breaking God's commandments.

By Friday, the weather cleared sufficiently to permit a picnic in the country. All the English pilgrims went, to get a little fresh air and exercise. Margery accompanied them, lecturing the while on their shortcomings 'and scharply sche spak ageyns hem' for sins and blasphemings. Fortunately, however, they did not have to endure long, for at a certain point, 'owr Lord Ihesu Crist' abruptly 'bad hir gon hom in haste to hir hostel', as a storm was approaching. They had hardly reached shelter when it broke. Margery's friends regarded this as a definite sign of God's favour. Perhaps the other side did, too. Had it not relieved them of a killjoy?

The next morning, her disciple ran to her, crying, 'Modyr, good tydyngys! We have good wynd, thankyd be God!' They hastened to the quay to book a passage. Cash was very short and they did not want to be delayed another week. But the only boat ready to leave was a miserable bark which looked to the priest as if it would sink under the first wave. Surely, he protested, it would be madness to trust oneself to such a craft. 'Modyr,' he urged, 'here is no schip.'

'Sone,' she reproved him, 'God is as mythy in a lityl schip as in a gret schip.' It was not Sunday. The wind was fair. What objection could there be? Heaven had decreed that they should start at once.

It must have been deceptively fine to begin with, or she would have stayed on shore, leaving it to God to pay the bills when the time came. After they had gone too far to put back into port, suddenly 'it began waxin gret tempestys and dyrke wedyr'. The bark wallowed alarmingly. The passengers thought they would surely sink. 'Than thei cryed to God', repeating the most efficacious prayers they knew. Luckily, it was only the tail end of the last week's storms and did not last long: 'anon the tempestys sesyd and thei had fayr wedyr' for the rest of the crossing. The next day, in the evening 'thei cam to londe' in East Anglia.

Now a great feeling of relief and joy overcame her. How many times in the past year had it seemed likely that she would not reach home again? She might have died in the Alps with William Weaver; or in Venice where she was so ill and her maid refused to nurse her; or in the Holy Land of exhaustion and fever; or on the Italian roads from attack by bandits; or in Rome of starvation. All these dangers she had triumphantly passed, for her courage had never failed. She 'fel downe on hir knes kyssyng the grownde'.

# CHAPTER XXXI

## Reunion

Even Margery was laughing and cheerful as they took the road to
Norwich. She had not experienced such spontaneous good
spirits since girlhood. It was true she had 'neithyr peny ne halfpeny
in hir purse', but they fell in with another party of pilgrims whom
she was able to entertain so agreeably by relating 'good talys' that
they gave 'hir iij halfpenys . . . and than was sche ryght glad and
mery'. She had something to offer at the altar of the Holy
Trinity in Norwich cathedral 'as sche dede whan sche went owt
of Inglond'.

Having spent the halfpence on candles and made their prayers
of thanksgiving, the entire party went on to St Stephen's, to find
the vicar, Margery's old friend and supporter. He was extremely
glad to see her again and took them all round to his lodgings 'and
mad hem ryth good cher'. No admirer of levity, he was rather
surprised at the general gaiety. 'Margery,' he said gravely, 'I
merveyl how ye can be so mery.' It would be more suitable, he
felt, to show signs of the great spiritual experiences she had
passed through. Also, her sheer physical stamina amazed him.

These were sentiments which, in the ordinary way, she would
have seconded with tears and appropriate quotations. But now
her joy at being safely in her own country was such that she
replied unaffectedly: 'Syr, for I have gret cawse to ben mery.'
Conversation continued agreeably until they left, the fellowship
starting on the last lap of their journey home. Margery remained
in Norwich for a few days to visit friends, in particular a certain
anchorite who had previously upheld her claims to holiness.

She was warned that other pilgrims passing through the town
had spread stories of her scandalous adventures on the continent.
These may have been her first fellowship, who had left Rome
before she did. They were East Anglians, perhaps even from
Norwich, or Lynn, for they knew her background before
embarking at Yarmouth. She never made a more implacable
enemy than the fanatical priest of that company who, with all the
fire of a passionate temperament, had convinced himself of her
kinship to the Devil.

The anchorite had been listening to some such person, whose truthfulness and theological opinions he respected. One of the wickednesses related of her was that she had had a child abroad. She had fallen from grace in a manner the anchorite felt unable to forgive. He did not wish to be connected with her any more. Margery was informed of this, but went to see him in the hope of winning him round. She would give him a chance of turning from evil to good, as she puts it. Besides, she could not leave these slanders unanswered.

The holy personage proved surly at their meeting. 'He wolcomyd hir hom schortly', as form required, and asked sarcastically after the baby. She had never done anything in foreign parts, she said warmly, which could possibly result in a child. But he would not listen 'for nowt that sche cowde sey'. He may have had revelations on the subject and thus been obliged to believe in her sin.

It would seem that he melted slightly, however, for she felt encouraged enough to mention the real object of her visit. She wanted licence to dress in white. So far, she had not been able to obtain this in England. Only the German priest in Rome had expressly allowed it. Evidently, she had not thought it safe to travel in unusual costume, in view of the great thunderings against heretics reverberating, at that moment, in Constance.

To her request, the anchorite replied: 'God forbede it.' She would attract undesirable attention. Also, he could not authorize a sinner to get herself up as a saint. She would not venture to argue with him, she said meekly, because God did not approve of disagreements between his servants. The best thing she could do, he answered sternly, would be to put herself entirely under his spiritual direction. He would receive her for the love of God.

She did not fancy the prospect and 'toke hir leve' of him. She had plenty of friends, including Jesus Christ and all the heavenly host. As a returned pilgrim from the Holy Land and Rome, she had an enhanced status. Everyone knew, and respected, her family. She would show that false anchorite what she could do.

First, she must borrow some money. 'Than went sche forth to a worschepful man in Norwich to whom sche was ryth wolcome.' They conversed agreeably about pilgrimage, saints, relics, foreigners and kindred subjects of which she now had a superb knowledge. Here was her man. She felt certain of it. 'Speke to this man, speke to this man,' muttered 'owr Lord ... in hir sowle.'

'Wolde God, ser,' she remarked, 'that I myth fyndyn a good man whech wolde lendyn me ij nobelys ... to byen me clothys wyth.' 'That wil I do, damsel, gladly,' he answered warmly. 'What clothys wil ye weryn?' 'Ser, sche seyde, white clothis, wyth the leve of God.' So he went out and bought a length of white cloth and had it make up at his own expense. If God said it was all right, who was he to object?

Resplendent in her new petticoat, dress, cloak and hood, Margery attended mass and received the sacraments. No one in authority made the least trouble. She had won the last round against her enemy, the fanatic priest.

In the course of these dramatic first days, John Kempe received word that his wife had arrived in Norwich and set off to fetch her. Margery draws a veil over their meeting. Beyond the fact that he enquired after her health, their mutual reactions are not recorded. We don't know how much gossip he had heard from returned travellers. With his experience, he can hardly have believed the story about the baby.

'And so (they) went hom togedyr to Lynne', Margery, we must presume, talking at a great rate of the wonders she had seen; of the fire of love and celestial music; of life on shipboard; of vendetta; of how she had always got the better of everyone in the end. She must have asked him to give an account of himself, particularly in regard to his religious observances. His replies were, evidently, not sufficiently interesting to remain in her memory. We only know, from subsequent events, that he had still not been successful in business. As Margery had spent her inheritance, they were very poor. In spite of this, and the vow of celebacy, they remained on good terms. Once, they had been deeply and satisfyingly in love and the bond was never entirely broken.

They settled down to their former life. 'And sche in schort tyme aftyr fel in gret sekenes.' During the past year, she had undergone enough physical hardship and emotional strain to weaken anyone. It is not surprising that she should have caught one of the many dangerous diseases endemic in medieval England, despite her wonderful constitution. Her life was despaired of. She received extreme unction. But the illness was not so grave that she wanted to die. She reminded God of her intention to visit the shrine at Santiago de Compostela. This would redound to his glory. It would also give her a new opportunity of suffering for his love. She knew that this pleased him. He had often told her so. There was nothing more spiteful, indeed downright dangerous, than a party of pilgrims, obliged to live a communal life day after day in discomfort. With any luck, she would find another uncongenial fellowship and, by their help, lay up huge treasures in heaven.

When he heard this, God relented, saying 'to hir in hir sowle that sche schuld not dey yet'. She could scarcely believe the divine words, 'for hir peyn was so gret'. However, she recovered gradually. The illness must have lasted a considerable time. It was autumn 1415 before she had fully recovered. Her debts had grown enormous, her income very uncertain. John Kempe was evidently hopeless as a support. 'Than it drow into wyntyrwarde, and sche had so meche colde that sche wist not what sche mygth do.' The white outfit was summer-weight. The fire of love could not be relied on to warm one at all hours of the day and night, like a bag of coal.

She could only endure and pray for an early spring. Poverty was easier to bear in Rome: the winter winds were not like those of Lynn, sweeping in from the North Sea with snow and icy rain, whistling through narrow streets and draughty houses. No doubt she had friends who asked her to lunch, as Dame Margaret Florentine had done, but the general public was not charitably inclined towards her. They objected to the white clothes and especially to the ecstatic scream with which she had been gifted in the church of the Holy Sepulchre at Jerusalem.

They had never heard anything like it before 'and many seyd ther was nevyr seynt in Hevyn' known to make such a hulla-balloo. Therefore, she must be possessed by a devil, they argued, or worse. 'Sum seyde', watching the violence of her fits, 'that sche had the fallyng evyl' and spat on her 'for horrowr of the sekenes'. Others declared her mad 'and seyd that sche howlyd as it had ben a dogge'.

'And al sche toke pacyently for owr Lordys lofe.' Insult and misfortunes were a source of personal satisfaction as well as an essential part of a life founded on Christ. She was much stimulated. The abominable scream re-echoed through the churches of Lynn more and more frequently. From once a month, it advanced to once a week and then to a daily occurrence. Though a few 'lovyd hir and favowrd hir' for this, most did not. 'Sum seyd sche had dronkyn to mech wyn.' Others cursed her for an evil thing and said she ought to be put to sea in a leaking boat.

Undeterred, she continued to enjoy 'hey contemplacyon' and an overwhelming 'swetnesse of devocyon' not only at shrines but 'sumtyme in the strete, sumtyme in the chawmbre, sumtyme in the felde'. Once, she let off the scream fourteen times in a single day. 'Another day sche had vij' visitations. She had a right to special behaviour. Had she not spoken to God in all the holy places of Jerusalem and Rome? Was she not the recipient of innumerable indulgences, covering every sort of transgression? She had pressed her lips against a host of famous relics and received their benediction.

# CHAPTER XXXII

## *The Year of Agincourt*

In spite of all this, the citizens of Lynn refused, with minor exceptions, to accept her pretensions. They had watched her antics for twenty years. She was an old and boring joke. She had squandered her money. Look at her now, going about in thin white rags. Who would take her for rich John Brunham's daughter? She had sunk right down in the social scale. They knew her husband and her children. What kind of a wife and mother had she been? She was the ruin of them. It was dangerous to have to do with her.

Friends began to detach themselves, making excuses, or even actually forbidding her the house. People who had had her to dine regularly 'for Goddys lofe now thei put hir awey' on account of the general feeling against her. It was said that she was leading the ignorant astray. The old charge of being a Lollard preacher hung over her, despite the certificate she held from the Archbishop of Canterbury.

Things had changed in England during her absence abroad. The attempted revolution in January 1414, led by Sir John Oldcastle, the arch-Lollard, after his escape from the Tower of London had frightened the authorities. In the subsequent inquiry, it appeared that word had been passed round the country and bands organized in the shires in a manner disagreeably reminiscent of the Peasants' Revolt of 1381. The itinerant preachers focused and led a discontent which simmered everywhere. For more than a generation there had been intermittent war; taxes had increased; agriculture had suffered; violence, riots and general disorder were prevalent.

The immemorial feudal system was gradually breaking down and a new world based on business and manufacture beginning to appear. A peasant could escape to the nearest town from the innumerable obligations and customs which, hitherto, had kept him at the plough. An energetic man could choose his occupation and make what he would of his life. Such people, often artisans and craftsmen, naturally inclined to a creed placing emphasis on a man's own efforts to interpret the scriptures and condemning subservience to a church regarded as corrupt even by its own adherents. Lollardy was essentially democratic. All the pure in heart could understand God's word directly. It was not necessary to be a prince, or a priest, to enjoy this privilege.

After the abortive rising in 1414, Sir John Oldcastle again escaped and was hidden by sympathizers. A new and more stringent law was passed against heretics by Parliament in April. It now became the duty of everyone actively to search out and denounce heretics to the authorities. It was essential that they should be thoroughly suppressed before the king began to implement his plans for the conquest of France. He would recover the old empire, once held by feudal right, across the Channel. He would emulate, indeed surpass, the exploits of Edward III and the Black Prince of famous memory. His battles would rank with Crécy and Poitiers. He would be one of the great potentates of Europe, far richer and more powerful than the Holy Roman Emperor, Sigismund. He might even reconquer Jerusalem.

Henry V was not a man to linger over projects. While Margery was travelling laboriously home through Germany, his ambassadors were in Paris, making impossible demands. As she lay ill at Lynn, he was pawning his treasures in the Tower of London and gathering an army at Southampton. On August 11, 1415, the fleet set sail, steering for the Seine estuary with the intention of taking Harfleur, to serve as a base for further conquests. The siege lasted over a month. Sickness prostrated most of the army and many died. But Harfleur was won at last, booty was captured, ransoms arranged and a certain number of French people put out to make room for loyal English settlers.

Since he was not strong enough to take Paris, on account of the depletion of his forces, Henry now planned to finish the season's campaign by marching north to Calais and there embarking for home. If he met the enemy, he was confident that a battle as renowned and successful as Poitiers or Crécy would result. His army, though small, was disciplined and professional. The French suffered from feeble and indecisive leaders. They were unable to make use of their great superiority in numbers and the fact that they were fighting on their own ground. Their day had not yet come: Joan of Arc was still a baby.

In October, as Margery contemplated a cold and poverty-stricken winter, the army started out from Harfleur with little baggage, marching lightly through the rain. They had not much to eat. On 25 October, 1415, wet, tired and hungry, they were confronted by an enormous French army at Agincourt.

They prayed for God's help, that they might not be overwhelmed. 'Every Englishemanne knelid doun and put a litille porcion of erthe in his mouth. And thanne saide the king with an highe vois' so that all might hear, 'In the name of Almyghte God and of Saint George, Avaunt baner, and Saint George this day thyn helpe!'*

Modern computations have put the English at about 6,000 and their enemies at 40,000. The good marksmanship and tactics of the English archers, combined with extraordinary ineptitude on the French side, allowed Henry to win one of the most famous battles in history. He had surpassed his ancestors of Crécy and Poitiers. 'And aftir this the king cam to Caleis and so into Englond, with alle his prisoners and was receyved with moche joie and worshippe.'*

Sir John Oldcastle was still at large, a desperate man now with nothing to hope for. He was reported here and there, and still had enough friends to save him from capture. He did not take the prudent course of fleeing the country, but lurked about the borders of Wales, planning mad revolutions with the help of Scots and Lollards. The authorities were instantly suspicious of anyone wandering round and appearing to deliver orations, addresses, harangues or sermons without proper licence from the church. While Margery stayed in Lynn, where everybody knew her, she was unlikely to suffer more than insults and inconvenience.

She remained at home for the whole of 1416, wondering how to collect enough cash to pay her debts and make the pilgrimage to Compostela. The trouble was, her friends complained, that she was senseless about money. No sooner was she given some than an irresistible feeling of charity overcame her. She was unable to deny herself the pleasure of giving away everything to the indigent. This showed her in a holy light, but plunged her

* The Brut, or English Chronicle, ed. J. S. Davis. Camden Society, 1861.

affairs into hopeless disorder. 'Wher schal ye now have so meche good as ye owe?' her acquaintance asked wearily. She could only reply that she trusted in God, 'for he fayld me nevyr in no cuntre'.

These problems, with visions and meditations on a variety of subjects, occupied her entire attention. She does not mention Agincourt, nor the Emperor Sigismund's visit to England in 1416. He came in the hope of arranging an armistice with France, because he fancied himself as a peacemaker and thought it would help at the Council of Constance if the English and French delegations voted together at his side. He was entertained with great pomp and expense at the Palace of Westminster. Everything was done to keep him amused and happy, though an armistice proved out of the question. In the late summer of 1416 he returned to Germany, having signed a treaty of friendship with Henry V who continued his preparations for a new invasion in the spring of 1417.

Margery faced another winter in reduced circumstances. Her supporters were few and tepid. In Rome, she had promised to meet Richard the Irishman at Bristol during Whitsun, 1417, to repay the money of his she had given away in an excess of devotion. There is nothing to show that she had heard of him since he left her service in a rage on hearing what had happened to his savings. He evidently regarded the debt as irrecoverable, or he would have stayed with her at least until he got some of it back. Yet, he had vague hopes that she would redeem her promise, for he sought her out in Bristol, as soon as he could. She knew he would be there. She had sworn in God's name to satisfy him; besides, she was an honest woman. Her whole story shows it. Nothing short of a miracle, it seemed, would enable her to start.

'And sodeynly cam a good man and gaf hir fowrty pens.' It was like manna from heaven. It showed God had not forgotten her. Greatly encouraged, she bought a fur coat with part of the money. Affairs took a distinct turn for the better. Perhaps she was tactful and tried to restrain herself in public, though she never found it easy to control emotional outbursts. Somehow or other, she compounded with her creditors and made ready for the new journey. From wide experience, she knew exactly what she would need under all circumstances.

Her friends relented to a certain extent. They wished her to pray for them at the shrine of St James in Compostela. When not too frightened, they believed in her powers. Prayers from such a woman, at such a place, could not fail to save them many years in purgatory hereafter. Also, it was quite usual to contribute to a traveller's expenses in return for this service: all prayers murmured by pilgrims had a special efficacy. One woman gave her £4. 13. 4 for the purpose.

By the spring of 1417, she was ready to set out. Funds were still rather short if Richard was to be paid in full, but she hoped to add to them by begging on the way. 'And than sche toke hir leve at hir frendys' meaning to start immediately, though it was 'seyd in Lynne that ther wer many thevys be the wey'. She was much alarmed, but no doubt reflecting that the country was full of thieves who might be met at any point on the road to Bristol, refused to postpone her departure. God would protect her. She said good-bye to John Kempe and the children since they declined to come. They just had no taste for pilgrimage.

Her courage was justified. No one molested her. The begging was so successful that there was plenty of money to satisfy Richard. On 26 May, 1417, she reached Bristol 'and ther fond sche redy the brokebakkyd man whech had ben wyth hir at Rome'. We are not told what they said to each other at this auspicious meeting. Perhaps some shadow of their old friendship returned. He had now the price of a passage home to Ireland, if that was indeed his destination. This crazy embezzler had made restitution. The account was settled. They never met again that we know of.

# CHAPTER XXXIII

## Before the Bishop of Worcester

Margery settled down in the pilgrim hostel at Bristol. It was to be six weeks before she could get a passage to Santiago de Compostela. Henry V had commandeered all the English ships to transport his army to Normandy for the campaign of 1417. The orders were 'to be redy at Hamptoun (Southampton) in the Wistunwike',* though the fleet did not actually sail until July. The king was absent three years and achieved his first ambition. The Treaty of Troyes in 1420 recognized him as heir to the throne of France and regent during the present king's life: Charles VI was incapable of government, being mad.

Owing to the international situation, then, Margery was put to a good deal more expense than she had provided for. However, there was nothing for it but to pay the hotel bills and hope a ship would soon appear. All the pilgrims were impatient and bored. Some 'went abowte fro port to port', following rumours which invariably proved unfounded. In the end 'thei cam ageyn to Bristowe', having accomplished no more than she had done by staying in the hostel.

As it was Whitsun, Margery roamed the town in great excitement, ignoring the risks of arrest as a Lollard. Such 'lowde cryngys and schrille schrykyngys' had never before been heard by the local people. Many objected strongly to the display, calling her worse names than 'ypocrit' and even making false accusations against her. But she was not afraid of enemies and bore it for the love of God and the peculiar satisfaction she got from misfortune. Also, she was a registered pilgrim, wearing the scallop shell badge of St James. Lollards did not approve of pilgrimage, saying that the money would be better spent on good works of a more socialistic kind, such as relieving the poor, or setting up schools.

On Corpus Christi day, she surpassed herself. As she followed the procession through the streets, her emotions at boiling point, confused 'holy thowtys' and visions whirling in her head, a woman said: 'Damsel, God gef us grace to folwyn the steppys of

* *The Brut.*

181

owr Lord Ihesu Crist.' For some reason, these words precipitated a crisis. She staggered, fell down as if in a sudden fit and had to be taken into a nearby house. There she lay screaming, 'I dey, I dey, and roryd also wondirfully'. Onlookers were astonished, 'havyng gret merveyl what hir eyled'. It did not strike them as a display of holiness.

In spite of the generally unfavourable impression she made on the people of Bristol, there were some who found her congenial. These 'haddyn hir hom bothe to mete and to drynke' and were happy to listen to improving and self-centred monologues for hours on end. Her closest friend was Thomas Marshall, of Newcastle in Staffordshire, also bound for Santiago. He fell completely under her influence. Tears of sorrow for his sins coursed down his cheeks, day and night. He would be overcome by his feelings when taking country walks. He felt 'as he had ben a newe man', he told her. He found it impossible sufficiently to regret a careless past in which 'he had ben a ful rekles man and mysgovernyd', as it seemed to him now. Sometimes, he fell flat on the ground under the burden of remorse. 'He blyssed the tyme that he knew this creatur', who appeared like an angel from heaven to save him before it was too late.

On the practical side, he was equally satisfactory. 'Modyr,' he said, 'I have here x marke. I pray yow that it be yowr as yowr owyn.' They would share it, penny by penny. 'Than, as it plesyd owr Lord', a ship put in from Brittany and began loading provisions for a voyage to Santiago. Thomas Marshall hurried to the quay and bargained with the captain for two return tickets.

The other pilgrims did not look forward to Margery's company on board ship. They thought it would drive them mad and also, if she were possessed of a devil, as some declared, it would have an adverse effect on the weather. They did not see why they should all be drowned in a storm on her account. A certain 'riche man of Bristowe' was adamant on this point. The woman was a heretic and stuffed with demons. It was impossible, he said to the captain, to allow such a passenger. 'Syr,' she answered firmly, 'yf ye put me owt of the schip, my Lord Ihesu shal put yow owt of hevyn.' He might bribe people on earth to get his way, but no payments whatever would open the gates of paradise to one who had insulted St Margery. She said other things as well, 'withowtyn any glosyng er flateryng'.

Shortly afterwards, enemies denounced her to the authorities as a Lollard. She was summoned to appear before the Bishop of Worcester who was staying at his manor at Henbury, three miles from Bristol. The ship was ready to leave with the first favourable wind. If she were detained while a long inquiry into her faith was made. she might very well miss it, as her fellowship devoutly hoped. She did not fear conviction on the charge. The bishop's court would give her a fair hearing. She had only to make it clear that she worshipped the saints, believed in miracles, confession, absolution, transubstantiation and the Pope's authority, to be acquitted at once. Anyone reasonable could see that she had no connection with political agitators. Besides, this bishop had known her father.

'Sche ros up erly on the next day' and covered the three miles to Henbury while the bishop was still in bed. It happened that an important man of Bristol also had business there. They got into conversation and found each other congenial. Margery lectured extensively, to their mutual benefit. Her new acquaintance invited her to breakfast before they went into the bishop's hall together to wait their turn.

Having already collected substantial witness for the defence, Margery entered the hall with some confidence. The room was full of the bishop's retainers, dressed in the latest extravagant fashion, their doublets elaborately slashed with coloured silks, their whole appearance gay as a flock of tropical birds. But an ecclesiastical household ought, in theory, to dress soberly, unostentatiously, thinking only to cover the body decently while the mind concerned itself with higher things. Margery stopped in her tracks and crossed herself emphatically. 'What devyl eyleth the?' enquired those who noticed. 'Whos men be ye?' she asked in return. 'The Bischopys men,' they answered shortly. 'Nay, forsothe,' she said in her downright way, 'ye arn lykar the Develys men.'

They were very angry and swore at her, not seeing why they should be lectured like this by a stray woman pilgrim. She was told to shut up and mind her own business and other things of the sort. A few, however, feeling slightly guilty, or else because her companion impressed them, were more receptive. These she continued to exhort, in the name of God, and obtained some response: they thanked her politely afterwards.

Thus time passed agreeably until 'sche went into the chirch and abood the coming of the bischop'. When he took his seat, she knelt before him and asked what accusation lay against her. She was a poor pilgrim, she said, hoping to take ship to Santiago. It would be a great disappointment, as well as causing extra expense, if she missed the boat through having to attend sessions of his court. Berths were so scarce on account of the king's invasion of Normandy. It might be another six weeks before she could get a second booking.

The bishop had made his enquiries. 'Margery,' he said mildly, 'I knowe wel i-now thu art John Burnamys dowtyr of Lynne.' There was no substance in the complaint against her. The case would be dismissed. She need not be alarmed about her intended pilgrimage. In view of the bad feeling at the hostel, it might be better if she put up in his household until her departure. He would be delighted to entertain her friend Thomas Marshall also.

Thus courteously, humanely, and as a gentleman, he dealt with John Burnham's obstreperous daughter, whose troubles were all her own fault. One can't help feeling it was a small sin that he allowed his retainers to overdress. Partly from good manners, perhaps, and partly to assure himself of her orthodoxy, he had long conversations with his guest on succeeding days. He grew to like her. She might be boring sometimes, but she was upright, faithful, a staunch believer in ecclesiastical authority. It was soothing to meet such a person in these difficult times when many were turning away from the church, either from worldliness, or else because they thought it corrupt and had been listening to abominable heresies, emanating from the Devil. He heard her confession himself and asked her to remember him in her prayers at Santiago. A holy man had prophesied that he had not long to live, and he felt it to be true.

When the fair wind at last blew, he gave her money and his blessing and ordered his men to escort her to Bristol. A delightful interlude had ended. Everyone had been kind, including the retainers, who had been obliged to listen humbly to her strictures since their lord favoured her. She had now to face her fellow pilgrims. They were extremely put out by the failure of their plot and the prospect of being exposed to evil influences uninterruptedly for a week at sea. They swore they would throw her overboard if they met a storm. Any dangers they might encounter would certainly be due to her spells.

These threats alarmed Margery. They seemed to mean what they said. She prayed with the greatest earnestness for calm weather. 'Yf thu wilte chastisyn me,' she implored, 'spar me tyl I come ageyn into Inglong.' Jesus stood by her, sending 'fayr wynde and wedyr so that they comyn to Seynt Iamys on the sevenyth day'.

The fellowship were calmed by the uneventful passage. Relations improved. Just as they would have attributed disaster to her supernatural powers, so they gave her credit for their safe arrival. On the journey to Jerusalem, the company had objected to her mainly as a troublesome woman who got on their nerves. Her new companions were less sophisticated: they believed she commanded strange forces and were afraid.

# CHAPTER XXXIV

## Santiago de Compostela

The shrine of St James at Compostela was one of the richest and most famous in Christendom. Pilgrim roads converged on it from all over Europe. It ranked in importance with Rome and almost with the Holy Land. Situated in northern Spain, on the Atlantic coast, not far short of Cape Finisterre, it seems, at first sight, a remote and uncivilized corner of the medieval world for the growth of so powerful a cult. There were, however, very special circumstances attached both to Spain and to St James.

Tradition relates that after Pentecost, when the disciples set out to convert the world, in accordance with Christ's last will, James chose Spain as his missionary field. He therefore took ship for that distant province of the Roman empire. Landing in Andalusia, he gradually worked his way north until he reached a small port near the later Compostela. His success in Spain was disappointing, even though the Virgin Mary, still alive, miraculously visited him on the banks of the Ebro. His converts were numbered in handfuls only. Nor did he persist very long in his efforts, but returned to Jerusalem where, in due course, he suffered a martyr's death.

His remains were carefully gathered up by two of his disciples. The most appropriate burial place seemed to them to be in the land of his missionary labours. This was far off, it was true, yet they were not daunted. Embarking with the holy corpse, they sailed the length of the Mediterranean, through the Pillars of Hercules, coasted the Atlantic shore as far north as the estuary in Galicia where Santiago was subsequently to be built. God must have directed them to come to this remote spot, otherwise, one supposes, they would have landed in Andalusia, in the south.

In spite of the apostle's efforts, the people of the neighbourhood were pagan and their queen actively hostile to Christianity. When the two disciples applied for permission to dig a grave, she imprisoned them at once. Fortunately, an angel helped them to escape.

Realizing that she had to do with the supernatural, the queen pretended to give way. They could bury their master, she said, on the slopes of a certain mountain. The two disciples did not know that this was the home of a celebrated dragon. The coffin was loaded on to a bullock cart and the party set off. As they reached the mountain, the dragon came out and prepared to eat them, but, at the sign of the cross, it fell down dead. Thereupon, for safety's sake, the queen became a Christian.

Meanwhile the bullocks, divinely inspired, had trundled some ten miles north-westwards, coming to a halt beside a ruin, perhaps a derelict tomb. This was evidently the appointed spot. The apostle was put into a sarcophagus and a small chapel built over him. The faithful disciples were buried beside him in their turn.

This delightful story is first recounted in the early ninth century, at the very moment when Christians in Spain needed supernatural help, a banner round which to rally in their long crusade against the Moors. For, in 711, the Moslems in their westward surge crossed the strait from Africa and swiftly conquered the whole Iberian peninsula. The Christians now found themselves second-class citizens in a state ruled by infidels. Many were converted. Others, though retaining their religion, adopted the Moslem civilization, which was vastly superior to that of Europe. The Caliph of Cordova became an independent sovereign and immensely rich. Magnificent buildings were put up, the arts and sciences assiduously pursued. Only in the north among the mountains and Atlantic capes did three miserable little kingdoms manage to retain their freedom. Their existence was clearly precarious: they were few, poor and barbarous, compared with the Moslem power. Even to keep what they held required a divine backing, superior to that of their adversaries. Driving the Moors out of Spain, the traditional occupation during the middle ages, was not finally accomplished until 1492. During Margery's visit, the kingdom of Granada, on the southern coast, was still unconquered.

It is, perhaps, not surprising, therefore, that in about 814 in the Christian state of Galicia a curious star was seen to shine persistently over a clump of bushes in a field. Investigation revealed an ancient tumbledown chapel containing a tomb in which, as was learned by revelation, were the remains of St James the Greater, apostle of Christ. This was sensational news. A church was quickly built and a monastery founded to honour the saint and engage his interest in local affairs. Eight centuries' scandalous neglect of his rites no doubt accounted for the infidel invasions. These measures worked. In 834, at Clavijo, a victory was won against an enormous host of Moslems with his help. The saint was seen, dressed as a knight, on a white charger, galloping through the air and killing thousands of Moors with his own hands.

Thereafter, his presence was felt on every battlefield, though he was not always visible. Compostela became internationally famous. A city developed round the original church and monastery, which were continually enlarged and enriched. Tourists brought money and there was also a special tax on all Spanish Christians. By Margery's time the relics were housed in a magnificent twelfth-century cathedral in the Romanesque style of southern France. The town contained innumerable souvenir shops, hostels and amusements for visitors.

St James himself increased in stature. In life he had been a simple fisherman. Now he was a knight, a god of war, prancing through the air on a mettlesome charger. Had not he and his brother John, the sons of Zebedee, been surnamed Boanerges, sons of thunder, by Christ Himself? Such a one would naturally gravitate to the title of Santiago Matamoros, St James, slayer of Moors.

In a confused way, too, he became in some degree merged with St James the Less, brother of Jesus. The exact position of this St James in the Holy Family was a matter of debate. If he was the twin brother, as certain people held, he would partake of divinity in the same manner as Christ. He would be, in fact, another aspect of God himself. Pictures of Santiago exist in which he is given the conventional features of Christ. Strict orthodoxy insisted on the distinction between the two, but Santiago had a particular effulgence as though he might indeed be, as it were, the son of God. No other saint had taken so firm a hand in laying low the infidels.

The feast of St James is on the 25th of July. Margery probably was there, taking part in the processions with 'many gret cryes', holding out her arms like a cross before the most precious and magical of the relics which were exposed on this occasion. She was not troubled by doubts as to the authenticity of these sacred objects.

Some pilgrims wondered whether any part of the apostle was really to be seen at Compostela. 'I desired with great presents, that they would show me the holy body', relates Arnold von Harff. 'They replied that anyone who did not believe truly that the holy body of St James, the Greater Apostle, lay in the high altar, but doubted and therefore desired to see the body, he would immediately become mad, like a mad dog.' For his own good, they declined to satisfy his curiosity on any account. As for those relics which were visible, he had already seen many of them in other churches during his travels. Yet, though disbelieving, he journeyed on, enduring dangers, hardships and expense; kissing supposed relics and feeling the better for it.

At Compostela, the main rite was the embracing of the great statue of St James above the altar. Carved in granite and brightly painted, it represented the apostle seated with a pilgrim's staff and bottle in his left hand. Steps were provided behind the image to enable people to place their hands on its shoulders while kissing the hood of its robe. One then confessed to a priest who spoke one's language and received a certificate conferring the official title of pilgrim to St James.

The round trip, for English visitors, was accomplished within a month and was much less fatiguing than for French, or Italians, who had to plod some hundreds of miles, perhaps, ending with the passage of the Pyrenees. Margery stayed 'xiiij days in that lond', enjoying herself tremendously after her own fashion. The return voyage to Bristol was uneventful, taking only four days. This was fortunate: who knew what her fellowship would have done had the boat been blown off course, or long becalmed? For they firmly believed the weather was under her influence.

# CHAPTER XXXV

## *The Mayor of Leicester*

She stayed in Bristol only long enough to pay her respects to the kind Bishop of Worcester and then set out for Lynn, escorted by the still admiring Thomas Marshall, and other pilgrims whose homes were in the midlands, or north country. On the way, she stopped at the Abbey of Hailes in Gloucestershire. Here was preserved a bottle of Christ's blood, presented by a patron in 1270, together with a guarantee of authenticity from Pope Urban IV. In the course of her wanderings round England, Margery had never yet visited this particular shrine.

The monks appreciated the fervour of her devotion and asked her to dinner. She found them very agreeable, except that they were somewhat given to swearing 'many gret othys and horryble' for which she was obliged to reprove them, showing a knowledge of the scriptures they had not suspected in a simple woman pilgrim. Some thought it not a suitable accomplishment, but others 'wer ryth wel plesyd, thankyd be God'. She did not want more trouble such as had befallen her at Bristol.

The party then continued safely as far as Leicester. Here an unfortunate thing happened. Entering 'a fayr cherch wher sche behelde a crucyfyx', Margery was taken with a very bad devotional fit. She screamed and shouted, writhed and wept 'ful hedowslyche'. The fire of love burned hotly in her bosom. The local people had never seen anything like it. Some were impressed, others scandalized. To the latter, she appeared a suspicious character. The Lollards were particularly active in Leicester and the midlands. Sir John Oldcastle was still at large, threatening rebellion from his secret retreat on the borders of Wales. It was the duty of all responsible citizens to watch over the security of the state, especially now while the king was away at the war. A complaint ought to be made to the mayor.

Unaware of the danger, Margery gradually recovered her senses and left the church. At the door 'a man toke hir be the sleve and seyd: Damsel, why wepist thu so sor?' His manner was not sympathetic and she refused to answer. However, she had met many disagreeable people during her career and thought no more of it, but went back to the hostel with Thomas Marshall, for dinner. 'Whan thei had etyn', she asked him to write a letter to John Kempe. It was unsafe for her to travel alone and Thomas was not going further in her direction than Melton Mowbray. John Kempe would have to come and meet her there.

As they were struggling with this composition, an ostler dashed into the room, snatched up her scrip, or pilgrim's satchel, and said she must immediately accompany him to the mayor. In spite of her natural self-confidence, she must have felt uneasy, hurrying through the streets to the guildhall. At least she need not fear that they would find incriminating literature in her scrip. The chief thing in it was a piece of Moses' rod, which she had bought in Jerusalem.

Called into the mayor's presence and told to give an account of herself, she said boldly: 'Syr, I am of Lynne in Norfolke, a good mannys dowtyr of the same Lynne, whech hath ben meyr fyve tymes of that worshepful burwgh and aldyrman also many yerys, and I have a good man, also a burgeys of the seyd town of Lynne, to myn husbond.'

To this the mayor replied: 'Thu art a fals strumpet, a fals loller, and a fals deceyver of the pepyl and therfor I shal have the in preson.' 'I am as redy, ser, to gon to preson for Goddys lofe,' she retorted, 'as ye arn redy to gon to chirche.'

The mayor became more violent, shouting and abusing, 'and seyd many evyl and horybyl wordys onto hir'. He appears to have been a thoroughly intemperate man and mindful of his own importance. This woman was not on her knees crying for mercy. No, she dared to answer back, to lecture, to talk down to him from spiritual heights it was assumed he was incapable of scaling. Moreover, people in the court were obviously impressed by her demeanour. She was getting the better of him on his own ground. He would have liked to burn her at once. She was undoubtedly a heretic and in league with the Devil, whatever she might say. Unfortunately, it was beyond the competence of his court. He could only remand her to prison until the next sitting of the Earl of Leicester's court.

'He comawnded the jaylerys man' to take her away. The gaoler was upset by the order. Her eloquence and honest manner had convinced him of her innocence. 'Ser,' he said to the mayor, 'I have non hows to put hir inne les than I putte hir among men.' 'I prey yow, ser,' said Margery, for the first time really alarmed, 'put me not among men, that I may kepyn my chastite and my bond of wedlak to myn husbond.' 'Ser,' said the gaoler quickly, 'I will be bowndyn to kepe this woman in safwarde tyl ye wyl have hir ageyn.' Here a man from Boston in Lincolnshire remarked that in his home town Margery was 'holdyn an holy woman and a blissed woman.'

The mayor was obliged to accept the gaoler's offer. He took Margery to his own house and locked her in 'a fayre chawmbyr'. It was not a severe detention. Trusting her promise not to escape, he allowed her to go to church whenever she liked and invited her to meals with the family.

The Earl of Leicester's court was presided over, on this occasion, by his steward, a man of the knightly class and an even more unsympathetic character than the mayor. He sent a man to the gaoler's house, ordering him to produce Margery. It happened that only the wife was in and she refused to let the prisoner be taken away without her husband's knowledge. They had to wait until the gaoler could be found. He then brought her to the court where a crowd had gathered, for the case had become celebrated. There were also 'many prestys stondyng abowtyn', for it was really an ecclesiastical matter and, if the accusations seemed well founded, would be referred to the Abbot of Leicester's court.

When Margery had explained who she was and denied the charges of being a strumpet, Lollard and deceiver of the people, the steward addressed her in Latin. 'Spekyth Englysch, if yow lyketh,' she replied, 'for I undyrstond not what ye sey.' If she had known Latin, it would have proved that she was not the poor pilgrim she seemed.

'Thu lyest falsly, in pleyn Englysch,' the steward translated. 'Syr,' she said calmly, 'askyth what qwestyon ye wil in Englysch and throw the grace of my Lord Ihesu Cryst, I shal answeryn yow reasonabely therto.'

'Than askyd he many qwestyonys' concerning her history, manner of life, beliefs; whether she went about preaching or distributing literature; the nature of her visions. To all, she gave satisfactory replies. He found it impossible to trip her up on any

Hermits in the wilderness. (From a Psalter belonging to Henry VI of England. Circa 1430. Cotton Domitian A XVII.)

Rome. (From *Le Trésor des Histoires*, selected historical anecdotes from the time of Adam and Eve to the middle of the 14th century. Cotton Augustus V.)

A lady in a horse litter. (From a collection of stories, verses and ballads by the poetess Christine of Pisa. Early 15th century, French. Harley 4431.)

point. The nature of her visions excited his curiosity particularly. How did she know whether they emanated from God or the Devil? She refused to go into this matter, fearing it might be a trap.

Determined to get to the bottom of it, the steward took her into another room and behaved as if he intended to rape her. 'Ser,' she begged him, 'for the reverans of almythy God, sparyth me, for I am a mannys wife.'

'Thu shalt telle me whethyr thu has this speche of God er of the Devyl, er ellys thu shalt gon to preson,' he said. 'Ser,' she replied scornfully, 'for to gon to preson I am not aferd . . . I pray yow doth as yow thynkyth the beste.'

Unable to endure the thought that she might get the better of him in the end, he came at her again 'and strogelyd wyth hir, schewyng unclene tokenys and ungoodly cuntenawns'. This time he frightened her. She began to explain how her visions came, in what they consisted and how she could not resist them, nor control the tears, screams and fits by which they were accompanied. As she warmed to the theme, her eloquence impressed him. He was amazed that anyone unlearned should have such command of language. Her voice rang with sincerity. Yet, he could not dispel a last doubt: the Devil could accomplish miracles of deception.

Finally he sighed, 'as many men had do beforn: Eythyr thu art a ryth good woman er ellys a ryth wikked woman.' The hearing was ended. It was clearly a case for the ecclesiastical court. The gaoler took her away again to his house, until the summons should come from the Abbot of Leicester.

Meanwhile, Thomas Marshall had been lying low in the hostel. He was much alarmed for his friend's safety, having gloomy premonitions that she would be burnt. We do not know whether he dared to attend either of the hearings, but he was brave enough to stay in the town. This he was now to regret. For the mayor, determined on a general clean-up, arrested him, and another pilgrim, at this point. There was no charge against them except that of being Margery's associates. It was generally felt that they were perfectly innocent. The impression was much reinforced the next day when a fearful storm broke over the town.

Something had to be done quickly both to save the mayor's face and prevent the city from being destroyed by thunder, lightning, flood, earthquake and God alone knew what else. The two prisoners were hurried to the guildhall and asked whether they were prepared to swear before the mayor and aldermen that Margery was 'a woman of the ryth feyth and ryth beleve, continent and clene of hir body, er not'. They at once deposed in the affirmative, as 'God shulde help hem at the Day of Dome', and were immediately released, fleeing in the direction of Melton Mowbray. 'Anon the tempest sesyd and it was fayr wedyr.'

A few days later, Margery was brought to the church of All Hallows, where the Abbot of Leicester and his chapter held their court. The case had become famous throughout the city. A great crowd gathered to watch the trial, those at the back standing on stools so as to get a good view of the prisoner. Everyone agreed that she was in touch with the supernatural. The only question was whether she represented the powers of heaven, or of hell. The audience stared at her with the most intense interest as she knelt in prayer while waiting for the abbot to open the proceedings. The mayor was also present.

When she had sworn on the Bible to speak only the truth, they asked her about transubstantiation: did she, or did she not, believe that the bread and wine miraculously became Christ's flesh and blood after the words of the mass had been said over it? The Lollards denied that anything happened, except in an allegorical sense. 'I believe,' she answered, 'that it is hys very flesch and hys blood and no material bred.' She also repudiated the heretical idea that a true priest must be a man of irreproachable character. Once ordained, a priest 'be he nevyr so vicyows' had been given the gift of working the miracle of the mass. He could not lose this power except by being unfrocked. To all the other questions, she replied in an equally orthodox manner.

Meanwhile, the mayor was becoming more and more angry. He was certain the woman had commerce with infernal powers and was connected with the network of Oldcastle's sympathizers who wandered about the country preaching sedition. How many Lollards had abjured their opinions, only to relapse into their former ways as soon as the coast seemed clear? 'In fayth,' he shouted suddenly, 'sche menyth not wyth hir hert as sche seyth with hir mowthe.'

'Sir,' the judges retorted, 'sche answeryth ryth wel to us.' The thought that he was not going to have the pleasure of putting her on a bonfire before the assembled citizens threw the mayor into a violent rage. She was not the respectable woman she tried to pretend, he screamed. She was full of demons, a witch and a strumpet and heaven knew what else.

'Sir,' she said with dignity, 'I take witnesse of my Lord Ihesu Crist ... that I nevyr had part of mannys body ... be wey of synne.' She had been perfectly faithful to her husband, 'be whom I have born xiiij childeryn'. She loved all men, it was true, but only in a spiritual sense: 'in God and for God'.

Thus far, she addressed the court in general. Now, with the authority of a prophetess and of a mayor's daughter, she turned and 'seyd pleynly to hys owyn persone, Sir, ye arn not worthy to ben a meyr'. God was watching his persecution of an innocent woman and had, in the scriptures, promised vengeance on wicked cities.

Undeterred, he next demanded to know why she wore white. In his opinion, she had come to Leicester dressed like this with the object of enticing 'awey owr wyvys fro us and ledyn hem' to her master the Devil for the amusement of himself and his demons.

Since the white clothes had caused so much suspicion, Margery felt obliged to answer this fantastic charge. It was obviously no good explaining revelations from God to a man like the mayor. Besides, his soul was not in a fit state to receive knowledge of sacred mysteries. However, she said, if the court was cleared of laymen, she would be happy to tell them, as it were in the confessional, everything they wished to know.

One can imagine a good deal of grumbling among the public as they were driven out at this exciting point in the story. While they waited outside with the mayor, Margery 'knelyd on hir knes before the Abbot and the Den of Leycetyr and a Frer Prechowr, a worschipful clerk' and confided the full history of her desire to wear white from the beginning and how she finally accomplished it. Her confessors in Rome and since in England had been so convinced, she said, it was the will of God, that they gave her the necessary licence, not daring to refuse as 'thei wolde ful gladlych' have liked to do.

She had by this time satisfied the abbot and his chapter that she was neither heretical nor a political agitator. In contrast to the secular courts, they had heard her patiently and fairly without prejudging the issue. One must suppose, also, that hers was not the first false accusation they had dealt with. She was a harmless woman and whatever colour she chose to wear did not affect her faith. Perhaps God had really instructed her in the matter. They called in the mayor and informed him that her confessor had ordered her to wear white and that was the end of it.

When the mayor saw that he had lost the case, he became very amiable towards Margery, putting on a generous face and expressing a Christian wish for reconciliation, in order to wipe out any idea in the Lord Abbot's mind that he had behaved in a disgustingly vindictive manner. No, since she had been proved innocent, he accepted the verdict with joy. He had acted simply in what he conceived to be the best interests of church and state. But, he said, drawing her aside, he could not be responsible for the fact that she was at large. It was not safe in these troubled times. He would not let her out of the city gates unless she promised to go to the Bishop of Lincoln, in whose diocese the town lay, and obtained a letter exonerating him, whatever might subsequently happen.

This she could easily do, for Lincoln was the very bishop before whom she and John Kempe had taken their vow of chastity. Though afraid to authorize white clothes, he had greatly admired her conversation and had urged her to write a book, then and there. But these were not days in which to be a controversial author.

'Ser,' she said to the mayor with some triumph, 'I dar speke to my Lord of Lyncolne ryth wel, for I have had of hym rith good cher afor this tyme.' The detestable man then 'gaf hir goodly wordys' with murder in his heart.

Margery must have been extremely anxious to leave this city of dreadful night, to flee ten miles without stopping, as Thomas Marshall had done. Never had she been in such mortal danger. It was necessary, however, to obtain a letter from the abbot to the Bishop of Lincoln, certifying that she had been examined on her faith and found orthodox. 'So sche went fyrst to the Abbey of Leycester into the chirche.' As she knelt, thanking God who had preserved her life, the abbot and some monks advanced down the nave. These men had saved her. They were like a vision of Jesus and the apostles. It was not a tactful moment for 'hy contemplacyon.' She ought to stand up 'as curtesy wolde'. Struggling to control her emotions, to avoid falling on the ground with a hideous epileptic scream, she hung on to a pillar and managed to gasp her request. They were very gentle, comforting her distress, which they found perfectly natural in the circumstances. While the letter was being written, she was taken into the monastery and given a drink of 'ryth good wyn'.

Meanwhile, Thomas Marshall had gone to ground in Melton Mowbray, at the house of a fellow pilgrim called Patrick. He was very worried about Margery whom he regarded with reverence as a holy woman and as his spiritual mother. Had she been burnt, or not? No one could give certain news. He dared not go back to Leicester himself after his own adventures there. He managed, however, to prevail on Patrick to go and 'inqwir and se how it stod wyth' her.

We don't know at what point he arrived in the city, but, on the happy conclusion of the trial, he made himself known and offered to escort her to Melton Mowbray. They set off gaily, cheered by a crowd of Margery's supporters, who were now numerous. She had been declared a genuine holy woman and they were sorry to see her go, feeling that a beneficent influence was passing away. If she would condescend to come again, they said, 'sche shuld han bettyr cher among hem' than had been the case this time. She does not record that she accepted the invitation.

Patrick had a good strong horse which they both got on to and thus rode under the town gate. They had not gone far before Margery suddenly remembered she had left her scrip, containing the relic of Moses, behind. 'Sche wold not a lost it for xl s.' Would the obliging Patrick gallop back and fetch it? She could wait here in this blind woman's cottage. He consented.

'Than went Patryk agen into the towne.' He found the precious scrip and was coming away when he 'happyd to metyn wyth the meyr' who demanded to know his business, threatened the terrified Patrick with prison, torture and burning and seized the scrip. Possibly, the intemperate mayor had him taken to the guildhall and put through his paces, for his absence was so unnaturally long that Margery realized something bad had occurred.

At last, she saw him coming down the road. 'Patryk sone,' she cried, 'wher ha ye ben so long fro me?' 'Ya, ya, modyr,' he said irritably, 'I have ben in gret peril for yow. I was in poynt to a ben put in preson for yow, and the meyr hath gretly turmented me for yow, and he hath takyn awey yowr scrippe fro me.' 'A, good Patryk,' she said soothingly, 'be not displesyd, for I shal prey for yow . . . It is al for the best.'

Without further conversation, he dragged her up on to the horse and they made for Melton Mowbray. There they found Thomas Marshall, who helped her 'down of the hors, hyly thankyng God that sche was not brent'.

# CHAPTER XXXVI

## The Archbishop of York at Cawood

She was kindly received by the Bishop of Lincoln's household, who remembered her, and a letter was at once sent to the mayor 'monyschyng hym that he shulde not vexyn hir' and requiring him to return her scrip. While she waited for an answer, an unusually bad storm broke over the neighbourhood. Many people said this was due to God's displeasure at her presence and intimated that she should leave forthwith. Who knew what misfortunes beyond flattened crops and burnt trees they might have to suffer if the evil influence were not expelled?

Since the bishop was on her side, Margery was able to refuse firmly. 'Sche wolde in no wise gon thens,' she declared, 'tyl sche had hir scryppe agen.' They had to put up with her for three weeks. The agitation must have died down, for Patrick remained faithful, in spite of his alarming adventures with the mayor. He even consented to be hired as escort to York where Margery wished to visit the shrine of St William* in the Minster to give thanks for her escape from death.

All this time, John Kempe was, presumably, keeping quiet in Lynn. We do not know whether Thomas Marshall ever completed and dispatched the letter, interrupted so unexpectedly by Margery's arrest in Leicester. One can only remark that there is no sign of the cautious John, as yet.

St William did not prove a very strong protector of his devotee. On reaching York, Margery went to see an anchoress she had known before travelling to the Holy Land. It was her intention to celebrate the eve of the Virgin's nativity by eating bread and water with the recluse. When she appeared at the cell window, however, 'the ancres wolde not receyven hir for sche had herd telde so mech evyl of hir'. Either she had been listening to malicious gossip, or else the news of Margery's arrest had preceded her and the holy woman thought her acquaintance inadvisable. Other people received her well and 'made hir rith good cher', but, on the whole, the atmosphere was chilly. She began to have pre-

* A Bishop of York, noted for miracles of healing. Two windows were put up to him in the Minster during the fifteenth century.

monitions. 'Dowtyr,' remarked God, 'ther is mech tribulacyon to thewarde.'

She could easily have averted trouble by keeping quiet. If she had refrained from haranguing people and thus giving the impression that she was an unlicensed preacher spreading dangerous ideas, her noisy devotions would not have mattered so much. The Lollards did not prostrate themselves before statues of saints. It was a habit they objected to as savouring of the worship of graven images. But nothing had ever been able to stop Margery's monologue as long as there was anyone present who understood English. No threat of death or violence by her fellow pilgrims had had more than a temporary effect. Why should she beware now, straight from a triumph over the mayor of Leicester? Anyway, she couldn't. If it was God's will that she should be persecuted by the false accusations of a wicked generation, she was happy to endure.

The prospect made her 'ryth glad and mery', giving her addresses extra vigour; her descriptions of hell more depth; and the sound of the choirs of angels who waited to greet her own ascension to heaven when the hour came, a serene reality. What wonder that people were astonished by her fluency? Some found it 'fruteful'. Others were not so entertained. 'Damsel,' enquired a priest in the Minster, 'how long wil ye abydyn her?'

'Ser,' she replied confidently, 'I purpose to abyden thes xiiij days.' She had a certain number of friends among the Minster officials, men who admired the hermits and anchorites and practised an emotional form of religion. One was a doctor of divinity and another a priest of the Chantry of All Saints, employed to sing perpetual masses for the souls of donors. In these congenial surroundings, Margery felt free to worship in the manner which gave her most satisfaction.

The opposition, however, grumbled ominously in the background, with occasional flashes of violence. One day, a priest appeared suddenly 'and, takyng her be the coler of the gowne, seyd: Thu wolf, what is this cloth that thu hast on?' 'Ser,' tittered the choirboys, who happened to be passing, 'it is wulle.'*

Margery thought it best not to answer, until he began swearing

---

* I don't know whether this is the earliest reference to the proverb of the wolf in sheep's clothing.

in a fearful rage. At that, she could not help reproving him. A man in his position ought to be careful of God's commandments. He was not soothed by this and they argued for some while. All at once, he had had enough and vanished among the pillars so precipitately 'that sche wist not wher' he becam'. It was as if he had been a devil, sent to trap her into damaging admissions.

She had further visitations: 'a gret clerke' appeared from the shadows and asked how the Biblical injunction, 'Crescite et multipliciamini' should be understood? Some heretics used it to justify an inclination to free love and perhaps there was a reference to this in the mayor of Leicester's allegations of immorality.

Margery had the right answer ready. It meant that marriage should be fruitful in the sexual sense and also, more importantly, that one should cultivate the virtues so that they grew and multiplied extravagantly. The great clerk was quite satisfied and went away.

If she had left at the end of the fortnight, probably nothing further would have happened. Those members of the chapter who thought her a suspicious character who ought to be investigated, could have been held off by her supporters until she passed into another jurisdiction, where they had no power to arrest her. 'Damsel,' said one of those who would have helped her, had she not been utterly impossible, 'thu seydest whan thu come first hedyr that thu woldyst abydyn her but xiiij days.'

Deceived into a false security by the mildness of his complaint, she replied that she had never said she wouldn't stay longer than fourteen days: 'I telle yow trewly I go not yet.' In that case, he answered, she would have to appear before the authorities in the chapter-house. He gave her the date fixed for the hearing.

Experiences of this sort had taught Margery that the more of the right kind of friends one could rally, the better the examination would go. The master of divinity promised to stand by her. Another, lesser, master hummed and hawed 'tyl he knew how the cawse shuld gon'. She had followers among the ordinary people and these, together with a large crowd of the curious, filled the chapter-house on the appointed day. The crush was so great that a priest had to take Margery's arm and batter his way through to the middle of the court.

She was relieved to see that several of the officials sitting beside the judges were acquaintances of hers and, as far as she could tell, well disposed. The case opened abruptly. 'Woman,' demanded the chief judge, 'what dost thu her in this cuntre?' 'Syr,' she replied, 'I come on pilgrimage to offyr her at Seynt William.' 'Hast thu an husbond?' he asked. 'Ya,' she answered.

Strictly speaking, she ought to have carried a letter containing her husband's permission to travel about the country alone. It was a kind of passport, identifying a woman and those responsible for her at law.

'Syr,' she protested, 'myn husbond gaf me leve wyth hys owyn mowthe.' No one had these letters in actual fact, as was well known. At that very moment, York was full of unauthenticated pilgrims. Let them examine her on her faith, which was the important thing. If 'I have seyd any worde otherwise than I awt for to do, I am redy for to amende it wyth good wille. I wil neithyr meynteyn errowr ne heresy.'

Then they put the usual series of questions and she gave the correct answers. Even so, the judge said, she must appear before the Archbishop of York, at Cawood, nine miles south, where he had his palace. They could not take the responsibility of discharging her. Everyone had to be careful of his duty in these days. Only a few weeks before the Scots had made a sudden raid into Northumberland. The archbishop himself had marched against them at the head of several thousand of his tenants. Oldcastle was still not captured. He might be in league with the Scots. It was part of the Lollard programme to unseat the government, if they could. The heretics in Bohemia were reducing the country to anarchy.

In short, the chapter felt it was impossible to let Margery go. She had not even any letters of identification – though this was a technical point, since there were people in York who had known her for years. Indeed, she had sufficient friends to stand surety now and save her from spending the next few days in prison. She needed support: a certain monk, a celebrated preacher, got up in the Minster and gave an address. He castigated wicked women in a manner indicating to his numerous congregation that he spoke of Margery. Her friends 'wer ful sory and hevy therof'. But she 'was mech the more mery', she records, at hearing these slanders and injustices directed at her in public. A delicious sense of martyrdom suffused her. These were the steps to sainthood.

Shortly afterwards, she and her sureties travelled to Cawood and put up at the inn, Margery being in no way restrained, though technically a prisoner. One of the archbishop's officials, scandalized by such laxness, pointed out that if she escaped, her friends would be responsible. They replied that they were happy to take the risk. The next day, she was duly produced in the archbishop's chapel, where the court was held. Some of his Grace's household amused themselves, while waiting for the proceedings to begin, by calling out 'loller' and 'heretyke' and looking forward to seeing her burn 'with many an horrybyl othe'. 'Serys,' she retorted, 'I drede me ye shul be brent in helle wythowtyn ende les than ye amende yow of yowr othys.'

'At the last the seyd Erchebischop cam into the chapel' with a numerous retinue. He was a man of abrupt and somewhat military manners, less patient and agreeable, though no less fair, than other ecclesiastics before whom she had appeared. A robust and energetic man, he had not hesitated to take the field in person in defence of his country against the Scots. He was extremely anti-Lollard, for he could appreciate the political dangers they represented.

'Why gost thu in white?' he demanded sharply of Margery. 'Art thu a mayden?' 'Sche knelyng on hir knes befor hym, seyd: Nay ser, I am no mayden. I am a wife.' His information was, he answered, that 'sche was a fals heretyke'. Let handcuffs be brought. At this very moment the Council of Constance was dealing with a certain beastly sect which went about in white, practising frantic austerities and screaming in ecstasy.

He then left the chapel. Margery stood and prayed for divine help. Seldom had she felt so intimidated. She trembled all over and 'was fayn to puttyn hir handys undyr hir clothis that it schulde not ben aspyed'. The public were very excited, speculating audibly as to whether she was a Christian or a Jew. Some declared her a holy woman 'and sum seyd nay'.

The archbishop returned and, this time, took his seat, surrounded by officials. During these preliminaries, Margery continued to pray with the greatest intensity of which she was capable. The near approach of possible martyrdom unnerved her. It was very different from brooding over it in imagination, dwelling with a delightful thrill on pain, torture, blood, screams, smoke, fire and ascension to heaven in a halo. The strain was too much for her. She had one of her seizures.

When she had recovered herself and the sensation had died down the archbishop shouted at her: 'Why wepist thu so, woman?' The day might come, she replied with dignity, when he would wish that he had wept for love of God.

She was then questioned on 'the Articles of owr Feyth', answering correctly and quickly to every point. The archbishop turned to her accusers, saying: 'Sche knowith hir Feyth wel anow. What shal I don wyth hir?' They said that they did not believe in her profession of orthodoxy. She was continually preaching to the people and had great influence over them. It would be best to expel her from the diocese.

'I am evyl enformyd of the,' said the archbishop to Margery. 'I her seyn thu art a ryth wikked woman.' His Grace had many personal qualities and habits which did not reach the high standards of meekness, austerity, chastity, wisdom and saintliness that a prince of the church was, theoretically, meant to embody. She could not resist saying quickly, 'Ser, so I her seyn that ye arn a wikkyd man. And . . . ye shal nevyr come in Hevyn les than ye amende yow whil ye ben her.'

'Why, thow wrecche,' bellowed he, 'what sey men of me?' It was time for caution. 'Other men, syr, can telle yow wel anow,' she said prudently. 'Pes,' said 'a gret clerke wyth a furryd hood' to her, 'thu speke of thiself and late hym ben.'

In spite of his furious temper, the archbishop recovered himself. He did not have her handcuffed, nor thrown into prison for a few days to teach her proper respect for her betters. 'Ley thin hand on the boke her beforn me,' he said merely, 'and swer that thu shalt gon owt of my diocyse as sone as thu may.'

But she began to argue. Either she took courage from the fact that he was fundamentally a just man who had been unable to find her guilty. Or else, recollecting the scene years afterwards as she dictated her book, she touched it up a bit in her own favour. 'Nay, syr,' she reports herself as saying, 'I pray yow, geve me leve to gon ageyn into Yorke to take leve of my friendys.' He gave her a day or so. 'Sche thowt it was to schort.' There were various people she had to speak to, she objected, and it was absolutely necessary to go on to Bridlington to consult her confessor, a holy man who had previously been confessor to St John of Bridlington.*

This was out of the question, said the archbishop, unless she swore on the book to leave off preaching to 'the pepil in my diocyse'. 'Nay, syr,' said the insufferable woman, 'I shal not sweryn.' She would go about speaking of God and reproving bad language until the Pope made a special pronouncement against it. She quoted several bits of the gospels supporting her contention that Jesus himself wished women to enlarge on holy subjects.

Some clerks here exclaimed that this proved her guilty. She had evidently been reading Wyclif's translations of the scriptures. One 'browt forth a boke' and read out St Paul's remarks on woman preachers. To him she replied that she never preached. 'I come in no pulpytt.' She simply conversed on improving subjects with friends and exhorted them to lead the good life, 'and that wil I do whil I leve'. Another cleric declared that she spoke against the church. 'Syr,' he said to the archbishop, 'sche telde me the werst talys of prestys that evyr I herde.'

The archbishop said he would like to hear this terrible story also. He was rather coming round to Margery. There was something robust and honest about her that appealed to him.

Margery did not need to be asked twice. She at once began to relate a fable of a priest who came on a beautiful pear tree in full bloom in the middle of a wood. As he admired it, a bear appeared, gobbled all the blossom and then, turning round, was very dirty. The priest was much upset for he could see that it was a symbolical happening of some sort. As he walked on through the wood, trying to work it out, he met an elderly pilgrim and asked his advice. The old man found the problem easy. The beautiful tree and the disgraceful bear, he said, were two aspects of the priest himself. By virtue of his office, he represented all that was best and most lovely. But, like some low, dirty brute, he gabbled the services, thinking only to end them quickly in order to go out with girls, get drunk, do business deals and so on. He administered the sacraments perfunctorily, his mind full of 'lying, detraccyon and bakbytyng'. What hope had the church of being fruitful under his guidance?

* Died 1379. Canonized 1401.

The archbishop said he thought it an excellent story. There was not a word of heresy in it. The criticisms were perfectly justified. At this unexpected reaction, the cleric hastened to say that he thought so too and sat down in some confusion.

The archbishop now had to decide what to do with Margery. He must discharge her, since she was innocent, but what with the Scots and the Lollards and the king being abroad, he could not have someone liable to cause commotions wandering about his diocese. At the same time, he did not want to prevent her going to York and Bridlington, as she wished. The best way of keeping her out of trouble would be to send an escort with her. 'Wher shal I have a man that myth ledyn this woman fro me?' he asked of his retinue.

Several young men, anxious to please their master and rise in his service, volunteered eagerly, saying: 'My Lord, I wyl gon wyth hir.' 'Ye ben to yong,' replied the archbishop. They would never be able to cope with the emergencies likely to arise in connection with Margery. Besides, it would not look sufficiently respectable. Someone responsible and steady was needed.

Finally, 'a good sad men' called John got up and asked what pay was offered for the job. The archbishop said five shillings. John didn't think he could do it under thirteen and fourpence. No woman was worth that, said the archbishop: 'Se, her is Vs, and lede hir fast owt of this cuntre.'

# CHAPTER XXXVII

## *The Archbishop at Beverley*

When Margery arrived back in York, she was congratulated by her friends on near escape from death. They had hardly hoped to see her again. God certainly had her under his especial protection. They listened admiringly to the story of the trial: how she had answered all the accusations and disputed with learned men on their own ground, refuting their quotations with others from different parts of the gospels. It seemed miraculous in one 'not lettryd'.

The journey to Bridlington was uneventful. If there were questions, John answered them with a flourish of the archbishop's seal. Having paid her respects to her confessor, she turned south-wards for home. Everything was calm until they reached Hull. Here Margery joined a procession and became very excited. An important lady objected to her behaviour and the crowd, taking their cue, began abusing her and saying she ought to be in prison. However, a decent man took her part and invited her to dinner.

No doubt the incident would have passed off, had not two Franciscans been somehow involved. Perhaps Margery had insulted them by relating, in their hearing, a fable like the one she had recounted to the archbishop. The result was that her host received threatening visitors during the evening. He had better get rid of his guest, they said. She would do him no good. The poor man was terrified. He might be arrested for harbouring heretics. He might be murdered, robbed.

Thus, not withstanding John's credentials, 'the next day at morwyn hir hoste led hir owt at the townys end'. He dared not do otherwise.

Abandoned at the town gates, Margery and John – who must have liked this five-shilling job less and less – went the few miles east to Hessle, where they proposed to take a ferry over the Humber. But, just as they were stepping into the boat, the two Franciscans, accompanied by two yeomen of the Duke of Bedford's forces, accosted them.

The Duke of Bedford was Henry V's brother. He had been appointed Lieutenant of England, to govern during the king's absence at the war in France. On hearing of the Scottish incursion, he had collected an army and marched north. On the way, he halted at Leicester for a short time, very soon after Margery's trial of strength with the mayor. Evidently the case was the gossip of the town. It was said she was one of the wickedest women alive, having obtained an acquittal by telling the abbot abominable lies and pretending to believe in the true faith.

When the two Franciscans made their complaint and it was realized that this was the same notorious woman of Leicester, great excitement prevailed. The duke's officials had not heard the next instalment of her adventures with the Archbishop of York. They ordered her to be arrested and taken to Beverley, where the archbishop was shortly expected to hold court.

'Owr Lord the Duke of Bedforth hath sent for the,' the two yeomen cried, seizing Margery and John whose documents they waved aside as forgeries. 'And thu art holdyn the grettest loller in all this cuntre er abowte London eythyr.' She was a marked woman and they had been on the look-out for her all along the road from Leicester. The duke would certainly give them a reward for having caught her; perhaps even as much as a hundred pounds.

The two prisoners, the two yeomen and the two Franciscans formed into a procession and set out at once for Beverley, some miles north of Hull. As they passed through Hessle, women came out of the houses brandishing their distaffs and shouting: 'Brennyth this fals heretyk!' The men of the countryside were more sympathetic, saying compassionately: 'Damsel, forsake this lyfe that thu hast and go spynne and carde as other women don, and suffer not so meche schame and so meche wo.' Religion wasn't worth it, they urged. The joys of this world were more certain than those of the hereafter. But she replied staunchly that she had not yet suffered as much for Christ as he had suffered for her and all mankind.

As they continued on their way, Margery discoursed to her captors and related improving stories. The Franciscans let her talk, one presumes, in the hope that she would say something incriminating. One of the yeomen was impressed by her eloquence. He began to regret having arrested her. 'Me semyth that thu seyst ryth good wordys,' he remarked uneasily. For her part, she said tactfully, she was 'ryth wel plesyd' to have had this opportunity of making his acquaintance. Such Christian forbearance made him even more unhappy. 'Damsel, yf evyr thu be seynt in Hevyn, prey for me,' he begged, trying to make the best of both worlds. 'Sir,' said she, feeling a little judicious flattery appropriate for the occasion, 'I hope ye shal be a seynt yowrself and every man that shal come to Hevyn.'

These sweet words seem to have had an effect, for, on reaching Beverley, she was not put into the common prison, but taken to the yeoman's lodgings and locked into 'a fayre chambyr and an honest bed therin wyth the necessarys'. The unfortunate John was not so favoured and was led off to the cells. His term was short, however, for the archbishop arrived later the same day and had him released at once.

He then appeared among the crowd outside Margery's upstairs window 'wyth angry cher, seying: Alas, that evyr knew I the.' 'Havyth mekenes and pacyens,' she advised soothingly, 'and ye shal have gret mede in Hevyn therfor.' He did not stay for further conversation.

Margery was never one to waste a chance of influencing people for their own good. Nor could she resist an audience, however unpromising. Here she was at the window, at is were on a rostrum. There, in the street, was a gathering, come to stare and jeer at a heretic. She began to speak. That she was a persuasive orator for those inclined to religious subjects, there is plenty of evidence. Being emotional, she must have made dramatic gestures to illustrate her fables and point the moral. She was practised, after many years' experience. Her mind was not pre-occupied with fears of death, for the archbishop was her friend. The result of it all was that those who had come to insult her stayed to weep, crying out in grief-stricken voices: 'Alas, woman, why shalt thu be brent?'

Margery was, by this time, very thirsty and called out to the yeoman's wife 'to gevyn hir drynke'. The woman replied that she couldn't do anything because her husband had gone off with the key of the room. The crowd were much upset. She was a martyr, such as the priests had told them of in sermons. Something must be done to alleviate her sufferings. It would dispose her well towards them after she had ascended to heaven in the smoke of a bonfire. They fetched a ladder and clambered up with a cup and a pint of wine in a jug, begging her to put them under the bed, or somewhere out of sight, when she had finished, so that the yeoman 'myth not aspye it'. Sorry though they were for her predicament, they had not the slightest desire to risk personal inconvenience on her behalf.

In spite of a brave front, Margery was very worried that night, lying in the honest bed. She would have justice from the archbishop, but the Duke of Bedford was the most powerful man in the country. He might imprison her for political reasons, simply to get her out of the way during a time when people were restless, inclined to listen to talk and riot. The Franciscans, of all the religious orders, hated Lollards most, for they came into direct competition with them.

Popularly known as the preaching friars, they were trained speakers and travelled the country giving sermons in churches and at market crosses. Weather permitting, they would often set up a pulpit in a churchyard under one of the large crosses which may still be seen in many places, and bring the word of God to the people in vivid terms. The Lollards entirely approved of this aspect of their work. They did the same themselves. What they objected to was corruption in the Franciscan order. These monks were not poor, as St Francis had intended. They might arrive on horseback with servants. Chaucer's blistering description of Friar Hubert embodies everything the Lollards disliked.

Hubert had a wonderful smooth tongue, a bold face, expensive clothes, a taste for drink, a bag of presents for girls, a number of bastards, a cheerful snobbery which prevented him from mixing much with humble people, though he was not above charming a widow's last farthing out of her pocket. All these faults the Lollard preachers were careful to avoid, and it is no wonder that they undermined the friars' influence and found ready listeners to their idea that the Church should be disestablished and monastic property be distributed among the tenants.

In these circumstances, the two Franciscans could be expected to make the most strenuous efforts to have Margery convicted on some count or other. As she lay thinking of these things, she drifted into sleep and, in her dreams, heard a loud voice cry: 'Margery!' rather as the infant Samuel's attention had been attracted by God. Having more experience than the youthful prophet, she knew at once that it was a divine summons and composed herself to receive the message. It was to the effect that she should be of good cheer, because God did not actually require her life at this time. The disgrace of imprisonment and notoriety for his sake was quite enough. Very special rewards were reserved for her in paradise. One hopes she slept well after this, for the next day proved a gruelling experience.

She was taken to the chapter-house of St John's church 'and ther was the Erchebischop of Yorke and many gret clerkys wyth hym, prestys, chanowns and seculer men'. As soon as he caught sight of her, the archbishop exclaimed: 'What, woman, art thu come agen? I wolde fayn be delyveryd of the.' He ordered her to be brought out into the middle of the court and then addressed those present saying that he examined her at Cawood and found her perfectly orthodox. Afterwards respectable men had come to him declaring her a good, pious, even holy, woman. 'Notwythstandyng al this I gaf one of my men Vs to ledyn hir owt of this cuntre for qwietyng of the pepil.' As they were going about their lawful occasions, they were suddenly arrested, his man imprisoned and Margery's money, rosary and ring taken away. 'Is ther any man can sey anythyng agen hir?' he demanded.

One of the Franciscans was pushed forward. She had spoken disparagingly of monks, friars and all priests. Her devotional fits and weepings were a fraud, put on to attract a crowd. He did not believe she had ever been to Jerusalem, Rome, or any other centre of pilgrimage. She would have been burnt years ago in Lynn, if the Franciscans had had authority there.

The two yeomen jumped up and said she was certainly a disaffected person, one of Oldcastle's messengers wandering round the country with letters inciting people to rebellion. They could not, however, produce the slightest evidence in support of their contention.

When her accusers were at last silent for lack of anything to say, the archbishop invited Margery to reply. Every word they said was a lie, she answered simply.

The archbishop then pointed out to the friar that Margery's reported conversation might be mistaken and slanderous, but it was not heresy. In spite of her protestations, said the friar, she was really a Lollard and the Duke of Bedford was determined on her conviction. He could not be a party to that, said the archbishop. In law, she was innocent. The friar would have to take her before the duke himself. But this was impossible, since she had been cleared in the ecclesiastical court. If she had been found guilty of heresy, then she would have been handed over to the secular authorities for burning, because the church courts could not impose the death sentence. The friar knew that the duke would never over-ride the archbishop's decision in a case like this.

He began to excuse himself and to back out, saying ingratiatingly, 'It fallyth not for a frer to ledyn a woman abowtyn.' However, the archbishop thought it not wise to discharge Margery at once. He ordered both parties to be detained so that he could look into the matter further.

Margery begged that she should not be put into the common prison, 'for sche was a mannys wyfe'. 'Nay,' said the archbishop kindly, 'thu shalt non harm han.' One of his men was detailed to look after her in his own house as a member of the family. She was allowed visitors and many people came to commiserate with her, since the archbishop's attitude made it safe to say openly that she was being persecuted by the Franciscans.

'In schort tyme aftyr, the Erchebischop sent for hir.' Accompanied by the gaoler, she passed through the great hall where his household were enjoying a hearty dinner. In the middle ages, apart from the communal hall, there were no proper reception rooms and the bedchamber served when privacy was required. Margery had been interviewed by Archbishop Arundel of Canterbury in the garden of Lambeth Palace, as it was fine and warm. The Bishop of Worcester had received her in his bedroom, he being in bed. Now she was taken to the Archbishop of York's bedside, for he wished to settle the matter quietly.

Before the proceedings began, Margery thanked him sincerely for his kindness towards her and for his uprightness and the justice she had received. 'Ya, ya,' replied he in his rough way, 'I am wers enformyd of the than evyr I was beforn.'

She said quickly, rather alarmed, that she would be happy to answer any number of questions. If she was found to have mistaken views, she would amend them at once. But the accusations, this time, were quite unexpected. A senior Franciscan appeared, a suffragan bishop, to whom the archbishop said: 'Now, ser, as ye seyde to me whan sche was not present, sey now whil sche is present.' 'Schal I so?' said the Franciscan, evidently taken aback. 'Ya, seyde the Erchebishchop.'

The friar then began a long story of how Margery had visited the Countess of Westmorland and talked at great length with more than a touch of heretical ideas. The countess had been taken in by the specious Lollard. Furthermore, and this was much worse, Margery had advised Lady Westmorland's daughter, Lady Greystoke, to leave her husband. All this had happened last Easter, he said, in answer to Margery's question on that point. He said many other disgraceful things about Margery also: 'it is not expenient to rehersyn hem', she remarks in her book.

When he had finished, Margery replied that she had not seen Lady Westmorland since before she went to Jerusalem. At that time, the countess had sent for her and they had enjoyed an agreeable conversation. As for the business of Lady Greystoke's separation, the subject was never mentioned between them. She was ready to go to Lady Westmorland and obtain an affidavit to that effect. But those of the Franciscan's party feared she would abscond. 'Late hir be putte in preson,' they cried, 'and we shal sendyn a lettyr to the worshepful lady.' If the answer supported what Margery said, she could be released immediately. Margery said she was willing to submit to this arrangement. 'Putte hir xl days in preson,' one of them advised brutally, 'and sche shal lovyn God the bettyr whyl sche levyth.'

The archbishop then asked what moral story she had told Lady Westmorland. It concerned, she said, a lady who went to hell for not loving her enemies, and a bailiff who forgave everyone and so was saved, though the world held him a wicked man. The archbishop said it was an excellent story. 'Lord,' cried the opposition, seeing they had lost the case again, 'we prey yow late hir go hens at this tyme and if evyr sche come ageyn, we shal bren hyre owrself.' 'I leve ther was nevyr woman in Inglond so fered wythal as sche is and hath ben,' his Grace remarked with amusement. 'I wote not what I shal don wyth the.'

She said that if she could have a letter, sealed with his seal, plainly stating that she was not, and never had been, a heretic, she would go straight to Lynn. Perhaps the man John would escort her over the Humber which was the boundary of the diocese. He agreed to this arrangement, but said that, before going home, she must journey to London and obtain a letter from the Archbishop of Canterbury, certifying her orthodoxy. For Arundel had died and Chichele held the see. Her old certificate was out of date.

Thus, she said good-bye to this remarkable man whom narrow-minded persons thought unworthy of his position because of a certain lack of saintliness in his private life.

As she left the room light-heartedly, some of the archbishop's men asked her to pray for them. The steward, on the other hand, observed: 'Holy folke shulde not lawghe.' But she could not help it, so great was her relief at danger escaped. Besides, holy folk did sometimes laugh: St Bridget had been remembered for precisely that in Rome. As she passed through the great hall, 'ther stod the Frere Prechowr that had cawsyd hir al that wo.'

# CHAPTER XXXVIII

*Retirement to Lynn*

We do not know whether the disgusted John was given another five shillings to conduct Margery over the Humber. Perhaps not, as it was a matter of less than ten miles. However, he performed his duty, leaving her at the ferry.

She had hardly set foot in Lincolnshire before she was seized as a suspicious character. Fortunately, a man came forward who had been present at her trial. He stood surety 'and so sche scapyed awey in the name of Ihesu', in company with a Londoner and his wife who were going via Lincoln. There she halted for a short time and had certain adventures, though nothing like as bad as previous experiences. She was a veteran of cross-examination now. Clerks marvelled at such ready answers in an illiterate woman. 'Of whom hast thu this cunnyng?' they enquired after she had given them quotation for quotation from the gospels. 'Of the Holy Gost,' she replied firmly.

Sometimes people came asking her to prophesy, but these were not propitious days for that sort of thing. Though 'gret lordys men' approached her swearing 'many gret othys' and demanding to know 'whethyr we schal be savyd er damnyd', she remained cautious, replying in harmless platitudes. 'As long as ye sweryn swech horrybyl othis ... I dar wel sey ye schal be damnyd ... And yf ye wil be contrite and schrevyn of yowr synne ... I dar wel sey ye schal be savyd.' 'What!' they protested, 'canst thu noon otherwise tellyn us but thus?' 'Serys,' she replied with dignity, 'this is ryth good, me thynkyth.' They went away in disgust, much to her relief.

At last she came safely to West Lynn and sent for some of her friends to cross the river from Bishop's Lynn, so that she could tell them her news. It was impossible to come home, she explained, until she had obtained the Archbishop of Canterbury's certificate. Would they please get hold of John Kempe? She required him as escort for the journey.

One cannot imagine that poor John Kempe was keen on the idea. He had never cared for travel and the scrapes Margery invariably got into terrified him. However, he found it impossible to excuse himself. She was, theoretically, his wife and his responsibility. On the pilgrimages abroad, she had been attached to regular organized parties. If she now demanded his inadequate protection he was obliged to assent, especially as, it seems, he had no business requiring his attention in Lynn.

They set out together on the journey to London. Nothing worthy of note happened on the road, which must have been a source of deep thankfulness to him. In a way, he admired her and accepted her claims to spiritual experiences. But there is no evidence that he had the least wish to follow her to those rarified heights where God spoke familiarly and without regard for the effect his immortal words might have on everyday existence.

It seems that no difficulties were put in their way on reaching Lambeth Palace. The interview with Archbishop Chichele went smoothly and they obtained the precious document which was to save their lives in future. Margery now had the highest possible references. During her stay in London, 'many worthy men' entertained her. It must have been a wonderful relaxation after the strains she had endured.

The return to Lynn was equally uneventful, until they neared Ely, when 'ther cam a man rydyng aftyr' them at a gallop. He had been informed that they were highly suspicious characters. It was his intention to take them to the nearest prison. 'He cruely rebukyd' them both, using a good deal of strong language.

What with the surprise of this sudden attack and the realization, as it seemed, of all his worst forebodings, John Kempe remained perfectly mute with terror. He did nothing until his wife ordered him to get out the archbishop's certificate and show it to the man. As he read, his fury melted away with extraordinary rapidity. 'He spak fayr and goodly unto hem', saying with reasonable reproach: 'Why shewyd ye me not yowr lettyr beforn?'

Thus happily passed off the last occasion on which Margery was arrested. She was now to settle down in Lynn where everybody knew her history and of her licence especially granted by the Archbishop of Canterbury. Also, in the winter of 1417, Sir John Oldcastle was at last captured, brought to London, tried before the Duke of Bedford and executed as a traitor and heretic. Thereafter, the Lollards ceased to be regarded as a public danger. Their political organization had been smashed. They continued to propagate their views by means of itinerant preachers and odd Lollards were burnt in succeeding years, but they never again had the cohesion to threaten rebellion. It was not found necessary to hunt them over the countryside, in the process netting many innocent persons whose eccentricities alarmed the ignorant; or people whose enemies thought this a good chance of doing them a bad turn; or those who were, in some way or another, a nuisance to their neighbours.

The citizens of Lynn perforce contented themselves with abusing Margery when she got on their nerves; or pouring bowls of dirty water over her from upstairs windows. Years passed, more or less peacefully. She had several serious illnesses, but mercifully recovered. There were brushes with priests on account of the disturbance caused when she screamed and had fits during mass. Yet, they dared not refuse her the sacraments, as they would have liked to do, on account of the Archbishop of Canterbury's letter.

Her visions continued unabated and in the same repetitive vein. She never made any progress in the spiritual life from first to last. Lacking the selflessness essential to the true follower of the contemplative way, her glimpses of the infinite, as related in her book at tedious length, are sadly banal. They consist entirely of day-dreams in which she imagines herself as a humble friend of the Holy Family, taking part in all their doings, as told in the gospels.

Jesus is always sweet and reassuring, pleased with everything his Margery does or says. Sometimes, it is true, lewd devils worry her with impure thoughts and horribly enjoyable visions of men, both heathen and Christian in a state of erection. But, it's only for her own good. Saints have to suffer these setbacks. It does not detract from their sainthood. She prays for the sins of the world; and particularly for those of the people of Lynn. It is revealed to her who among her acquaintance shall be saved, and who damned. Yet, there is nothing malicious in these divine communications. Immature they may be, and full of self-esteem, but never spiteful.

In the first years, she was unpopular. The old charges of heresy and devil worship were remembered. In spite of her certificate, she could not find a priest who would do more than permit her to attend his mass. She longed for someone with whom she could have discussions on sacred subjects, a literate man who could read her the works of hermits, recluses and saints.

At last a stranger came to Lynn and lodged in the town with his mother. On seeing Margery in the street, he was agreeably struck by her demeanour. He made inquiries and, discovering that she was the local holy woman, invited her to his rooms. The conversation seemed to him delightful, his visitor remarkable. After she left, he asked his mother's opinion. The old lady strongly approved the new acquaintance. That settled it. They became firm friends. He braved her many enemies and undertook to read out all the books then in vogue among the pious, translating from the Latin where necessary.

Thus, they perused 'the Bybyl, wyth doctowrys therupon'; St Bridget's *Revelations;* the lives of saints now hardly remembered, such as St Elizabeth of Hungary and St Mary of Oignies, written by their confessors; books of instruction in the mystical way of life by English practitioners famous at that date. They must have read them all many times, for the association continued 'vij yer, er viij yer'. The priest 'wolde not a lokyd at' half these works, had she not insisted on hearing them. Notwithstanding his natural indolence, he became learned and, in the end, had cause to thank her for his forced labours: he found he had qualified himself for promotion and obtained a very nice living.

In other ways, too, she proved his true friend. When he fell very ill, some years later, she bought comforts out of her own money, as long as it lasted. Then she went round her acquaintance begging alms, so that he might not want. By this time her friend, the holy vicar of St Stephen's in Norwich had died. Prayers at his grave were found particularly efficacious. She went to Norwich on her priest's behalf and prayed in such an emotional manner that several persons present were sorry for her and took her into a tavern for a good drink to cheer her up. Thanks to the vicar's efforts in heaven and Margery's on earth, the patient recovered his health completely.

During these first years of return, life was not altogether easy. Though many respectable citizens endorsed her claim to holiness, she had too many enemies for comfort. Thanks to the archbishop's certificate, they could not do much harm, but they were a source of annoyance and inconvenience. She was obliged to move out of the matrimonial home and live separately in another part of the town because sceptics refused to believe in her chaste life. Who knew what went on once the doors were shut and the lights out, they said insinuatingly. Perhaps John Kempe was grateful, for he seems to have continued unregenerate to the last, refusing to follow his wife in her extravagant career, failing in his business. He must have written off his marriage long ago. There is no evidence that the frightening course of improving lectures to which he had been subjected were of the slightest benefit to his character.

From her new home, which must have been humble in view of a chronic lack of funds, Margery continued her determined career as a saint. One of the things she most enjoyed was to go to sermons. This was not then such a dismal form of entertainment as it has subsequently become. In order to hold the audience's attention and make some impression on illiterate memory, the church, especially the travelling friars, used particular forms of address. Books of these sermons have come down to us. First there is a story, of knights and dragons, of ambush by thieves, unfaithful wives, miracles done by saints, tales from history, or from certain immemorial collections originating in India at some date hardly now to be determined. These last were used by clerk and layman alike. They can be read not only in medieval com-pilations for the use of priests, but in Boccaccio, the Arabian Nights, Chaucer and Shakespeare. They are stories of love, magic, princes and princesses, battles with strange demons; some are set in Rome among the Caesars; some in the strange lands visited afterwards by Sir John Maundevile.

As may be imagined, the Christian moral drawn at the end of the tale was short, strained and subsidiary. The dragons are the Devil. The good emperor is Christ. The faithful lady is the Virgin. The oracle is a holy recluse. Let every man pay his tithes and be careful to avoid heresy, lechery, avarice, slander, vanity and pride. The travelling preacher was really an itinerant story-teller. He stood in a pulpit, or under a cross, instead of on a box in the street. He addressed the same people as his rival and held them by the same methods. Theological reasoning and a high spiritual tone were equally absent from his discourse. These were reserved for schoolmen and doctors, the educated class of monastery and university.

Great excitement prevailed in Lynn, therefore, when it was announced that a famous Franciscan was coming to one of the monasteries in the town. 'Hys name and hys perfeccyon of prechyng spred and sprong wondyr wyde.' 'Margery,' cried her friends, bringing the news, 'now shal ye han prechyng anow, for ther is comyn on of the most famows frerys in Inglond.' Everybody rushed to St James's chapel, where he was to give the first oration.

This man was accustomed to breathless attention while he spoke. His gestures, his matter and manner of delivery held the congregation spellbound. The resident priest of St James's had a feeling that he would not take kindly to Margery's vociferous interruptions: during her screams the speaker would be obliged to stop until she calmed down. So he begged Margery to restrain herself, if she possibly could, on the one hand. On the other, he went to the friar, explaining that she couldn't help being noisy. It was a gift from God and came on with particular violence at any mention of the Passion; 'But it lestith not longe,' he said propitiatingly.

Sure enough, at a vivid description of Christ's sufferings, Margery 'braste owte wyth a gret cry and cryid wondyr sor'. The friar endured in patient silence. But when he found that she attended all his sermons and caused the same diversion at each, it was too much. 'I wolde this woman were owte of the chirche, sche noyith the pepil,' he said angrily. 'Sir,' replied Margery's supporters, 'have hir excusyd. Sche may not withstand it.'

The friar retorted that she was obviously mad, or a fraud. 'If sche come in any chirch wher he shulde prechyn,' he repeated, 'and sche made any noyse as sche was wone to do,' he would curse her from the pulpit. Even the solicitations of a Carmelite, several priests and a prospective mayor failed to move him, though they supported their arguments with a bottle of 'wyne to cheryn hym'. The Augustinians, the Dominicans and the Carmelites all bore with her for the love of God, they pointed out. One had only to wait a little until she had quieted sufficiently for one's voice to be heard. 'Sche hath a devyl wythinne hir,' replied the friar to everything they could say.

He conceived a great hatred of Margery and as his following grew in size and enthusiasm, so did the general feeling against her. The few who remained faithful to her were afraid she would be run out of the town. She did not dare to go publicly to mass, but had to receive the sacraments from a friendly priest in some secluded chapel where her sobs were more or less muffled. She even managed to control herself to some extent and relaxed the severity of her fasts and penances. The only relief she had was when the friar went on a preaching tour, accompanied by a crowd of his most rabid admirers.

She had scarcely a friend except God. 'Dowtyr,' he said stoutly, 'yf he be a preyste that despisith the, knowyng wel wherfor thu wepist and cryist, he is acursyd.'

# CHAPTER XXXIX

## The Great Fire of Lynn

It was not until the great fire at Lynn in 1421 that Margery was able to make any headway against the friar. This catastrophe occurred in midwinter, starting in some unexplained manner in the guildhall. The flames quickly took hold and it seemed likely that the whole town would be burnt to the ground. What with narrow streets, thatched roofs and no fire brigade, the conflagration spread round the guildhall, becoming hotter and fiercer, despite the united efforts of everyone with buckets of water and flails to beat out flying sparks.

While the people worked with despairing energy, Margery 'cryed ful lowde many tymes that day', praying for 'grace and mercy to alle'. Men who had cursed her as a noisy hypocrite now begged her to continue. Only a miracle could save their property, they felt. Perhaps she could obtain one. Those who believed in her powers as a holy woman might be right. Who could tell? The ways of God were very mysterious. The friar might not have penetrated them all. So they urged her to scream louder and have more frequent fits, to draw God's attention to their plight and cause him to send them a deluge.

The sky remained perfectly clear. As Margery knelt in St Margaret's 'sche beheld how the sparkys comyn into the qwer throw the lantern of the cherch'. The priest in charge asked whether she would advise him to take the blessed sacrament out and hold it up before the flames, saying the words of the mass. 'Ya, ser, ya,' she cried, 'for owr Lord Ihesu Crist telde me it shal be ryth wel.' So he went out singing and perambulated round the fire. Margery accompanied the procession, crying 'wyth a lowde voys and great wepyng'. 'Sende down sum reyn er sum wedyr that may thorw thi mercy qwenchyn this fyre and esyn myn hert,' she shrieked. As the door opened for their return, sparks entered with them and 'fleyn abowte the cherch'.

Margery now prayed with all the vigour of which she was capable. Her reputation and, indeed, her future in the town, depended on a miracle. If she won, she was safe for ever, no matter what heretics arose, or friars declaimed. As she pleaded with God to excuse the sins of everyone in Lynn, not to consume the city this time, wicked though it was, 'iij worschepful men' with snow on their coats rushed in shouting, 'Lo, Margery, God hath wrowt gret grace for us and sent us a fayr snowe to qwenchyn wyth the fyr.'

They got the flames under control with the help of the blizzard. Everyone agreed that it was entirely due to Margery's efforts and not a natural storm. It came too suddenly for that. One minute the sky was 'brygth and cler', the next it was full of 'clowdys and derkys' and enormous swirling flakes.

From this time, her supporters began to outnumber those of the friar. Priests who had forbidden her their churches were converted. Her holiness was acclaimed at the next annual meeting of the Dominicans in Lynn. Precedents for her behaviour were found in the lives of saints and approbation in books written by hermits and other respectable authorities. Such was the swing of opinion in her favour, that preachers felt it an honour when she deigned to attend their sermons and were happy to interrupt their remarks as long as she wished to demonstrate. For, being imbued with sacred influences, she was a beneficent presence, bringing good fortune wherever she went. It says much for Margery's sterling qualities that she was not carried away by her new position. Her egoism became no worse than it had always been. The cosy chats with an admiring God did not grow more ridiculous than before. She seems not to have gone about boasting of miraculous powers, or, indeed, to have done anything except try to model herself on what she conceived of as the ideal, as she had always done.

There were still, of course, people who refused to admire her, being bored by her moralizings and temperamentally disinclined to violent piety. But these were gradually silenced. People began to ask her to prophesy whether, or not, they should set out on long journeys; to weep over dying friends and relations in the belief that it would speed the way to heaven. Rich ladies sometimes sent for her and invited her to explain the holy life for the edification of themselves and their household. She was called to a poor mad woman, afflicted after childbirth, as she herself had been so long ago.

'Sche knowyth not me ne non of hir neyborwys,' said the

distracted husband. 'Sche roryth and cryith so that sche makith folk evyl afeerd.' She was so unmanageable that her wrists were manacled. Her screams continued day and night. This got on people's nerves to such an extent that she had to be taken to an isolated house on the outskirts of the town, 'and ther was sche bowndyn handys and feet wyth chenys of yron'. Only Margery could calm her. Other visitors made her worse, for they were accompanied by crowds of devils, she swore. Whereas Margery had angels floating in the air beside her.

Every day Margery came and harangued her on improving subjects, no doubt at considerable length. As the platitudes and clichés rolled on and on, the lunatic was soothed. Here was something to hold on to in confusion. Every day the same voice, same subjects, expressions and manner of delivery. No one else was kind and unafraid. Gradually, whether by the passage of time, or Margery's prayers, or a combination of the two, her madness abated. She became calm, sensible, reliable and, finally, was conducted to church by her saviour to be purified.

Many people thought it 'a ryth gret myrakyl'. Of all the lunatics they had known this woman had been the most violent and given the least hope of recovery. Yet, there she was now, 'sad and sobyr', for all to see. Who would dare admonish Margery as she followed the processions on saints' days, waving her arms, staggering, writhing and screaming at the top of her voice? Besides, she was by no means unique. Only the most extreme. Numbers of the pious believed themselves possessed by divinity on these occasions.

Even when she expressed a strong desire to kiss lepers because they reminded her of the wounded Christ, her confessor could merely protest feebly that if she must do it, she had better confine her attentions to female lepers. 'Kyssyn no men,' he said faintly. In the days before her conversion to the holy life, 'ther was nothyng mor lothful ne mor abhomynabyl to hir' than the lepers. She had fled from the mere sight of them. Now, with morbid eagerness, she made special visits to the women's lazar-house and kissed several of the inmates, remarking that their illness was a good thing really as it assured them of a place in heaven, if they bore their pains in a suitably grateful spirit. She returned often to pray for and comfort one of the women who was upset by certain

Pope John XXIII presents the Emperor Sigismund with a golden rose. (From the *Chronik des Ulrich Richental*. Circa 1460.)

The King and Queen of Naples at Mass. It was immediately after the rebellion in Rome following the accession of this king in 1414 that Margery entered the city with Dame Margaret Florentine. (From a Book of Hours belonging to Alfonso V of Aragon and Naples. Circa 1442. Additional 28962.)

Belehrung des Burggraven
Friedrich von Nürnberg mit
der Markgrafschaft Bran-
denburg.

A nobleman's suite at Constance. (From the *Chronik des Ulrich Richental*. Circa 1460.)

A court hearing. (From a 15th century copy of Valerius Maximus, with notes and supplementary material by two Masters of Theology, in French. [Valerius Maximus was a Roman of the 1st century. His book contains episodes from Roman history and was intended for use in the schools of rhetoric.] Harley 4375.)

vivid dreams. In real life she had never sinned – 'sche was a mayde' – but all sorts of wild orgies with devils passed through her head. Here again, Margery had had similar experiences as a result of prolonged chastity. She knew what it felt like and how best to defeat it. These tips she passed on to her leper friend, who was much relieved, she said.

Thus, Margery pursued her local round, absolutely uninterested in anything outside her own affairs. If she mentions a national event, such as Henry V's death, it is strictly in connection with her prophesies. While she kissed lepers and consoled lunatics, the protestant revolution began in Bohemia and resisted all efforts at suppression. The extraordinary episode of Joan of Arc took place across the Channel. She, also, had visions of God and the saints, spoke directly with divinity and prophesied. The same religious background inspired them both.

But no two women could have been more different than the garrulous, middle-aged busybody of Lynn and the strange young warrior of Domremy, whose dream it was to set her country on its feet again and who achieved her aim, at the cost of her own life. Joan, too, was accused of commerce with the Devil, of heresy, fraud and using supernatural powers in a manner forbidden by the church. Here, the slight comparison ends. Joan had been bought by the English from her captor, the Duke of Burgundy, for a fortune in gold crowns. A fair trial before a just and humane bishop was felt impossible to allow. She had cast too strong a spell over the French. The Bishop of Norwich was present at her burning in 1431.

It may be that Margery did follow the news to a certain extent, but thought it not relevant to a book the object of which was to elevate and instruct less fortunate souls. For she had the true missionary spirit. It seemed to be her business in the world, as far as she understood heavenly instructions, to draw the heedless to a sense of their spiritual predicament by constant precept and example.

During this time, also, while Joan was fighting for her life, Margery was extremely preoccupied. John Kempe was now over sixty, 'a man in gret age' for those times. He had lived alone for years on account of the gossips who refused to believe in Margery's chastity while they spent the nights under one roof. They had even abandoned short local pilgrimages in each other's company, because cynical persons accused them of making for the nearest 'woodys, grovys er valeys', there to enjoy themselves in seclusion.

One night John, getting up in a hurry to go downstairs 'barfoot and barlegge', slipped 'er ellys fayled of his fotyng' and crashed to the bottom on his head. The neighbours, hearing the noise, rushed in to see what had happened and found him on the floor half dead, covered with blood and his head twisted under him. They picked him up and sent for Margery. He had five wounds in his skull so deep that they had to be plugged. He was very ill for a long time and no one expected him to recover.

Some people blamed Margery for the accident, saying that if she had looked after him as a wife should, it would never have occurred. She was practically his murderer, they said, conveniently forgetting that it was their own malicious gossip which had obliged the two to part.

At last he was better, more or less, but not quite right in the head. He declined into a hopeless senility and incontinence and 'as a childe voydyd his natural digestyon in hys lynyn cloths', sitting by the fire 'er at the tabil . . . he wolde sparyn no place'.

Margery was always ready to suffer dramatically for the love of God, but shrank from the care of an invalid who might linger for years. He would require attention and supervision every minute of the day and night, not to speak of the continual 'waschyng and wryngyng' made necessary by his dirty habits. What about her daily meditations, sometimes lasting hours at a time? Her round of visits to admiring friends and disciples? All the talk and scurry and excitement of a holy woman's life?

Yet this man, whatever his failings, had always been good to her. She had known the delights of love with him. His complaisance had made possible her subsequent career. Conversations with God confirmed her feeling that she could not abandon him to strangers in his last clouded days. So she struggled on, denied the luxury of 'hy contmeplacyon', running up enormous fuel bills in order to heat water for the constant washing, enduring his vagaries. Sometimes, she felt she couldn't stand it any more. At other times, she reflected on the fittingness of this long penance: he had caused her 'ful many delectabyl thowtys, fleschly lustys and inordinat lovys to hys persone'; and he enabled her to pay for that sinful period. With these thoughts she endured her fate 'mech the mor esily'.

Such right conduct must have helped to sway popular opinion in her favour. When she could get away from her duties, nuns and important ladies were glad to receive her. As her reputation increased, so must the alms she was given. That would enable her to hire help to look after poor John and free her a little from household chores for which she had never had the slightest taste. She began to go on short pilgrimages again, visiting favourite shrines. Her position became so secure that she even thought of writing a book showing how God had favoured her over the years and promised the honour of sainthood to his faithful servant. Poverty prevented her from founding a religious order, but in authorship, at least, she could rival St Bridget.

# CHAPTER XL

## The Erring Son

Only one of Margery's fourteen children is mentioned individually in the autobiography, a certain son. As a boy, he was subjected to endless exhortations and checks on his natural gaiety. It is hardly surprising, therefore, that on becoming 'a tal yong man', he broke out into fine clothes, jocular conversation and a strong desire for the company of girls. No matter how his mother warned him of the place to which his sins would surely lead him, he persisted in his errors.

He took service with a merchant of Lynn, trading with the Hanseatic ports on the Baltic. When not journeying abroad for business, he lived in his master's house. He must have dreaded these periods in his home town, for Margery would waylay him in the street, beseeching him, with great emotion, 'to leevyn the worlde and folowyn Crist', to turn his thoughts to heavenly things, stop swearing and dressing up like a dandy. What wonder 'that he fled hir cumpany', bolting round corners at the sight of her? Once she caught him and cursed him, in the name of God: if he ever again went to bed with a woman not his wife, terrible punishment would befall him.

It must have been a great relief to the beleaguered young man when his master sent him, as agent, to one of the Baltic ports, perhaps Danzig. Once safely there, he determined to enjoy himself with the women of the town. As a result, he came out in sores and blotches on his face. Venereal or a skin disease seems a possible diagnosis in the circumstances, but this was not his opinion. He thought he had been stricken with leprosy on account of his mother's curse. His friends thought so too. They may have been almost right. The symptoms might have been psychological.

On his next return to Lynn, he was sacked, 'for no defawte' except 'hys visage' which appeared to be that of a leper. Though Margery pitied him sincerely, she did not feel it proper to lift the curse until he first came and begged forgiveness. Even in his extremity, he found it difficult to humble himself so much. He must have tried prayer, confession, penance, clean living, doctors.

As he had suspected, nothing had the least effect on the ugly sores, at the sight of which people fled, as from an evil spirit.

'So at the last . . . he cam to hys modyr', confessed his misdeeds and asked for her blessing. When she had assured herself of his genuine repentance and administered some 'scharp wordys of correpcyon', Margery consented to pray for him. One feels the interview must have proved quite as formidable as the miserable young man had feared. However, this was his last trial. Gradually, his face healed. His master took him back. He returned to his post in north Germany, married a local girl, had a child in due course and settled down to a blameless life. At intervals, he wrote to his mother, who thanked God for singular blessings and had a strong desire to see her daughter-in-law and grandchild; though it seemed an impossible ambition, as she notes, on account of the distance dividing them. Nevertheless, she had a feeling that, somehow or other, they would meet.

Some years later – possibly after John Kempe's accident – the son came on a visit to his aged parents. They were surprised by his sober deportment, plain dress and elevated discourse. 'Benedicite, sone,' exclaimed Margery, 'how is it wyth the that thu art so chongyd?' He had been converted, he replied, and hoped his mother would condescend to instruct him in spiritual matters. This must have been a moment of great pride and satisfaction for Margery. The boy was following her footsteps exactly. Had she not once been gay and worldly, amorous, heading for hell, pulled up, just in time, by a dangerous illness? Perhaps he, too, would become a saint. St Bridget had been the mother of one.

Fearing it was too good to be true, she watched him carefully at first 'for dred of symulacyon'. Observation convinced her that here was a genuine case. 'Sche openyd hir hert to hym.' He listened devoutly, remarking only that he considered himself unworthy to hear such holy mysteries expounded. Now the eloquence from which he had once fled uplifted him. The precepts impatiently flouted in younger, sinful days, seemed right and fitting, sure guides through the dangers of a wicked world. He, too, would make expensive pilgrimage to far-off sacred places. Margery can hardly have said anything he had not heard a thousand times before, yet then he had been deaf to its significance.

He left for Rome soon after and, on his return home, spoke in such high and reverent terms of his mother, that the young wife was curious to see this sainted old relative. He therefore wrote, asking if Margery would be good enough to prophesy whether they should take ship at Danzig, or come overland to Flanders. Having consulted God, Margery replied that they would arrive safely, whatever way they travelled.

So they confidently booked in the next suitable ship, meaning to bring some goods with them and do business in England. Hardly had they put to sea, when a fearful storm blew up. Their faith in the celestial message rapidly evaporated. Evidently there was some mistake. God did not intend them to sail. They disembarked and made arrangements for the long trek to the North Sea. Even though the storm must have blown itself out before they were ready to start, they dared not ignore a manifest sign of heavenly displeasure.

A temporary home had to be found with friends for the baby who was too young to stand the rigours of the roads. All their previous arrangements had to be changed. Yet, they did not abandon the idea of the journey to England. It was like an important pilgrimage. They would probably not have another chance of visiting Margery, now elderly and widely accepted as a holy woman. Her blessing would certainly have a beneficial effect on their lives, both business and private. She had expressed a strong desire to meet her daughter-in-law. This almost amounted to an order from heaven. Also, John Kempe, now sitting daft and incontinent beside the fire, might not last long.

The journey seemed uneventful. There were no particular wars in the countries they passed through. But, somewhere on the way, young Mr Kempe picked up a fatal germ. The day after his arrival, at a welcoming dinner, 'he ros fro the tabyl and leyd hym on a bed'. His illness lasted about a month, at the end of which time he died in a very decent manner, fortified by the rites of holy church. Margery notes especially that she only prophesied a safe return to Lynn and nothing further.

A little later, John Kempe also died, passing 'the wey whech every man must gon', as his widow remarks philosophically. Her conscience was clear. Theirs had not been a conventional relationship, but it had lasted till death and they had stood by each other at all important crises.

The two widows lived together for the next eighteen months. Margery must have made strenuous efforts to instil proper ideas into her daughter-in-law, but there is some evidence that the younger woman was not entirely responsive. She found her sainted relative too dominating, it seems. She did not want to settle down as an apprentice holy woman in a foreign country. Besides, she had left her baby behind. So when letters came from her family in Germany asking her to return, Margery was obliged to consent. Arrangements were quickly made. A young man travelled on the next ship from Danzig to Ipswich and hurried to Lynn to fetch her.

Before leaving on a journey, it was customary to make full confession and receive absolution and a special blessing. Who knew what dangers and hostile ghosts one might meet with on the sea, or on foreign roads? It was essential to be spiritually prepared. As Margery waited in the choir of St Margaret's while her daughter-in-law knelt before the priest, she suddenly thought: 'Lord yf it wer thi wille I wolde . . . gon wyth hir ovyr the see.'

She had always had such a taste for travel. John Kempe's death left her free to do as she pleased. She might never have another opportunity to see the world and all its famous shrines. Age would soon prevent it: she was already sixty and somewhat lame. There were certain difficulties, of course. The thought of a sea voyage made her hesitate, for one thing: she had a horror of being drowned. People would say she was too infirm to stand the hardships of so extensive a pilgrimage. Her daughter-in-law would be dead against it. Jesus agreed that it would be best not to mention the subject during her own confession.

As they were leaving, the priest asked who would chaperone the young woman as far as Ipswich. It was not fitting that she should travel alone in a young man's company. 'I shal gon wyth hir myself,' said Margery at once.

The priest replied that that was impossible. She had recently damaged one of her feet and she was 'an elde woman'. 'Ye may not gon,' he ended firmly. She, however, insisted. God would look after her. But who would actually escort her to the port and back, enquired the priest, trying another tack? There was a young hermit attached to the church, she answered. He would do very well. Thus it was arranged.

During the few days left before departure, Margery had further doubts. It was against the rules to go on pilgrimage, especially abroad, without licence from the church. She would certainly not be given permission on account of age, poverty and her daughter-in-law's opposition. It was impossible to make preparations for a voyage because everyone would then guess her intentions. When she reached Ipswich the daughter-in-law would persuade the captain not to give her a passage, saying the most terrible things in German to him and frightening him out of his wits with stories of Margery's connections with the Devil.

Yet, she had an overwhelming desire for one last adventure, before enforced retirement to Lynn. She still had the strength. God was in favour. 'Yf I be wyth the, ho schal ben ageyns the?' he said. This amounted to a divine command. How could one disregard it in safety? She, at any rate, was not prepared to run the risk.

As there was still time in hand, it was decided that they should go to Ipswich via Norwich and Walsingham, where the shrine of Our Lady was internationally famous. One could not have too much heavenly support during such a dangerous voyage. It was early in the year and storms might be expected. Thus they set out: Margery, the junior hermit, the daughter-in-law, the young German, with luggage and provisions for two beyond Ipswich.

As they journeyed, Margery still secretly debating, news came that a famous friar was due to preach at a 'village a lityl owt of hir wey'. Everyone for miles around was attending. Margery joined the crowd. What was her astonishment to hear the friar emphatically repeating: 'Yf God be wyth us, ho schal be ageyns us?' He said it 'many tymes' in the course of his dissertation. It was a clear sign from heaven. She was much relieved.

At Norwich, she confided the plan in a trustworthy priest of her acquaintance, explaining how she had received direct orders from God. The whole business worried her, she said. There was her daughter-in-law's certain opposition when she learned of the project. Also, her advanced age and fear of the sea made it prudent to evade the divine command, if possible.

The priest fell into the trap. In no circumstances, he cried, could one question the voice of the Holy Ghost. She had no choice. She must go. 'Sche was meche comfortyd wyth hys wordys' which amounted to formal ecclesiastical permission to make a pilgrimage abroad. She must have been excited by her secret plans as the party continued to Ipswich. God would provide clothes, food, money, health and strength, as he had often done before in similar situations. He would protect her on sea, land and among the foreigners.

When they reached Ipswich, the ship was ready to sail. Margery at once went to the captain and asked for a passage. Evidently she had enough cash for this at least. The captain was agreeable. None of the other passengers demurred. The daughter-in-law, taken by surprise, could only make ineffective protests. 'I must abeyn the wil of God,' Margery said firmly to all objections.

The young hermit was much upset by the turn of events. He had been ordered by his superiors to escort this overwhelming woman to Ipswich and back. If he returned without her, there would be trouble. He would be held responsible for her escapade. But she only repeated, in answer to his entreaties, that the journey was not her own idea. A nervous woman like herself would never have conceived of such a thing, especially without the full approval of her confessor. No, the matter had been taken out of mortal hands. The hermit would have to explain when he got back to Lynn. She gave him a tip to cheer him on his way.

Since nothing would dissuade her, he was obliged to acquiesce and left the quay full of forboding. Sure enough, his seniors were extremely angry when he got back. The story caused quite a sensation. Some said Margery was an old fool; some that it showed extraordinary goodness of heart to accompany her daughter-in-law even into her own country; some that it was inexplicable, being the will of God.

The ship sailed on the Thursday of Easter week, 1433, as near as the year can be judged. Almost at once, she was struck by a violent storm. It was impossible to do anything except drive before the wind and hope for the best. Margery prayed long and earnestly for deliverance from 'the perellys of the see'. Her life was in particular danger: if the sailors began to think her in league with the Devil and the cause of their distress, they might pitch her overboard forthwith. 'Why dredist the?' God enquired. 'Why art thu so aferd? I am as mythy her in the see as on the lond.' The saints to whom she applied were equally re-assuring, 'geving hir wordys of gret comfort' which she reported to her shipmates.

'In schort tyme aftyr' they saw the coast of Norway and managed to slip into the calm waters of a fiord, making fast before a small town. Here they spent the weekend, going ashore on Easter Sunday to attend service in the local church. As the cross was raised at noon to symbolize the Resurrection, Margery's visions were equal to any she had had 'at hom'.

On Easter Monday, a fair wind blew and they continued their voyage. The captain was extremely grateful to Margery for having saved the ship by her prayers, 'and was a tendyr to hir as sche had ben hys modyr'. She ate at his table and borrowed warm clothes from him 'for ellys sche myth a deyd for colde', being totally unprovided against the bitter North Sea weather. Yet, such was her appetite for travel, that she has no word in her book of regret for these unnecessary hardships. She was a born tourist.

# CHAPTER XLI

*Adventures in Northern Europe*

She stayed in Danzig 'abowte v er vj wekys', made a certain number of friends and enjoyed herself, after her own fashion, though the daughter-in-law continued morose. A few English people were resident there for purposes of trade, as Margery's son had been. However, the time came when, prompted by the daughter-in-law, no doubt, she had to think of going home. She had had enough of 'the perellys of the see', but it was not prudent to go overland all the way, on account of a war between the King of Poland, supported by five thousand abominable heretics from Bohemia, and the Teutonic Knights, which was raging in some of the countries she would have to pass through. Another difficulty was that she could find no escort, not even a beggar, like Richard the Irishman.

As always, she overcame the worst of obstacles triumphantly. She advertised her needs and 'went into a chirche and mad hir preyerys'. These methods had worked on previous occasions and did not fail now. She was approached by a man intending to make a pilgrimage to Wilsnak in the Mark of Brandenburg. In 1383, the village and church had been burnt to the ground. This proved a great piece of good fortune. Among the ashes were discovered three hosts on the altar, unscorched and sprinkled with miraculous blood. There were some who doubted the story, but not enough to matter. Wilsnak became rich and famous from that time.

Margery's new friend – John was his name – proposed that she should join his party as far as Wilsnak. He was ready to go on with her to Calais, if she paid his expenses. They would start off by sea, coasting as far as Stralsund in Pomerania, in order to avoid the King of Poland's forces. A boat had been hired and the provisions embarked when the authorities of Danzig refused Margery permission to leave because 'sche was an Englisch woman'.

The city of Danzig was a member of the Hanseatic League, a mercantile association of Prussia and north Germany. Hanseatic merchants had trading privileges in many European ports. The Steelyard in London was their best-known depot in England. At this time, they were being subjected to what they considered unjust taxes and customs dues by the English king, Henry VI. They retaliated by harassing English people in their territories. Margery must have been asked to pay a large sum in order to obtain an exit visa. She did not know what to do, or how she would ever reach home again. At last, 'throw the steryng of owr Lord' a certain 'marchawnt of Lynne', resident in Danzig took up her cause. After 'gret labowr' and, we must suppose, some expense 'this good man' fixed it.

She went on board and they set sail in very light winds. Margery thought it a delightful voyage: 'ther ros no wave on the watyr.' Her companions were of a different opinion. They would never reach Stralsund at this rate, they complained. Soon, the breeze freshened. It became rather rough and the boat went along at a spanking pace. Though 'hyr felaschep was glad and mery' at the change, Margery 'was hevy and sory for dred of the wavys'. She found it impossible to emulate St Bridget's courage in this respect. As an elderly woman, the saint had endured shipwreck on the way to the Holy Land with perfect equanimity.

They reached Stralsund safely and disembarked. Margery was extremely glad to feel the ground under her feet again. Not so her guide. He was afraid of robbers, ambush, stray soldiers, supernatural events and Margery's conversation. The job of escorting her across Europe began to seem very unattractive, no matter what spiritual rewards he might receive hereafter. One had to contend with this world day by day, after all. His demeanour was such that Margery feared he would abandon her in the midst of these hostile foreigners. 'Many tymys sche spak as fayr to hym as sche cowde', reminding him of his obligations and of the important fact that God was on their side. Under this protection, it was impossible for any bandit to harm them. Indeed, God spoke so firmly and kindly that Margery was overcome by emotion, sobbing, wailing, screaming 'ryth boistowsly'.

Far from being encouraged or edified, John began to feel more urgently than ever that he must get rid of his charge as soon as he decently could. He started walking at a great rate in the hope that age and bad feet would oblige her to fall behind and he could vanish round the next corner, as it were unconscious of the fact that she was no longer with him. Margery panted after him, begging him to moderate his pace. He dared not, he said. The forest was full of thieves. She would be raped unless they hurried, and he be beaten up and robbed. 'Sche comofrtyd hym as well as sche cowde', for lack of breath. No one would dare touch them, she repeated. God had promised: 'Dowtyr, I browte the hedyr and I shal bryngyn the hom ageyn into Inglond.' Hardly had she spoken when 'a tal man' fully armed and very fierce looking stepped out from among the trees in front of them.

'Lo!' cried John in terror, 'What seyst thu now?' 'Trust in owr Lord God and drede no man,' she replied in her practical way. So they said prayers and stood their ground. The Lord God did not fail them. The man went by in peace.

The two companions continued their journey at great speed, John walking long stages in the hope that Margery would fall by the way. He must have cursed his tender conscience which would not allow him to abandon her in a straightforward manner, once and for all. Often she begged him to slow down; to wait a moment while she rested; to consider her age, 'abowtyn iij scor yer,' and the fact that she was not accustomed to such violent exercise. But 'he had no compassyon of hir', remaining deaf to pleas in the name of humanity, of God, revelations, prophecies of divine retribution and other persuasions to a better course of conduct. It may be, too, that he found the volume of her conversation much reduced if he kept her continually short of breath.

As the hard days passed, Margery's strength began to fail. Her guide must have felt his deliverance near. He was to be disappointed. It was evidently not God's will that he should escape this burden. One evening, they reached a miserable inn. There were no beds, only straw on the ground. Margery thought this was the end. She would not be able to start in the morning and he would set off rejoicing without her. By great good fortune, a fearful storm broke the next day. It was impossible to travel in such torrents of rain. She lay on the straw for twenty-four hours, recovering somewhat.

The people of the village were scandalized at the treatment she had received from her supposed protector. What way was this for one pilgrim to behave to another? Weren't they supposed to be joined in Christian fellowship? They could not understand her language, but she seemed a very decent sort of old woman, perhaps even rather saintly. There she lay, flat out on the straw, utterly exhausted. It was a shame. The wretched John found himself obliged to hire a wain on her behalf.

They arrived at Wilsnak on the worst of terms and there adored the miraculous blood, found among the ashes of the church fifty years before. Even yet, the unwilling bodyguard could not abandon his charge. Public opinion, and, it may be, fear of what God would do to him, should he default, kept him at his post. After the holy blood, Margery was, of course, excited and much worse, from his point of view, than before. They had a wain each by this time and were on the road to Aachen.

At a certain point, they had to cross a river. A crowd of travellers waited at the ford, as roads to many places met there. Among them was a disgraceful monk, 'a ful rekles man and evyl governyd', accompanied by a party of young merchants. They came from Danzig also and called out to John, 'schewyng hym rith glad cher'. He was delighted to see these friends. In this congenial company, Margery would be diluted.

Once over the ford, they set out gaily 'alle in felaschep togedyr'. It was a thirsty day. At the nearest monastery, they stopped for a drink. Margery refused to go in, saying nuns would have been all right, but to drink among men, even religious, was hardly correct. So they brought her out a good jug of wine.

Everything would have passed off, had not some friars from the monastery invited them in to view 'the blisful sacrament' displayed in a crystal vessel for Corpus Christi week. Margery could not endure the idea of missing such an inspiring sight. Sure enough, on reaching the altar where it stood, she 'wept and sobbyd wondyr sor'. Her companions were not impressed by a proper sense of her holiness in behaving thus. As her transports grew, so did their disapproval. With belated prudence, she tried to restrain herself, but was filled with 'so mech swetnes and devocyon' that she could not.

As soon as they had left the church and were getting into the wains, the monk turned on her, abusing her with 'many an evyl worde'. 'Hypocrite' was one of the kinder names he called her. Always ready for argument, Margery trotted out several scriptural quotations in support of her own views. The monk and his friends were in no mood for scholastic disputation. They were just not going to be afflicted by a lugubrious old chatterbox on the road to Aachen. One needed to be gay and have diversions in order to support the hardships of travel. Why did their friend John put up with her? He had no need to. Anyone could leave a job if it didn't suit him. John saw their point Perhaps he had been too scrupulous.

Margery, seeing that the worst was bound to happen, begged him at least not to abandon her on the open road. 'Wyth gret preyer and instawns', she made him reluctantly agree to accompany her to the next town, where she might hope to find another band of pilgrims, who would prove more congenial. So they continued to jolt along in the wains, everyone out of temper.

Hardly had they passed under the gates of the town before Margery was told she must now make her own arrangements. John counted out her money and offered to lend her more, for his conscience still troubled him slightly. 'Iohn,' she said with sad dignity, 'I desiryd not yowr gold. I had levar yowr felaschep in these strawnge cuntreys than all the good ye han.' God would be better pleased if he performed his promises to her in Danzig than if he walked to Rome barefoot. 'Iohn,' she added further, as these remarks had small effect, 'ye forsakyn me for non other cawse but for I wepe whan I se the sacrament and whan I thynke on owr Lordys Passyon.' He could neither deny it, nor face the prospect of her company further. Besides, it might not be safe to do so. The monk declared her piety false. She might be a heretic, or otherwise connected with the powers of hell. He left her there, in the twilit street of a foreign city.

'The nyght fel upon hir and sche was ryth hevy.' Where should she lodge and with whom continue her journey next day? She did not know German, though it seems she must have picked up a smattering during her travels. With her excellent memory and ready eloquence, she had a certain gift for languages. In Rome she managed to conduct necessary business when abandoned by her fellow countrymen. So now, she found a hostel, booked a bed and made enquiries about pilgrims going to Aachen.

It was not an agreeable evening. The English were unpopular in those parts. A number of priests came into the hostel and jeered at her 'and spokyn many lewyd wordys'. If she had no escort, they leered, she could come with them. They would entertain her, English devil that she was. In a great fright, Margery begged the mistress of the house not to put her in a room by herself. 'The good wife assygnyd tweyn maydenys' to share her bed. The unfortunate girls cannot have had much sleep, for Margery remained awake and prayerful 'al that nygth'. But perhaps they were young enough to snore through it.

Margery's prospects seemed equally dismal next morning. While paying the bill, she asked the host whether he knew of any pilgrims she could join. He did not. There remained only God. She went to the nearest church. Outside it were gathered a company of extremely poor pilgrims, ragged, dirty, more like a crowd of beggars than anything. In her desperate situation, she could not afford to be snobbish. These people, she found on enquiry, were going to Aachen. They were astonished that a woman of her class, and in funds, should wish to join them. 'Why, dame,' said one, 'hast thu no man to gon wyth the?' 'No, my man is gon fro me,' she replied simply.

In some ways, the new fellowship was very satisfactory. They did not object to extreme behaviour. Indeed, being more or less destitute, they welcomed a chance of attracting attention and alms. Though so needy, they were perfectly honest and respectable. Margery's money and person were as safe as with previous escorts.

On the other hand, they were begging their food and lodging along the road. This delayed progress considerably. They might have to spend several days begging in a town before collecting enough to continue the next stages of the journey. Meanwhile, Margery was obliged to hang about, spending money without getting on. She was put, she remarks, to 'meche mor cost than sche shulde ellys a ben'.

For lack of the price of a clean bed, the fellowship were obliged to live in the most insalubrious slums during their sojourns in the towns. Their clothes and hair became the nesting places of every sort of vermin, 'betyn and stongyn ful evyl bothe day and nyght'. These were a further cause of delay. On reaching the privacy of fields and woods again, they would stop, take off their clothes 'and, sittyng nakyd', carefully pick out every bug. Hours might pass before they were ready to dress and go on. The halt was the more galling for Margery in that she felt unable to follow their example. She had to wait until they were comfortable and suffer

A storm at sea. (From a collection of stories, verses and ballads by the poetess Christine of Pisa. Early 15th century, French. Harley 4431.)

One of the mourners from the Earl of Warwick's tomb in St Mary's,
Warwick. (15th century.)

the fleas and lice as well. However, the pace was restful after her experiences with John.

At length, they came to Aachen. The begging pilgrims had saved her in a difficulty, but she was glad to say good-bye to them. We do not know what they thought of her: whether they respected her as a holy woman; or pitied her as mad; or believed she accompanied them as a penance; or had been unjustly abandoned by her friends. It was only possible to communicate in a limited fashion, for they spoke no English and heaven knows what sort of German they used. At Aachen, they pass out of history. What was their destination, or where they had come from, remain unanswered questions.

# CHAPTER XLII

## *The Worshipful Woman of London*

Aachen was full of pilgrims for it was on the road to Rome and, also, certain unique relics were publicly shown in the west tower of the minster every seven years. One could always view a fine collection of bones, blood, bits of saints and their belongings. In 1433, one could see in the west tower of the great church 'owr Lady's smokke' worn during the birth of Christ, the infant Jesus' swaddling clothes, a piece of cloth in which John the Baptist's head had been wrapped, the loin-cloth worn by Christ on the cross. These four items drew enormous crowds from all over Europe. For they were magical objects, imbued with divinity in the highest degree. A beneficence came from them, bringing the delights of paradise within a worshipper's grasp.

Margery was able to take part in the ceremonies 'wyth a monke of Inglond' who had halted there on his way to Rome. It was a wonderful relief, she notes, to have someone to talk to again. During her stay, she looked round for a fellowship to which she might attach herself for the journey to Calais. By good fortune, there happened to be among the visitors a rich widow, come from London with a large party of retainers for the septennial show of relics. Margery approached 'this worthy woman', explaining her awkward position. The lady was extremely affable, said of course she could join them, asked her to dine, 'and made hir ryth good cher'. She seemed like another Dame Margaret Florentine, who had been such a good friend to Margery at Assisi and in Rome.

She turned out not to have the same simplicity of character. The more she saw of Margery, the less she cared for her. She could not endure the thought of travelling in company with this crazy old pseudo-saint, or heretic, or Devil's adjutant, whatever she was, yet lacked the courage to say so. There was only one thing to do: on the day of departure 'the worschepful woman sped hir fast owt' of Aachen before dawn.

Margery expresses no surprise in her book at this perfidy. The same sort of thing had happened too often for that. Saying good-bye to the English monk, she jumped on to a wain with some other pilgrims who were going part of the way in her direction, 'and pursuyd aftyr the foreseyd worthi woman as fast as sche myth'. But the other had got such a start that it was impossible to overtake her.

After a time, the wain turned off the Calais road and Margery applied to two passing Londoners returning home. Yes, they said, she could join them, but they were in a great hurry and she would have to keep up. They couldn't afford to wait if she lagged behind. She had no option except to follow 'aftyr hem wyth gret labowr'.

At the next town, she met more English pilgrims, coming back from Rome. Perhaps these would proceed at a more moderate rate. They also were willing to receive her, adding that she must be prepared to travel long stages because they had been robbed by the way and could not afford many stops. In spite of this, they seemed, on the whole, to offer better comfort than the two Londoners. So she said good-bye to them and joined the new fellowship for dinner.

Next to her at the table sat a friar with no plate in front of him. The reason for his abstinence, she found on enquiry, was that the bandits had taken his every penny. 'We wer robbyd as wel as he,' said the others firmly, 'ych man must help hymself as wel as he may.' No, they did not feel inclined to go hungry for his sake. Christian principles were all very fine in their place, but one had to keep up one's strength. 'Wel', said Margery, dividing her provender in half, 'he shal have part of swech good as God sendith me.' She gave him wine also and made suitable reflections on the situation.

Having rested, the party started out. Again the pace was hot. 'Sche was to agyd and to weyke' to keep up, though 'sche ran and lept as fast as sche myth'. They refused to slacken speed. Then it occurred to her to hire the destitute friar. He could have board and lodging and wages also, she proposed, if he would escort her to Calais, at that date an English town. 'He was wel content and consentyd to hir desyr.'

Letting the others go on ahead, they 'folwyd softly as their mygth enduryn'. 'I knowe thes cuntreys wel anow', remarked the friar, 'for I have oftyn tymes gon thus to Rome.' There was a very nice hostel just ahead where they could get a drink and refresh themselves after their recent exertions. This seemed to her an excellent suggestion. They halted.

The mistress of the house proved most respectable. So much so as to be upset by the idea of a woman of Margery's age and decency tramping the roads alone with a friar. Margery explained about the worthy Englishwoman with whom she had hoped to travel and how she had been obliged to make what arrangements she could after being stranded at Aachen.

What a piece of luck, the woman exclaimed, looking down the road. Here was a wain approaching full of pilgrims of her acquaintance. She would get Margery a seat in it. Perhaps she would be able to catch up the worthy woman who could not really have meant to abandon her friendless among foreigners. There must have been some misunderstanding about the hour of departure. Margery was inclined to this opinion, on account of the lady's kind and respectful manner to her, right up to the last.

She paid off the friar, therefore, and climbed on to the wain. Her fellow travellers were sympathetic, gladly making room. Perhaps fortunately, they did not have long in which to enjoy her company and improve their souls under her direction; for soon they came to a town where Margery saw some of the worthy woman's suite. So she called on the driver to stop, took leave of her companions and settled the fare. The wain trundled off. It was not halting at that place.

Margery at once approached 'the worschepful woman's' quarters, convinced that matters could be explained and the rest of her journey comfortably and respectably arranged. But the lady was horrified to see her again. She thought she had dodged this incubus successfully. Besides who knew what sort of old witch she was? She directed 'rith scharp langage' at poor Margery, enquiring sarcastically what made her think she could attach herself to superior people.

Thus, Margery shortly found herself once more standing in a foreign street alone. 'Sche knew no man ther ne no man knew hir.' How she regretted having parted from the friar. He might not even be coming this way. But, in the evening, as she watched the road with great anxiety, she saw him trudging towards the town gates.

She hurried to him, explaining the situation. The friar didn't seem much surprised. It was all God's will, he said philosophically. He advised against lodging in the town that night. It had an evil reputation. They continued on the road to Calais, looking out for a wayside hostel or farm, where they might sleep. The countryside seemed uninhabited, but at last 'thei parceyvyd an hows er tweyn'.

The people were unwilling to receive them. They never let rooms. They did not keep a hostel. The pilgrims would have to push on. Margery did not feel she could go another yard. Couldn't she lie down on that heap of ferns in the shed, she implored? She would pay. If they allowed the friar to shake down in the barn, that would be paid for, too. Finally, after much persuasion, these terms were agreed on. The travellers congratulated themselves on having secured a roof over their heads, at least.

The next two days they spent struggling through the sand dunes outside Calais. Few people lived in those parts and lodgings were not easily come by. Weakness and overstrain worked on Margery's nerves. She expected brigands at every turn and could scarcely sleep at night for fear of being ravished. Whenever possible, she shared a bed with at least two young and beautiful maidens. Thus protected, she could doze between her prayers.

They reached Calais safely. At the hostel, she paid the friar what she owed for his invaluable help and 'gaf hym reward' besides. This loyal man now passes out of history. Evidently he was not bound for England, for they said good-bye 'and departyd asundyr'.

While waiting for a ship, Margery made some friends in the town, which was an English trading and military post at that date. 'Ther was a good woman', for instance, who gave her a bath and a new smock. 'Other good personys' invited her to dine. Certain pilgrims, whom she had known previously, turned up at the hostel. It is possible that they were connected with the worthy woman. These were suspiciously agreeable, she thought, in view of past events. Her caution was soon justified.

After 'iii or iiij days' boats put into the harbour and these pilgrims slunk off to book a passage without telling her or offering to deal with the captain on her behalf. Determined not to be outdone, she 'spyid as diligently as sche cowde' and discovered their ship. But when they found her on the passenger list, they secretly changed to another boat. Either they could not endure the thought of her company even for so short a voyage, or else they feared her presence would cause disastrous storms.

This plot, too, she frustrated, by the grace of God, though at the cost of leaving part of her luggage in the first ship. She appeared on deck triumphantly as the sail was set 'and ther was the worschepful woman of London'. Margery doesn't find it necessary to describe their mutual feelings in words.

The crossing proved rough, and Margery prayed that she might be spared the humiliation of being sick before an unsympathetic audience. 'Hir desyr was fulfillyd.' While everyone else was 'voydyng and castyng ful boistowsly', she remained quite unaffected. The worshipful woman was particularly ill and Margery devoted herself to her comfort, praying, reassuring and holding the basin. She was actuated purely by feelings of love and charity, 'other cawse had sche non'.

At Dover, the pilgrims dispersed to their homes. Though the London widow's party was going in Margery's direction, they would not permit her to join them. She trudged the road to Canterbury alone. Soon, however, she came to 'a powr mannys hows'. Here she could hire someone to escort her. It was so early in the morning that 'the good powr man' answered her knock with his clothes still unbuttoned, dragged on anyhow as he got out of bed. He consented to take on the job. They set off together, Margery dropping 'many a devowt teer', for she need not ingratiate herself with so humble an employee.

The journey to London was otherwise uneventful. There, she paid off the man and made her way to the house of friends in order to borrow money, for she was now destitute. As she crept along, ashamed of her shabbiness, a group of people she had known in Lynn came round the corner. 'Sche desiryng to a gon unknowyn' until she had obtained the price of a decent dress, held a handkerchief before her face. But they recognized her. 'It was Mar Kempe of Lynne,' they exclaimed, the false hypocrite who had once refused herrings at table with a penitential air, and afterwards been discovered tucking into 'good pike'.

This story dated from the earliest days of her conversion and had never been forgotten. It seems there was something excruciatingly funny about it to the contemporary mind. People would laugh over it at the end of meals when rather drunk. Here was a saint, they would shout, sending away the lowly herring in order to eat more delicately in the name of religion. No matter how often she explained that she had a passion for herrings, far preferring them to pike, she was never able to live it down.

She stayed in the city for some weeks, lodging with 'a worschepful wedow' and receiving food and alms from various other ladies, some quite rich. London behaviour did not meet with her approval. There was much too much swearing, cursing, lying, sharp practice and ostentatious dress. The anti-Lollard agitation had now died away. It was safe to speak one's mind. 'Sche sparyd hem not, sche flateryd hem not', even though it meant throwing away an invitation to dinner. Many agreed with her opinions and admired her courage. The priests in charge of churches, on the other hand, were not so keen on this high moral tone: her strictures tended to be directed against the more well-to-do members of the congregation. They also objected to noisy devotions. 'Therfor sche went fro on chirch to another, that sche shulde not ben tediows on to hem.'

From London, she made an excursion to the convent of the Brigitine Order, founded by Henry V at Sheen in 1415 and later moved to Mount Sion nearby. His sister was Queen of Sweden and it was natural that he should lend his support to St. Bridget, already well known in England. The nuns of Sion were ascetics, dreamers of heavenly dreams, prophetesses, subject to trances, fits, supernatural visitations and all the other marks of holiness considered desirable in the fifteenth century. As an order, they had not yet been corrupted by wealth, laziness and lack of a sense of vocation.

Margery blossomed in this congenial atmosphere. Her grief and remorse for a sinful life – as she chose to regard it in these circumstances – were so extraordinary, that a certain young man was 'mevyd thorw the Holy Gost' to approach her. 'Modir,' he said earnestly, 'thow I be yong, my desir is to plesyn my Lord Ihesu Crist.' Never had he seen such 'plenteuows teerys' or heard anyone 'so boistows in sobbyng'. He had an inclination for the religious life. Would she condescend to instruct him in the ways of God?

She received the new disciple 'wyth gladnes of spirit', discoursing at great length on divine affairs, illustrating her remarks by copious autobiographical references. The young man drank it all in with avidity. For as long as she remained at Sion, he accompanied her everywhere, like an acolyte.

Lammas Day 'was the principal day of pardon' when pilgrims gathered to receive the comprehensive indulgences offered. As she observed the ceremonies in the church, Margery suddenly saw among the crowd the hermit who had been deputed to escort her to Ipswich and back, when she was supposed to be seeing off 'hir dowtyr-in-lawe, as is wretyn beforn'. Here was the solution to a problem which had worried her: where to find someone willing to accompany her on the road to Lynn.

'A, Reynald,' she cried, 'ye arn welcome! I trust owr Lord sent yow hedyr.' As he had been selected to lead her out of Lynn, so would he take her back. 'The ermyte schewyd schort cher and hevy contenawnce' in answer to her overtures. She had got him into bad trouble with his superiors, he said. He had been blamed for letting her go abroad without proper licence. He did not care to mix himself up in her affairs again. 'I pray yow getith yow felaschep wher ye can,' he finished bitterly. 'I wil no mor.'

'Sche spak fayre', begging him not to be angry. She had many friends in Lynn. They would stand by her on her return, 'for Goddys lofe'. She would soon pacify her confessor. The hermit need not fear. Also, she would pay his expenses on the homeward journey. 'So at the last he' consented to take on the job, having carefully considered the matter. Soon after, they set out for London and, from there, went on to Lynn. Both their souls benefited greatly during the march which gave opportunity for much improving conversation.

# CHAPTER XLIII

## The Book

We now come to Margery's real achievement in life, that which gives her a permanent place in history and inclines a fellow-author, five hundred years later, to choose her as a subject. The danger of being prosecuted for heresy had passed. The Lollards had become a quiet underground sect, unimportant politically and so left in peace. She had made her way as a holy woman in Lynn and, to some extent, in other parts of the country. It was the accepted thing for saints, hermits and recluses to write books describing their spiritual adventures and the grace accorded to them by God as a reward for a life devoutly spent in his service.

Such reminiscences were intended to inspire elevating thoughts in the reader and to lead him, if possible, to abandon or, at least, greatly to moderate, the pursuit of worldly love, money, position and ostentation. For the persons addressed were mainly those of the new middle classes: merchants, aldermen, mayors, master craftsmen, artisans. These people were commonly literate by the fifteenth century, since business required it. They and their wives and daughters seem, in many cases, to have had almost insatiable appetites for improving literature.

Of a serious and practical turn of mind, used to thinking for themselves in everyday transactions, they did not feel their deepest questions on the nature and characteristics of God sufficiently answered by the stereotyped replies of the organized church. They wanted something more personal than a set of dogmas and pronouncements. They longed for God to be on their side, as a friend in the struggle to wring at least a modest fortune from their trade. Surely God did not only speak only through idle monks and doubtful friars, bishops and higher dignitaries? It seemed a very reasonable and logical idea that the pure in heart should have equal, if not superior, privileges in this respect.

The pious laity were not the only audience Margery could hope to address. Her orthodoxy had been fully attested under the Archbishop of Canterbury's seal. Nuns and other religious persons could safely read her book. As convent life was fundamentally boring to many inmates, Margery's autobiography must have purveyed a welcome tang of the outside world; of battles fought and won on the roadside; of foreigners, natives, infidels and sinners of all kinds defeated on their own ground. True, there was not much in the way of miracles recorded, but what a wealth of God's conversation: his advice so apposite, his attention so fully engaged by the problems on which he had been consulted. Here was not a remote God speaking only in the words of the mass, or of the scriptures. He was like an elder brother, or an ideal husband: simple, direct and dependable.

Margery's friends must have encouraged her to write. St Bridget had done so at enormous length. Many years before, indeed, the Bishop of Lincoln, Repingdon, had exclaimed in a moment of enthusiasm that such rare experiences as hers ought not to go unrecorded for posterity. At that time, however, she had felt it an unwise suggestion to pursue. The dissemination of writings would have increased the gravity of her position during the various trials for heresy.

It is not certain when she began her autobiography, which is in two parts, each dictated to a different scribe; the first died while the work was only two thirds done. The last event described in Book One is John Kempe's accident. This occurred a few years before his death in 1431, or thereabouts. The second scribe was not definitely engaged until 1436, after her return from Danzig, although he had been approached some years earlier.

Her first choice was a man who, though English, had lived long in Germany, married there and had a family. This description fits her son, the merchant of Danzig, and it has been thought that he was the person referred to.

There are reasons that make this ascription impossible, I think. If it were her son, one would expect Margery to say so. More cogently, the son is said to have sickened the day after his arrival and died a month later. No mention is made of any previous long visit to his mother. It is hardly likely that a dying man could have written 220 pages of rather small print in three weeks, at the most. For it is not as if the scribe was a practised writer, dashing off sentences and paragraphs without effort. On the contrary, 'the booke was so evel wretyn' his successor in the job reported, that it was scarcely possible to read it. Not only were the letters 'not schapyn ne formyd as other letters ben' but the language used was some extraordinary lingo, 'neithyr good Englysch' nor yet German, though it had some resemblance to both.

Margery was not a quick worker either. Everything had to be read over to her several times to be quite sure it was right. When describing her visions, she was liable to go off into a trance and remain in it for hours, dictation being interrupted until she came round. Nor were the sessions conducted in a businesslike manner, the atmosphere neutral and appropriate in one who wished to get through as much as she could while her secretary still had the strength to follow. Far from it. She would be overcome by emotion during the relation of her adventures. 'Holy teerys' would course down her cheeks; the fire of love, 'ful hoot and delectabyl' flame in her bosom; celestial music and song fill her ears. The scribe, also invaded by the divine, would sob uncontrollably.

Since these were her methods of composition, it seems most probable that the first secretary was a friend of her son's, a colleague among the merchants of Danzig. He was, perhaps, sent with an introduction to his friend's holy mother. He must have become her favourite disciple, or she would not have confided in him the story of her adventures, or asked him to participate in this last great task, the crowning achievement of her life as an apprentice saint. Unfortunately, he did not live long enough to finish the work.

After his death, she took the manuscript to a priest she had known many years, asking whether he would continue. Her reputation was now such that he was inclined to undertake the job. The date may have been 1431, or 1432, when she was widely regarded as the saviour of Lynn after her prayers had prevented the town from being burnt down.

But, on opening the book, it seemed to him that no man could read such fearful writing, nor disentangle such grammar except with the help of the Holy Ghost. Nevertheless, he agreed to try, even 'to copyn it owt and wrytyn it betyr'. He had not got very far, however, before the continuous debate in Lynn on Margery's claims to holiness took a hostile turn.

The famous Franciscan preacher who had forbidden her his sermons had been defeated, rather than reconciled, by her prowess at the fire. He fulminated against her in the pulpit 'whethyr sche were ther er not'. All his many followers remained her opponents. The town seems to have been divided into two camps on the matter. Some took sides with the Dominicans who voted her a true holy woman. Others preferred the Franciscan view that she was a beastly fraud.

A few of the more thoughtful tried to judge the question from an intellectual standpoint and read carefully through such books as the biography of St Elizabeth of Hungary, a thirteenth-century princess, lovingly recorded by her confessor with the help of her maids; that of Mary of Oignies, a young lady of the same date, who had left her husband for an anchoress's cell and concerned herself with lepers. They studied the hermit Richard Hampole's book on the fire of love and a composition erroneously attributed to St Bonaventure, entitled *The Prykke of Lofe*. All these Margery's priest manfully perused in an effort to get things straight; while the great argument raged outside his window, now one side and now the other having the advantage.

He was very nervous. This woman had a terrible history. Life was full of ups and downs. He had no aspirations to martyrdom. He gave back the manuscript and for 'iij yer or ellys mor' refused to listen to her, though pestered continually. 'He wold not, he seyd, put hym in perel therof.' He wanted to remain uncommitted. Why should he have to say definitely whether, or not, she could control her hysterics?

But at last he was convinced by his own strange experience in church. As he opened the gospels, he suddenly burst out weeping and couldn't stop. 'He wett hys vestiment and ornaments of the awter.' He could hardly stand. Then he believed that her tears were heaven-sent, exactly as described in the books he had been reading.

Even after this he did not fancy the job. It was too much work. How could anyone read such stuff? He advised her to go to a man who had known the first scribe well and had been accustomed to read his letters, sent from abroad.

'This good man wrot abowt a leef' and then stuck. 'The boke was so evel sett and so unreasonably wretyn.' The priest began to feel it must be heaven's will that he should undertake the task. Margery promised enthusiastically to 'prey to God for hym and purchasyn hym grace to reden it and wrytyn it also'. Thus encouraged, he 'red it ovyr beforn this creatur every word, sche sumtyme helping where any difficulte was'. Once he got started and the writing became familiar, he found it not such uphill work as he had feared.

Yet, on the whole, he was still reluctant and would have liked to get out of it, if he decently could. What better way, in the circumstances, than a supernatural hindrance? Something had happened to his eyes, he reported. In ordinary matters he could 'se wel a-now', but the moment he took up the manuscript, his sight mysteriously clouded and he was prevented from writing, or even mending his pen. 'He sett a peyr of spectacles on hys nose', thinking to overcome his disability, 'and than wast wel wers then it was befor'. How could he go on?

The trouble was due to the Devil, said Margery firmly, who was trying to frustrate his goodness from envy. This book had been specially ordered by God. If he wavered, it would be a great sin. He would have succumbed to the infernal powers. She spoke with intense conviction. There was nothing for it except to try again. So he abandoned his protest, saying merely that he could now see as well as ever 'be daylyth and be candellygth bothe'. No doubt it was a miracle.

Notwithstanding the importance of the task, the divine encouragement and liberal payment, her scribe was not so obedient, or as diligent, as he should have been. He was always wanting her to prophesy whether, or not, a certain course of conduct would advance his affairs, and threatening to strike if she didn't oblige. Then there was the business of the 'fayr feturyd, wel faveryd' young stranger, who appeared from heaven knew where with a hard luck story.

This 'amyabyl persone' had taken holy orders, so he said, but, having unfortunately killed a man 'er ellys tweyn' in a fight, had had to flee his part of the country. Now he was destitute, for he could not be fully ordained without a special dispensation from Rome. He required money with which to obtain it. He had many good friends, he continued, but dared not approach them until the furore had died down. Anxious to help a deserving case, the priest went to a merchant of Lynn whose wife was particularly charitable.

Margery thought the young man a fraud and couldn't bear the idea of his receiving special alms. She warned the merchant's wife to have nothing to do with him. The priest was very angry. His protégé was charming, educated, well dressed, nice mannered. How could one disbelieve his story? He would lend him money himself. 'Medyl ye not wyth hym,' Margery repeated, 'for he shal dysceyve yow at the last.'

The young man took the priest's loan with the deepest gratitude. His benefactor would excuse him if he left the town for a few days on business. He would be back very shortly. He said an affectionate farewell and vanished.

The priest was much abashed after this adventure. Perhaps he applied himself to his literary work in order to make up. Certainly, he was more cautious when approached by a doubtful person who said he had a fine breviary for sale, very cheap. It had belonged to a priest who had charged him, on his deathbed, to sell it to someone deserving. The purchaser would, no doubt, pray for his soul. No, the scoundrel said, he hadn't actually got the book on him, but would bring it immediately on receiving the very modest price he asked. It was laughable, really, considering the quality of the goods.

'Syr,' said Margery succinctly, 'byith no boke of hym, for he is not to be trustyn upon and that shal ye knowyn yf ye medyl wyth hym.' This time, he took her advice.

Thoroughly subdued, he now saw it was impossible to turn back. God was with her. He knew it for a fact. This labour would be rewarded in heaven, far beyond the wages Margery dispensed. Sometimes, he also was overcome by emotion and felt the divine spirit enter the room as they worked. This was no ordinary literary production.

Under these auspices, they began their labours and somehow managed to carry through to the end. Two thirds had already been written, but it took the priest the best part of two years to make a fair copy. First, he had to read it out for her revision. Many long discussions, digressions and arguments must have taken place during these sessions, one feels. Was this what she had really meant? What about the order of events?

Here, they stumbled, particularly in the opening chapters. She had a wonderful memory, but her career had started long ago and 'sche had forgetyn the tyme and the ordyr whan thyngys befellyn'. All they could do was to put everything down 'lych as the mater cam to the creatur', during dictation. This did not, she carefully notes, affect the veracity of her story: 'sche dede nothing wryten but that sche knew ryght wel for very trewth.' Whenever her narrative can be checked against events and persons otherwise known to history, one finds that this high standard of accuracy has, indeed, been adhered to.

The second redaction must have seemed almost easy compared with her struggles over the previous draft. Now she had a man accustomed to reading and writing, though somewhat lazy. Then, she had had the help, if such it can be called, of someone scarcely more literate than herself. Yet, he must have been loyal and persevering. For they covered the ground, she creating the form and content of her memoirs; he laboriously scribbling in some language halfway between English and German. It is not surprising that she 'seyd fewer bedys for sped of wrytyng than sche had done yerys beforn'. Perhaps she could not have gone on without God's encouragement. 'Dowtyr,' he said, 'be this boke many a man shal be turnyd to me.' It would be a famous work, preserving her name to posterity. So it has happened, though we read her now with a different interest from that which she intended to arouse.

Though illiterate, Margery had a thorough knowledge of contemporary devotional literature. She had a retentive memory and must have known most of her favourite authors almost as well as the Bible, from which she could quote extensively. These books, mainly by fourteenth-century recluses, such as Richard Rolle, or Walter Hilton, were meant as handbooks for aspirants to the spiritual life.

Such works had been produced throughout the middle ages, often with some special audience in mind: the novices of a particular monastery, for instance, or a convent of nuns. In them are described the various meditative exercises to be performed by those wishing to come close to God: how to compose oneself in readiness for the Holy Spirit; the signs by which one can know that one is following the right path; the gradual increase of enlightenment.

The best of these writers, such as Walter Hilton and the author of the famous *Cloud of Unknowing*, emphasize the necessity of total abnegation of the self. They regard the fire of love, celestial music and vibrations before the eyes as mere phases to be passed through, or adventures met by the way during the quest for God. The less intellectual, like Richard Rolle, were inclined to wallow in these marvels, believing they indicated that the desired union with God had taken place. These books were autobiographies in a limited sense, since the various stages of the contemplative life described in them had been personally experienced by the authors.

It was Margery's intention to produce a treatise after this pattern. She thought she had gone through all the prescribed grades and qualified for sainthood. She wished not only to teach people how to arrive at her blessed state, but also to set out her credentials. The most important chapters, in her view, were those containing long accounts of her visions and conversations with God and the saints. To us, these are naïve and tedious to a degree: God comes down to Margery's level; she does not rise to his.

Fortunately, there was another, quite distinct literary form with which she was familiar. This was the popular sermon. It was useless to address an illiterate and restive crowd in abstract terms. 'Merelaus regnyd a wise Emperour,' the preacher might begin, 'and he had weddid to wife the kyngys dowter of hungery, the which was a faire woman and full of werkis of mercy.'* The emperor set off for the Holy Land and the empress entered on a series of appalling adventures, including torture, servitude, murder, kidnapping, attempted rape, shipwreck. The source of her misfortunes was her beauty and steadfast refusal to have any of the men wishing to make love to her. Finally, she ended up as a holy woman in a convent on an island where, by an extraordinary coincidence, the emperor and all the men who had wronged her arrived to pay their respects. Everything ended happily, with her return to her husband at last and the confusion of her enemies. Chaucer was so taken with this story that he used it for the Man of Law in his *Canterbury Tales*.

One can understand how it was that sermons were a favourite entertainment in Margery's day. The fact that the emperor represented God and the empress the human soul adrift among the

* *Gesta Romanorum*, ed. S. J. H. Hertage, Early English Text Society, 1879.

temptations and sufferings of the world didn't in the least inter-
fere with the narrative. There were hundreds of such histories.
They must have been as well known to everyone as the lives of
the saints and the plots of the miracle plays.

Besides being full of drama, these pulpit fables were often
peopled by characters as realistic as any in Chaucer's pages: they
desire to look big; to drive a hard bargain; to sell something of
which, strictly speaking, they are not the owner; they are prostrated by love in all its violence, contradictoriness and absurdity;
they are deceivers, liars, cheaters in a way everyone could recognize as true, for it was culled from quotidian experience. The rich
oppress and the poor get by on their cunning. The conversations
are sharp and knowing. Virtue, by contrast, is rather wishy-
washy, though, of course, it always wins in the end.

Thus, it is not really surprising that Margery shows a considerable grasp of the novelist's technique. She had a gift for
words and a lifetime's practice in composing, or adapting,
stories from which to draw an appropriate moral. Her style is
not polished, for that was beyond her, but how clearly, and with
what economy she brings her characters before us. Here is the
fifteenth century in all its complexity: the Archbishop of York at
Cawood and at Beverley, so suitable and so unsuitable as a
prince of religion and embodiment of justice and mercy; Dame
Margaret Florentine, credulous, superstitous and good-natured;
the worshipful widow of London, treacherous and mean, or,
perhaps, frightened by the force of Margery's personality, sus-
pecting devils at work. Then there is the whole range of her
travelling companions, willing and unwilling, her hired escorts
and John Kempe, the prototype of all henpecked husbands. We
meet a great variety of priests, worthy and unworthy, arrogant,
silly, timid and easily imposed on.

All these vivid portraits, which carry the imprint of truth, are
given to us by a woman wrapped up in herself and her visions,
opinions, prejudices and importance to an amazing degree. Yet,
wherever she turns her attention to the world about her, the
egocentric dream recedes and we hear the very voice of her
contemporaries.

Finally, we are given a unique picture of an apprentice holy
woman, a career it was possible to take up without having to

submit to the disciplines of a recluse or anchoress. Indeed, in-discipline is the keynote of Margery's life. Though respectful of the church and those of its officers she approved, Margery owned no master, not even God. The Deity comes along behind clapping, as she pursues the path to sainthood. Courageous, shrewd, pious and overwhelming, nothing can deflect her from the goal. Who shall say she was wrong, or misguided? She extolled the virtues and practised them as far as her nature per-mitted. How harmless was her aim: to draw people to an ap-prehension of the joys of heaven. Irritating and conceited she may have been, but not malicious, or even bad-tempered. In spite of her moralistic outlook, she was tolerant, for she had met the world, both high and low, and few things surprised her much in the end.

Perhaps her philosophy could even have embraced her book's curious posthumous adventures. Evidently quite popular, it was copied, it may be more than once. In the early sixteenth century short extracts were printed as a pamphlet. These, by their selection and owing to their being given out of context, lent a spurious air of wisdom and holiness to Margery's thought. All self-esteem, all excess, were removed by the editor with remarkable effect. These seemed to be the broodings of a holy anchoress.

At some later date, the original manuscript, no longer read or consulted, disappeared. For hundreds of years it lay forgotten in one library or another. The holy anchoress, Margery Kempe, passed into oblivion until 1934, when she was suddenly dis-covered in a country house in Yorkshire. There was great excitement: a major writer of the fifteenth century had been found. There was equal disappointment: she was not a saint after all, nothing like one.

But many saints have written books, whereas only one member of the medieval public has had the industry, self-confidence and will-power to describe for us the everyday life and vicissitudes of a mayor's extraordinary daughter.

For one cannot help being impressed by the frankness of her testimony. In describing her misfortunes, she intended to show that her opponents were always wrong, inspired by the Devil, subject to the crass stupidity and blindness which is the common lot of humankind. Under these pressures, they called her hypocrite, meaning an hysterical and deluded woman. Yet, how often can we see from her ingenuous account that they were right. That she was the victim of religious mania, deceiving herself as to the nature of her dreams and hallucinations.

Though shrewd enough in other matters and penetrating in her judgements, about her connection with the divine she remained obdurate. She knew how to be tactful. She was alert, intelligent and a woman of the world in many respects. But when the religious mood came on her, she lost all control and could not be persuaded by any number of dangerous misadventures that some, at least, of her critics might be justified. Her story thus descends from the heights on which she intended it to rest and becomes the tale of a woman we can understand and with whom we can sympathize across the gap of five hundred years.

So we leave her, in 1438, madly dictating to her friend with swoons, with horrible roarings, cryings and shriekings; with arguments as to whether she had really said what he had written down. For it was not as if these were mere human words. Far from that, they emanated directly from on high. Christ himself was co-author.

# BIBLIOGRAPHY

D'Anglure, Seigneur. *Le Saint Voyage de Jherusalem*, 1395. Société des Anciens Textes Français, 1878.

Atkinson, William C. *History of Spain and Portugal*. Penguin, 1960.

Bennett, H. S. *Chaucer and the Fifteenth Century*. Oxford, 1947.

Borenius, Tancred. *Italian Painting*. Avalon Press, 1945.

Bridget, St. *Revelations of St. Birgitta*, ed. W. P. Cumming. Early English Text Society, 1929.

*Brut, The, or English Chronicle*, ed. J. S. Davis. Camden Society, 1861.

Capgrave, John. *Chronicle of England*, ed. F. C. Hingeston. Rolls Series, 1858.

Capgrave, John. *Ye Solace of Pilgrimes*, ed. C. A. Mills. Frowde, 1911.

Castro, Americo. *The Structure of Spanish History*. Princeton, 1954.

Cecchelli, Carlo. *Vita di Roma nel Medio Evo*. Palombi, 1960.

Chambers, P. F. *Julian of Norwich*. Gollancz, 1955.

Chaucer, Geoffrey. *Canterbury Tales*, ed. Skeat. Frowde, 1894.

Clay, R. M. *The Hermits and Anchorites of England*. Methuen, 1914.

*Cloud of Unknowing, The*, ed. P. Hodgson. Early English Text Society, 1944.

Colledge, Eric. *The Medieval Mystics of England*. Murray, 1962.

Creighton, M. *History of the Papacy*. Longmans, 1882.

Evans, Joan. *English Art 1307-1461*. Oxford, 1949.

Fabri, Felix. *Book of the Wanderings of Felix Fabri*, tr. A. Stewart. Palestine Pilgrims Text Society, 1892.

*Fourteenth Century Verse and Prose*, ed. Kenneth Sisam. Oxford, 1950.

*Gesta Romanorum*, ed. S. J. Hertage. Early English Text Society, 1879.

Green, A. S. *Town Life in the Fifteenth Century*. Macmillan, 1894.

Green, V. H. H. *The Later Plantagenets*. Arnold, 1955.

Gregorovius, F. *History of Rome in the Middle Ages*, tr. A. Hamilton. Bell, 1894.

Grollenberg, L. H. *The Atlas of the Bible*. Nelson, 1956.

Harff, Arnold von. *Pilgrimage of Arnold von Harff*, ed. and tr. Malcolm Letts. Hakluyt Society, 1946.

Hillen, H. J. *History of the Borough of King's Lynn*. Norwich, 1907.

Huelsen, Christian. *Le Chiese di Roma nel Medio Evo*. Firenze, 1927.

Jacob, E. F. *The Fifteenth Century*. Oxford, 1961.

Jorgensen, Johannes. *Saint Bridget of Sweden*. Longmans, 1954.

Jusserand, J. J. *English Wayfaring Life in the Middle Ages*. Methuen, 1961.

Kempe, Margery. *The Book of Margery Kempe*, ed. H. E. Allen and S.B. Meech. Early English Text Society, 1940.

*The Book of Margery Kempe*, a modern version by W. Butler-Bowden, World's Classics, Oxford, 1954.

Kendrick, T. D. *St. James in Spain*. Methuen, 1960.

Ker, W. P. *Medieval English Literature*. Home University Library, 1912.

Knowles, David. *The English Mystical Tradition*. Burns and Oates, 1961.

Knox, R. A. *Enthusiasm*. Oxford, 1950.

Ludolph. *Description of the Holy Land and of the Way Thither*, 1350, tr. A. Stewart. Palestine Pilgrims Text Society, 1895.

Maundevile, Sir John. *The Marvellous Adventures of Sir John Maundevile*, ed. Arthur Layard. Constable, 1895.

*Mirabilia Urbis Romanae*, ed. and tr. F. M. Nichols. Ellis, 1889.

Myrc, John. *Festial*, ed. T. Erbe. Early English Text Society, 1905.

Myrc, John. *Instructions for a Parish Priest*, ed. Peacock. Early English Text Society, 1868.

Myers, A. R. *England in the Late Middle Ages*. Penguin, 1952.

Newett, M. M. *Canon Pietro Casola's Pilgrimage to Jerusalem*. Manchester University Press, 1907.

Oman, C. *The Political History of England*. Longmans, 1910.

Owst, G. R. *Preaching in Medieval England*. Cambridge, 1926.

Owst, G. R. *Literature and Pulpit in Medieval England*. Cambridge, 1933.

Paschini, Pio. *Roma nel Rinascimento*. Bologna, 1940.

*Paston Letters, The*, ed. J. Gairdner. Macmillan, 1904.

Petry, Ray, C. (ed.) *Late Medieval Mysticism*. S.C.M. Press, 1957.

Poloner, John. *Description of the Holy Land*, tr. A. Steward. Palestine Pilgrims Text Society, 1894.

Power, Eileen. *Medieval People*. Penguin, 1937.
Prescott, H. F. M. *Jerusalem Journey*. Eyre and Spottiswoode, 1954.
*Select Documents of English History*, 1307-1485, ed. S. B. Chrimes and A. L. Brown. Oxford, 1961.
Starkie, Walter. *The Road to Santiago*. Murray, 1957.
Thurstan, Herbert. *Surprising Mystics*. Burns and Oates, 1955.
Wey, William. *Itineraries to Jerusalem*, 1458. Roxburghe Club, 1858.
Wilson, R. M. *Three Middle English Mystics*. English Association, 1956.

# INDEX